The Path of Relationship

The Life and Work of Drs. Hal and Sidra Stone

To Anne,
My first editor +
my first fan. Thank you
for all your help.
Warmly,
Dianne

Dianne Braden

Dianne Braden's website: www.diannebraden.com

Voice Dialogue International website: www.delos-inc.com

ACKNOWLEDGEMENTS

Where to begin?

I can hardly begin to list the people who have contributed to this project without saying directly thank you to Anne Brennan, my faithful editor over the first two and a half years of writing. To say this wouldn't have come about without her is true, but too trite to cover the rollercoaster of battles as well as high fives of congratulations over the months of developing *THE PATH OF RELATIONSHIP, the Life and Work of Drs. Hal and Sidra Stone.* Little did I know I would need more editors, nor did I know I could find them nearby in such quality. My thanks also go to Laura Walter, whose insight, perspective, and ability to see my whole project has been invaluable. Also, to my dear friend and colleague Mark Winborn, PhD, who simply can't read a manuscript without editing. A lucky circumstance for me.

My list of friends whose support has never wavered is long and makes me more grateful as I look at it. Bonnie Pfeiffer represents the bookends around this project. It was she who first called to the writer in me, inviting me to Kauai for a writer's retreat which birthed the first shaky transcription of the book. It was also she who read the final draft, helping me close the doors on a labor of love and commitment. It was her loving energy and support that simply kept checking on me, softly "wondering how the book was going." My oldest and dear friend Iudita Harlan has also been invaluable as the kind of artistic support I didn't know I needed. Her

1

patience and understanding of the creative process has carried me through the best and worst of times.

My friends Gabrielle and Martin Pollecoff have added their support and comment in this work's early stages, as well as gently encouraging questions along the way of "and how is the book?" I am also indebted to all the Voice Dialogue facilitators who generously passed the iPhone around at the 2014 Colorado Convergence. To all of you who escaped my editors' pens, and those of you who didn't, I thank you for your memories of the good old days of Voice Dialogue's infancy. Other supporters have been my friends Jonah Koslen, a creative cohort and web designer, Dale Lappert, who celebrated the completion of my first draft as if it were her own, and William and Kirsten Lynch, MD. Sadly Bill did not live to see the end of a project about which he was so very enthusiastic. Wherever he sits on the other side, I hope he knows it is finally done and his encouragement appreciated. Patti Ferris closes the list of friends who have patiently listened to me run up and down the scale of emotion surrounding this project, with patience and encouragement. Thanks to you all, it's here.

I also want to thank my Jungian analysts, Stanton Marlan, PhD, Janet Dallet, PhD, and Del McNeely, PhD, who helped lay my Jungian foundations and saw me as the analyst and writer I've become. I also thank my training analyst James Hollis, who first saw a writer in me, and my former supervisor and colleague, analyst Paul Kugler, PhD, for encouraging me to tell this story a year before I could begin work on it. This is not to forget my colleague, analyst Paulette Toth, who wins an award for enduring patience and attention to my writing process. And last but not least, I thank my friend and colleague, analyst Carolyn Bates, PhD, whose quiet and reflective encouragement always appeared magically when I most needed it.

2

I am also indebted to the Washington Street Diner outside of Chagrin Falls, Ohio who generously let me monopolize booths for hours at a time, always telling me, "No, you're fine. More coffee?" In the same category, I offer a shout out to The Tame Rabbit, Specialty Coffee and Roaster, also of Chagrin Falls, who offered the best coffee and background music I could ask for, and an atmosphere of welcome on the last leg of this journey.

For his wisdom and skill in the world of IT, I can't thank Jeffry Gonzalez enough. Although this book wouldn't have been possible without so many friends and supporters, it truly couldn't have taken flight if it hadn't been for Jeff. Many thanks my Guru, my friend.

At the end, I add my sincerest thanks to J. Tamar Stone, Hal Stone's daughter, who spent considerable time with me on the phone, and patiently read, not once but twice, the story of her own life contained in the tale I tell of her father and Sidra. And lastly, my deepest thanks go to Hal and Sidra Stone, who granted me access to their personal worlds and so generously gave me their time, support, and their love. Back at you always, Hal and Sidra.

Contents

ACKNOWLEDGEMENTS..1

PROLOGUE..6

INTRODUCTION 10

CHAPTER ONE..14

CHAPTER TWO..28

CHAPTER THREE...41

CHAPTER FOUR..52

CHAPTER FIVE..65

CHAPTER SIX..76

CHAPTER SEVEN 90

CHAPTER EIGHT...105

CHAPTER NINE 123

CHAPTER TEN..139

CHAPTER ELEVEN...152

CHAPTER TWELVE 168

CHAPTER THIRTEEN 180

CHAPTER FOURTEEN 206

CHAPTER FIFTEEN...221

CHAPTER SIXTEEN..244

CHAPTER SEVENTEEN 269

EPILOGUE 272

PROLOGUE

It was March 31st, 2014, 11:55 am, Eastern Standard Time. There was a note on my waiting room door that read "Running 5 minutes late. We thank you for your patience." I sat in my consulting room in my usual chair. My associate was on the couch, silent. We were waiting to pray for Hal Stone.

I had received word from Sidra that Hal had been hospitalized with a serious infection. The word "serious" seemed superfluous. Hal was already eighty-six years old. Any infection was serious. I hadn't had time to reminisce, bring up fond and funny memories, to adjust to the immediate reality that he could die. Their children had been called. I was heartsick. It was bad.

There had been no word since a quick "Thank you for thinking of us. We love you," email several days before. The number of times a day I checked my iPhone for another exceeded my personal best. I was beyond worried.

By the end of the week, there had been an email from two people in the Voice Dialogue community. East Coast therapists, Abbey Rosen[1] and Ruth Berlin[2], requested that all of us, at an appointed time in our respective time zones, spend five minutes in meditation and prayer for Hal's recovery and healing. The thought, even now, brings tears. Within hours, dozens of emails came through to the list serve from all around the country and the world. People who love Hal and Sidra were getting on board like an energetic convoy headed for his hospital bed. The community came together in a virtual embrace and stood firm.

Email responses varied in length and language, but never in content. Hal and Sidra Stone are beloved. People wrote openly about their love and gratitude, how they were forwarding the request to their communities, how they would be there at the appointed time. We would all meet in the ethers and send our love and support.

The day after I heard that Hal was ill, I had a dream. In the dream, I was at their home in northern California, facing the house. I was in a large circle of people holding hands, surrounding the house. Everyone's gaze was directed through the windows. We were silent. The dream ended.

I thought about the dream as I waited for the clock to reach twelve. The minutes dragged by with a heaviness whose importance grew as the second hand of my office clock crawled around the clock face. Reality seemed porous as I sat in the space where the dream and the Voice Dialogue community met in real time. The effect was startling. I was expanding and contracting simultaneously, feeling alone and worried, and in touch with every prayer traveling through the mists to Hal's door. Then it was noon.

I let my mind settle into a quiet I reserve for listening to a dream. I saw an image of Hal lying in his hospital bed, Sidra seated beside him. I let my heart open to the Intelligence in the universe, and God, the Buddha, and anyone else out there whose ear I might reach if they could help. I prayed for Hal's suffering to lessen, for his recovery to begin. So did everyone else.

While I was at it, I explained, privately, that I hadn't finished the book about them yet … that I wanted Hal to read it. It was about them, after all. What kind of bad joke would it be if they didn't get to see it while Hal was alive? Then I simply felt how scared I was that he wouldn't make it. Although I'm not much of a joiner, in that moment I took my place in the ranks of a collective. We were on this. If love were enough to cure, Hal would surely live forever.

Whatever one thinks about prayer, and I've been on many sides of it, the experience of so many hearts energetically reaching out to Hal and Sidra with love was spectacular. I could feel all of us. When the allotted five minutes were up, I wanted to linger in the psychic space we'd created, it was so deep and filled with sweetness. I can still feel it.

But I had clients waiting. It was a workday, like others, except, of course, it wasn't. This was *the* workday when I understood that love, though often invisible, has no real limitations; that it can be strengthened, not diminished by joining others. Moreover, with concentration and mindfulness, love can sometimes change the order of things, the twists of fate, and the direction of illness. Hal began to recover that afternoon. I have no doubt that the community prayer made a difference. I was part of that. I ask you, how impossibly wonderful is that?

We live in a world where the shadows and difficulties of our humanity get a lot more press than our nobility. This effort and the continuing community meditation on Saturdays, at the exact same time everywhere, remind me we are individually and collectively incredible souls. When we struggle with our cruelty and tendency toward destruction, perhaps in the end our capacity to love in this way will count for something, redeem us in the eyes of future generations who will surpass us in compassion and self-control. At least I hope so. It only takes five minutes.

The people who awaken this kind of love, who inspire us to pull together-rather than apart, fascinate me. I'm curious about how the Stones managed this feat. What they contributed to consciousness, where their work fits in consciousness literature, and how they created a worldwide loving community is contained on the rest of these pages.

Let me share the story with you.

INTRODUCTION

My name is Dianne Braden and I am a Jungian analyst. What that means, for those who aren't familiar, is that I am trained to work with people therapeutically in analytical psychology. That is the work of Swiss psychiatrist Carl Gustav Jung. In my private practice, I work with peoples' inner lives; their dreams, fantasies and creative projects, that yield meaning to a personal process of psychological growth. Jung believed that these experiences come from the vast unconscious, or that part of the psyche about which we know nothing. Establishing a dialogue with this valuable structure is the work of a Jungian analysis.

My own analysis offered me such experience and my passion for the work grew. I became entranced by the beauty and power of dreams; the dimension they added to my understanding of my humanity. Jung had a gift for understanding the psyche in a way that made sense to me. Finally, I decided to become an analyst myself. My training surrounded me with analysts dedicated to that which fascinated me. Although Jung himself died long before my interest in his work awakened, I listened to and learned from analysts who actually trained with him; men and women who remembered him personally, who first brought his work to this country. I was hooked and grateful.

But my process is only a part of the story I intend to tell here. Some years after I entered analytic training I had the good fortune to meet and work with Drs. Hal and Sidra Stone, two California psychologists whose joint experience in the field of psychology spans more than eight decades; in fact, it covers a time in this country when there literally was no such thing as psychology. Further, Hal Stone was a Jungian analyst who analyzed and trained with that first generation of people who actually met and trained with Jung himself.

Combining their separate experiences and an amazing relationship, Hal and Sidra created a body of work called Voice Dialogue and the Psychology of Selves, a process that rests solidly on both Jungian and Cognitive Behavioral foundations. I am indebted to them both personally and professionally, and through the last years of my analytic training, and after it ended, I spent many hours in retreat and study with them, embracing their work. As my relationship with them deepened, I found the story of their lives and how their work developed from it, as fascinating as a long and beautiful dream about love and how it changes consciousness. Hal and Sidra are interesting, eccentric and gifted people. They have brought a gift to the world of relationship.

Buoyed by the prospect of a series of interviews with the Stones and a lot of ambition, I undertook the writing of a book about them. I began to wonder about who Hal and Sidra were personally, how their love for one another supported and contributed to their process and the creation of their work; and how their work contributed to consciousness in general. Because I'd not undertaken a project of such magnitude before, the book seemed more than daunting on many levels. Then I had the following dream.

I was part of an oceanic construction crew. I was being transported on a vehicle I'd never seen before, like a great hovercraft, skimming over the sea at great speed to a construction site already underway. I arrived and looked up at the ironwork skeleton of an enormous building of blimp-like shape that seemed to hover over the platform. It was all rafters and beams and long wooden walkways. I had never seen anything like this. I wasn't sure I knew how to work on a structure such as this. But I picked up the small black dog

11

travelling with me and disembarked, adjusting the little protective cone the dog wore around its neck to keep it from bothering a wound that was healing.

When I awoke I was filled with the kind of energy that comes from contact with the numinous. Like the ancient Greeks, I felt the nod from the gods. The dimensions of the construction in the dream were otherworldly, as was the vehicle transporting me to it. Naturally the dream ego (me in the dream) had doubts about how to proceed, a condition that was matched by my conscious ego to be sure, but what followed was a shock. As if carried by the huge swells of ocean waves, from that moment on, I had direction and purpose. I broadened my perspective and added my own voice to the material. I answered for myself the questions I asked of the Stones: What influences people who make significant contributions to consciousness? How did the work evolve? Finally, what does it add to our notions of consciousness, transformation, and spiritual experience?

My understanding of what it takes grew exponentially as I poured over interviews, email exchanges, dreams and recollections. I became a storyteller of a different kind than I had initially imagined. The book carried me while I was writing it, forcing me to walk the beams and rafters of the dream construction site. As I hovered above a platform floating on the dream's seascape, I longed for "sea legs" to stabilize my labors.

While life in such a liminal space may have its drawbacks, it has its perks. I have been invited into intimate contact with people I admire, with an open invitation to talk about their lives. I'm charged with presenting their work to a broader audience. I do so in the hope that it offers a dimension of relationship pointing toward a future of real connection with each other, in spite of a worldwide race toward substituting technology for that experience.

12

Hal and Sidra Stone have straddled eight decades collectively. How they discovered and developed Voice Dialogue, the Psychology of Selves, the Aware Ego Process, and each other is a great story. How they approach consciousness and where they think their work with it will go is as interesting as how they came to it in the first place. They are a lesson in the *tension of the opposites*[3] and the *transcendent function*[4] of the psyche as Jung understood it. Add to that a love that refused to be ignored, times in this country when consciousness was redefining itself, and the stage was set.

I have charged myself with this work for several reasons, not the least of which is that the Stones graciously agreed to allow it. But I also feel a debt to the future. I think we should preserve the stories of the people who brave the discomfort of changing consciousness, who pay the price in time, health, and relationships to make a contribution to something larger. We must not forget to honor the souls that walk through the fires before us, nor avoid learning from and finding comfort in the many turns and twists they endured for our benefit.

And last, but not at all least, this is a love story. That means I include the peaks and valleys and the stumbling climbs of love, work, and the creation of something new. It means this story contains the truths and illusions of pioneers, and the suffering of transformation. The story of Voice Dialogue and the Stones also treats the costs of surrendering to a process. There are plenty. Hal and Sidra don't shy away from taking responsibility for them. As they model now how to grow old with some consciousness and dignity, they have allowed me to tell the story of how they weathered the journey. I offer readers the joys and shadows of contributing to consciousness as it happened to them, with the hope we still remember how to do this going forward.

13

CHAPTER ONE

THERA

I'm sensitive to the spirit of place. I like to remember first how it felt to be in different locations, how their energies affected me. I have the same interest in peoples' homes or properties, or vacation spots and professional offices. I'm attentive to what energies float about in my consulting room, my own, and the ones that play and work with me there. I thought long and hard about the art that decorates my walls, and what the masks, antique windowpane, and framed degrees speak to about me, and the space I welcome people into.

The places I visit more than once all seem to have something in common: they influence my energy in a powerful way, and I say powerful, and not positive, intentionally. I'm less interested in "nice" times and "sweet" places than in important stays and powerful experiences. I want to feel deeply into things and be moved by them, try on different feels and looks, imagining myself in new ways as long as I can. I'm not going to live forever. I don't want to waste what the Buddhists rightly call "a precious human birth."

I return to Thera, Hal and Sidra Stone's home in northern California, because it does that for me. It calls me into deeper parts of myself than other places. I often wonder if the climes of Mendocino will call me in quite the same way when Hal and Sidra are not there. But I'm sure I'll never be there without thinking of them, so the point is indeed moot.

Then, there's the name, Thera, which is a kind of perfect blend of Hal's love of Greek mythology and Sidra's deep connection to Greece. The land of Thera, the namesake, stands surrounded by the waters of the Aegean Sea. Farther south, the same waters mingle with the Mediterranean Sea, winding its way toward the Gulf of Sidra. Thera itself is an island, according to classical Greek mythology, once inhabited

14

by Theras, an important hero whose family tree boasts Cadmus in its ancestry. You remember Cadmus, who followed the bull and slew the dragon whose teeth created an army that slew itself. Great story! If you haven't read it, look it up. The image of a space surrounded by the waters of the unconscious, decorated with the touch of masculine and feminine, and offering retreat, would apply to the Thera that greets you when you drive down Middle Ridge Road. Its spirit of place hits you the minute you see it.

It's a long drive. It takes a good three and a half hours from San Francisco to get to Albion, which is the small town you'd blink and miss if you were on your way to Mendocino, a much more upscale, artsy, northern California getaway kind of place. The coastline is breathtaking and the color of the water an almost indescribable blue … but of course, everyone tries to describe it. The dark coastal rocks offer contrast, and something for the ocean to push against in a constant tango of advance and retreat. I love the trance it offers me when I can just sit and watch. That is, naturally, why people go there.

It's hard to keep my eyes off the coastline when I come up the hill approaching the road leading to Thera. I have to force myself to watch the turns and curves that continue after leaving the ascent and descent around the great hills leading out to the coast.

I turn down Middle Ridge Road. It always appears just after I think I've missed it. The sun flashes on and off my windshield as I pass under the great trees. They exude such an ageless depth, it seems they give but brief permission to pass underneath, and then close over the road again, after I pass by. I try not to look at my rearview mirror, just in case.

The road is paved until I come to the llama farm with its great mahogany-looking gates in stylized, curved, artistic design to my right. The llamas look up. If the farm dogs aren't out, I sometimes stop and pull fresh grass for the little ones, who

15

have followed the elders walking sedately to the fence. They pretend they don't even want the handful of grass, just to keep me in my place. Then as a favor, they delicately pull a few strands at a time out of my offering fist. The pavement stops right after the llama farm. The dirt road and its layer of dust and potholes force me to slow down. The air of privacy that the residents have created is clear. The houses are mostly hidden behind high fences or deep woods.

After some dips and turns, I come to the top of a slight hill. Thera spreads out before me. There's a lovely meadow dotted with grasses and taller plants, often hosting a flock of wild turkeys, or small bands of deer. There's a solar panel installation now that pays for itself and testifies to Hal and Sidra's attention to the environment and resource conservation, and then a couple of wells for water.

It's hard not to stop and just look. A panorama would offer weathered wind horses on the left, their faded Buddhist flags on the tall poles having sent prayers out to the universe for many years now. Right at the fence, there's a lovely bed of short grasses, with an imposing standing Buddha statue looking out over the meadow and outbuildings. The effect is spectacular. I can feel my spirit expand and soften.

On the far right, I can see the two apartments guests stay in when visiting Hal and Sidra. Tucked under massive trees, both apartments offer a retreat experience: one with its deck facing a seated Buddha statue under an old apple tree, and woods into which the deer and turkeys disappear in the evening. The other apartment is larger. Its morning view opens to the entire meadow through a big picture window. Both spaces have a feeling of calm and containment in the evening, as the silence of the forest folds around you like an old friend. I can't wait to settle in.

As I approach the driveway, a large stone head of a third Buddha statue rests comfortably against the tree that shades the parking lot. A modest tile sign announces that the Stones live here. I turn in, and the front porch of the house opens to me overlooking the meadow I've just passed, and a small pond with lily pads and trickling

16

water. The view grows in beauty and serenity as I check out the placement of different items that move from season to season, or following seminars held outdoors when it's warm. Picnic tables and chairs play checkers with each other, moving in groups or small circles, telling the tale of the last Intensive or family visit.

There are apple trees everywhere. In the fall, the deer are attuned to the sound of a single apple falling, like a Zen koan they've figured out as they rush to dispatch it. Under one of the apple trees by the smaller apartment, the seated Buddha's very presence drops me into meditation when I sit on the porch with my coffee, watching the morning mists burn away.

Behind the main house, protected from the deer, is Sidra's garden. It's a world of its own. The flowers supply the amazingly colorful and fragrant arrangements she creates and places around the house. When the ginger blooms, color and scent combine in the house in a way Sidra would call delicious. Hal's more abstract stone sculptures rise up out of the lawns and other clearly well-chosen places that contribute to an aesthetic that is uniquely theirs. There are no vistas at Thera that aren't beautiful, deep, and inductive into the spirit of the place. When the visual tour is over, the front door opens. The journey renews itself with the presence of Hal and Sidra Stone.

There are times when the energetic connection that people have with one another is more palpable than others. It's one of the perks of being human, this kind of linkage to another that yields such a feeling of belonging. It is one of those things I sometimes don't recognize until I'm losing it, or it's gone all together. This is not a sad thing. Goodbyes aren't always permanent. Connections, of the valuable kind, can be reestablished if tended to and, repaired, if need be. Or, energetic connections can simply be rediscovered and enjoyed all the more for their history and the sweetness of memory.

When I was in my forties, the wisdom of the spheres brought me to a kind and strong analyst. I sat before him for a long time, not really knowing what to do, or why I was there specifically, until the energetic connection was established. Jungians call it transference; spiritual pundits call it devotion and a number of other things. What I understand about this experience now is that it's the energetic linkage that is fundamental to a good analytic relationship.

In the late 1980's, I busied myself driving to my analytic appointments, a couple of hours each way. I would do this faithfully for the next eight years. I would sit in the waiting room listening to pretty awful music and wait for my analyst to open the door. I felt the usual uneasiness, that mix of excitement and dread, in case I hadn't had a dream to explore. In essence, it was none of those things that seemed as daunting on the front side of my appointments, as what I faced leaving. What I realized when the hour was over, was that I had been so well held and attended to, I was filled with an energy both wonderful and terrible. I knew as I started my car, it would be another week before I felt loved like that again. That's energetic linkage.

This early understanding of connection created a space in me that could only be filled energetically. I sought out analysts who carried that ability, and more importantly for this book, I found it in Hal and Sidra Stone, ramped up by a million gigahertz. (I learned to exaggerate from Hal. It's contagious.) By simply walking into their offices for my first sessions, I recognized the real thing and never looked back.

The first time I worked with Hal is a good example. It was the early 1990's. His office looked then like it did when I sat with him for the interviews in the fall of 2011. It feels like walking into a personal study.

As I come through the doorway, my eyes first travel the short distance across his large desk, and to the view out the window. My gaze refocuses on the meadow sprawling out toward some distant pines that hide a neighbor's house. I take in the apple trees, some sculpture, maybe a deer or two, before my eyes return to the small room holding Hal's energy and aesthetic.

Flanked on both sides by smaller windows, his workspace sings with openings and multiple points of view. To my right sits a very impressive, intricately carved, wooden dragon. Its curling neck and serpentine tail pull me toward the precise detail of his scales and teeth, making me linger in appreciation of his beauty and the power of the archetype he represents.

The small bookcase beneath the dragon contains the volumes that now interest Hal. Many concern near-death experiences and volumes of Swedenborg and Steiner populate the group. Other titles of a more philosophical nature assure me that even if I try to remember what they are and explore them privately, they might elude my understanding. I can tell from the titles.

If I let my eyes wander in a counterclockwise direction, I find a complicated-looking phone setup and photos of Hal's grown children, sprinkled with grandchildren's faces and a large, hi-tech Apple computer. Hal once told me people so loved their Apple computers one guy had a wedding ceremony for it when it arrived. He told me this with tears streaming down his face, he was laughing so hard, while acknowledging he could completely understand how the guy felt.

Moving on I would see another wall, filled with old photos that defy my vow to mind my own business. They're nestled in between sacred objects and small pieces of art whose energy must delight Hal, or they wouldn't still be there. To be sure, it's about the energy to be in Hal's office.

Below the wall used to be a very large, overstuffed soft leather couch, whose depths pulled me in when doing facilitations with Hal over the years. In fact, it was so soft and comfortable, I had a hard time getting out of it. Talk about putting yourself in a self and staying there … the device was perfect, although I doubt that was the intention.

It's gone now, that old couch. Hal's opted for space these days, and more maneuvering room around the chairs. But it was a look and an experience for many an awkward or glorious moment working with him. Let me tell you about the first time.

I sat in a chair opposite Hal. I was nervous. His direct gaze made me squirm no matter how hard I tried to quiet my suddenly twitchy body. I thought I should cross and uncross my legs a few times, for warm-up purposes, preparing to feign a casual comfort I couldn't find. I was in training to become a Jungian analyst then, so, naturally, I wanted to appear like I already was one. I hoped he would see my obvious depth, my serene expression, alluding to my clear and constant grasp on consciousness. Instead, I started to sweat … noticeably.

Hal cleared his throat loudly, and said, "Let's just be together energetically for a few minutes, shall we?" I nodded less in agreement than a sudden and very real inability to speak at all. Also, I didn't really have a firm grasp on what "being together energetically" meant exactly. I intuited it might mean continued looking at each other, which was already causing me some distress, but I nodded again. The twinkle in his eye disappeared. His easy smile went with it as he locked his gaze onto me. He didn't suddenly become unfriendly. The shift was not visible in that way, but it was palpable. The change in the connection between us, and the power and seriousness of it drove my false courage down onto the floor and sent it crawling out the door.

I looked out at him from behind my disintegrating defenses. I was amazed at the great mass of white hair that adorned his head. Younger men would envy the thick and wavy silver that allowed his head to reflect the soft light in his office. He ran his hand through his hair often, as if to enjoy the feel of it himself now and then. Hal was taller than he is now, and taller than I was at the time on every level. He sat easily in his swivel chair, both hands resting softly on the arms, his legs crossed at the ankle. He took a deep breath.

I looked at his eyes from a distance that was fading in spite of myself. They were cloudy even then, his eyes, like a mist was moving in behind them while he watched me. I was distracted by the questions that kept popping into my head about whether he could really see me, and if he could, what was he looking at specifically, and worse yet, did he think I was fat. I sucked my stomach in. No worry about him finding my inner depth. It was nowhere to be seen.

I looked away to my right, trying to avoid the discomfort I was feeling when my eyes locked onto the wooden dragon. It was about two feet tall but seemed twenty in the moment. It was so accurately carved I could feel its power and aggression. Its open mouth hosted an impressive array of pointed teeth. Its scale-covered tail wrapped back over its back, seemingly caught in mid-attack by the carver's blade. I found little comfort to my right. I returned my gaze to Hal.

He was sitting just as I had left him, waiting quietly for me to reorganize myself and come back into contact with him. My eyes locked with his and I understood something I'd missed before. The process was not really about what I saw. I began to feel something between us that was new and beautiful, except I didn't know what new and beautiful meant at the time. I began to look for the feeling from my inside out.

Years later I worked with an analyst who only had her peripheral vision due to macular degeneration. When I was talking away early on in my work with her -- I did finally figure out how to talk when someone looked at me directly -- I thought she was listening intently because my issues were so interesting and complicated. Much later I discovered she couldn't see me at all when looking straight at me; she had to turn her head to the side to see me seated in front of her. I looked away time and time again when she did this, thinking she was distracted by something I couldn't see. And I was right. She was distracted by something I couldn't see. It was me, and my flaming inflated shadow, but I didn't get that at the time.

21

In any case, as I became more comfortable in Hal's space, in my chair across from him, and in my own skin, I began to feel something new in the space between us. At first it felt warm, gently moving toward me, and then slowly I could tell it was touching me, somewhat impossibly, deep in my body and being. I started to want to look at Hal, to feel more comfortable looking at him than looking away, and I began to melt into a silent intimacy I didn't really know what to do with.

"Okay," he said. "I'm going to do some chakra work with you, just energetically. Would that be alright?" I nodded again and almost immediately felt the shifts in my chakras, aware that whatever meditation I'd done in the past -- and I thought I'd done some -- had not awakened this in me. I felt like a lifeline had been created between us, or the silver cord people talked about seeing when they left their bodies ... except that I wasn't one of those people. I was so completely vulnerable I was afraid to be this close, but just as afraid to lose the connection.

Hal wasn't speaking at all. We sat together like this for maybe twenty minutes until I "let" myself move into my crown chakra. I felt my psyche open up. I expanded into a place that felt immense in dimension and vista. Just as I was feeling smug about my capabilities, defusing as I was with everything around me, Hal said firmly, "Don't space out." I landed back in my body with a thud, only to be caught up again gently by Hal's energetic connection, that kept me in touch or in tow, I wasn't sure which until he took a deep breath and showed me how to turn the dial down on the energetic bond between us.

When the session was over, everything in me screamed "What the hell was that?" As I silently tried to return to myself and act like I'd done this many times before, everything in me screamed "How can I get back there?" I was bonded to Hal like an imprinted chick. Being separated from him energetically was palpable and difficult, like the energetic cord that had connected us had been cut. I missed him even though I sat with him in the same space. It was some time before I learned how to manage these new energies within me. I was exploding with feelings and

22

information about them, like I'd finally landed on the magic planet I'd been looking for and Hal had just handed me a map he wasn't using.

As fantastic as this was, it was a long time and many sessions later before I had any agency over my energy with Hal. The largeness of his gift and the intensity of his connection with other layers of consciousness make him a master of the art. It's just hard to sit close to someone whose energy is so much larger than one's own. But this was the beginning for me. Then he said gently, "Well, my dear. That's enough for today, don't you think?" I let my feet metaphorically touch the ground again and agreed, hoarding the little piece of bliss I took with me as I left the office.

Now with Sidra, the energetic story goes in a different direction. It begins in her office and continues to other dimensions of connection. But I'll start right there, in her office. The space has an entirely different feel. The feminine energy she exudes has a lot to do with it, accentuated in contrast to Hal's obvious masculine. Naturally, it's more than that. As expansive and broadening as the entrance into Hal's office is both concretely and metaphorically, Sidra's space is just as expressive of her. Before I enter, my eyes find the warmth and color of a fire in the fireplace, which is always burning, unless the summer heat prohibits building one.

The truth is, I think Sidra so loves the aesthetic of a fire, there may not be a season in her world when a fire wouldn't be just the thing to set the mood. That's exactly what hits you first about Sidra herself. Her warmth is palpable, energetically, concretely, and metaphorically once you cross the threshold into her world.

There's an enormous, thick canvas glove that rests to the left of the fireplace tools. Sidra dons it like a small-fisted firefighter when a log needs retrieving or restacking in the fireplace, even if the log is burning when she picks it up. I always wince when she does this, even now. The sight of her talking casually to me while holding a burning log is so Sidra. It just isn't Dianne Braden, who would likely opt to hover around her, worrying about her safety. Of course, she wouldn't allow that. So, she brushes aside the risk with an air of years of practice, laughing at whatever she's thinking about or contemplating what she was saying before the fire needed tending.

A big window also opens over Sidra's beautiful wooden desk. She loves that desk like a pet and talks about its beauty with the proud appreciation of a mother catching you up about her child. My eyes catch the apple trees and the small pond with lily pads, a couple of out buildings and a deer or two lying down comfortably by the pond near the house. If it's spring there will be wild turkeys in the meadow, the males preening and showing off for the females who ignore their strutting, busily foraging in the green grass for seeds.

Sidra's desk sports an Apple computer like Hal's, and pictures in brilliant colors drawn by her grandchildren move silently on the screen's wallpaper. Then there's a chair … a white wicker rocker that looks like it was made for Sidra alone, it so fits her demeanor and style. Her back to another window looking out on the porch, which has a fountain, Sidra works quietly with the sound of water falling in the background. It's hard to imagine her elsewhere, she so fits in the space she created in her home.

There's a small table on the other side of the doorway, next to a straight-backed chair, then a small alcove in which used to rest a couch. Like Hal, Sidra has since cleared her office of larger furniture, opening things up to more light and space. She glows noting the change, claiming who she is now in comparison.

Then a bookcase draws the eye, filled with volumes saved from her college days, favorite novels worn by rereading, and poetry in more than one language. The space is loaded with wisdom, welcome, and a warmth Sidra exudes when she ushers you in. It feels like home even if you've never been there before. But the first time I met with Sidra by myself, I noticed none of this.

I had arrived in Albion during an impressive rain storm. My session with Sidra was scheduled for that evening. It poured rain all afternoon and I watched a stormy landscape in a dreary mood. I had planned to do relationship work with them, but my relationship was falling apart. I was there alone and angry. The long drive in the rain had disconcerted me. Driving back inland to their home in the woods, in the dark, in heavy rain, was scary. Sidra didn't know when she greeted me at the door that she was welcoming a wet and irritable mountain lion into her home. But the big cat was there to be sure and she wasn't purring.

There was some light banter between Hal and Sidra that night as they settled into their evening. Sidra would work with me first, to be followed by a session with Hal the following day, in a pattern that would continue for the rest of the week. They poured tea, offered me some which I refused, and we settled in. I was unfamiliar with their work in any intimate way, and given my mood, I was unwilling to let go of my trusted analytic experience. I was a candidate in training, remember. I couldn't help wanting to look good. Sidra made several attempts to offer facilitation, (the actual dialogue with parts of us that help us manage our lives) but I couldn't stop explaining how things were for me; how I understood them analytically; how doggedly I wanted to present myself as on top of things.

It was, of course, a huge dodge. I didn't want Sidra to see how vulnerable I felt, how abandoned, or how angry I was at my situation. As my attempts at cover up failed one by one in the face of Sidra's kind but deliberate focus, I began to talk about my trip thus far.

Given the weather, I'd spent a lot of time in my hotel room. Restless and bored, I finally decided rain or shine, I was taking a walk by the ocean. I was in Mendocino, right? Go look at the ocean! So, I took myself into town and turned my collar up to the wind, and walked along the ocean, somewhat miserably, but I had done it.

25

As I finished this pronouncement, Sidra got very quiet. She looked directly at me and in a low and very ominous voice, she said, "Ohhh. You shouldn't do that this time of year. The ocean is very dangerous. We have what are called Rogue Waves. They come out of nowhere, these huge waves, and wash up on the shore. People who turn their backs on the ocean can get washed out to sea without warning. It's very dangerous and every year someone loses their life this way."

Although her tone never wavered, her message stopped me short as I awakened to what she said. It scared me into consciousness with a jolt. The only sound in the room was the crackling of the fire as the danger she described sunk in. The room was warm, but I felt a chill come over me. I had walked to the edge of something in myself I didn't know was dangerous, and Sidra didn't miss it.

Suddenly the gates were open. I saw I was awash in my own life and finally telling someone about it. I dropped the language and the reflective stance of a trained professional and wept for the first time in months about my confusion and pain. I became open to the work and allowed Sidra to guide me. Instantly connected to her irresistible energy, I saw how I'd taken myself to the edge of my own sea and then abandoned myself there. And I hadn't once looked back to see if anything or anyone was behind me.

There are warning signs posted along the beaches of the coast in Mendocino. At certain times of the year, they warn tourists to never turn their backs to the ocean. They alert people to the Rogue Wave dangers. There had been such signs along my way the afternoon in question. I had not seen them. With Sidra's unwavering caring and energetic support, I explored the parts of my personality I didn't recognize. Her soft-spoken questions opened me to a shocking consciousness. Who was it in me that didn't care about my safety? Who thought it okay to walk on the edge of the land in the pouring rain? Who was so restless that any exercise would do and what was she running from? And most of all, who was so busy looking down, she never saw the warning signs on the edge of the ocean?

That night next to the fire, held in Sidra's gentle but steady energy, I felt like she tossed me a life preserver just as I risked getting too far out. Sidra was the first to say, "I've got you," and she meant it.

My week with Sidra and Hal that year continued at a depth I hadn't plumbed before. The West Coast warning of never turning your back on the ocean became a metaphor for never ignoring the waters of my unconscious, and for years after, Sidra reminded me about the Rogue Waves, whenever my attention drifted, or I seemed careless about how I walk by the beaches of my soul.

I left her office that particular night with much the same question I had asked myself when I left Hal. "Who ARE these people?"

I am about to tell you.

CHAPTER TWO

The Ground We Stood On

What I've always loved about reading Jung's autobiography, *Memories, Dreams and Reflections,* is how it identifies the seeds of his later work imbedded in his childhood experiences. Although it might not have been the specific intention, certain bits and pieces of his reminiscences surface more brightly than others. I am forced to reflect on the things that shaped me in my history, lessons and influences whose roots go deeply into my early years, and rest there, supporting or stressing my life in the present. I have some understanding of the important relationships and studies that make becoming an analyst, a writer, and a student of consciousness literature, a logical conclusion as choices go.

I often think of my thirty-year love affair with horses, watching how they carry themselves, as the precursor of my fascination with psyche's wanderings. Or perhaps it was my boredom with routine as a child that was the catalyst for my intense need to find new ways to look at things, new languages in which to express my discoveries. Or were the days I spent wandering the hills and valleys out in the country on horseback, the incentive to explore larger and larger spaces in the minds of others? Asthma, too, plagued my youth, and could surely have been a troubling inspiration for the need to breathe deeply in the world, to find a place in which I could fill my lungs and soul with spirit.

I think this is how it is with most creative processes and with the Stones' work as well. I came to them filled with curiosity, wondering how they came to be who they are. As they opened their worlds to me, complete with stories, dreams, and memories, I felt like a tourist in a new landscape. Our conversations were at first glimpses into an era before my time. I knew nothing of pre-war American cities. I've not been part of a war effort that rang with the patriotism of the time when Hal was a young boy. So, the story of his beginnings was fresh for me, filled with unfamiliar images that came to life in the telling.

Before Thera, before Hal and Sidra were a couple, and before, in fact, either of them lived in California, they were separate. Not quite ten years apart in age, they were individually ushered into life in very different places and times. I waited restlessly on the first morning, like the audience before the play begins. Hal leaned back in his office swivel chair, musing about the late 1920's in Detroit, Michigan, a time and culture he now connects with only vaguely.[5]

"Growing up in Detroit was, for me, a five-star nothing burger!" he said with a wistful smile followed by a chuckle. "I guess to an outsider it might look interesting, but for me, it really holds very little." As he continued to share his early history, a very different picture would emerge than the one I had expected from the man I had known over the years.

Detroit was a tough place to live in during the late 1920's. Hal's parents owned what was called a beer garden[6] in those days, located in the black section of the city. Although we tend to think of the West as wild and wooly, there was nothing gentrified about the larger cities of the Midwest at the time Hal was growing up. "They had to have special police in the area, because there was a lot of rowdy drinking and dancing," he said. "The nightlife during those years was rough and dangerous."

Hal's parents protected him from most of that life. He had little memory of the time until age five, when the family relocated to what was then suburban Detroit, and more at the center of things. "Although my parents continued to have that beer

29

garden through my entire childhood," Hal said, "they commuted to it. My life was entirely separate from it, at least geographically."

Like many children of immigrant families, Hal's knowledge of and relationship to his ancestors was sketchy, at best. Victims of the Holocaust, most of his relatives were killed before he knew them. Hal's mother, Ethel Gross, came to the United States from Czechoslovakia, now Hungary, at the age of fifteen with an aunt of hers. Hal's father, Sam Stone, travelled alone from the Poland-Russia border area to New York at the age of thirteen. When he settled into life in this country, he also stayed with relatives here. He went to work very early and was very soon on his own.

"I don't really know much about how he grew up," said Hal. "What I do know was that by the age of nineteen, he was the manager of a small hotel in the New York area." Like many of that generation of immigrants, Hal's parents carried a very strong work ethic. "My father was a very good-hearted man," he said. "He always worked. He was always responsible and kind. But he drank alcohol, and drinking was an issue in his life. It affected all of us."

The picture Hal paints of his early relationship with his father leaves a lot of blank space on the canvas. There's a lasting picture of a very physical, non-verbal, strong man. Hal described him as built like a Greek wrestler. "But I have no memory of him even talking to me," he said. "Once I think he was mad at me for throwing a clock at my brother. This was when we were still living in the original house in the black section of Detroit, but I have no clear memory of any other time. He just wasn't a talker. Since I never had that with him, I didn't miss it."

Hal acknowledges that like the rest of us, there was plenty to work through with his family of origin. His father was also a very sexual man, and Hal had many judgments about his father's drinking and infidelities. He reflected that it wasn't until his first Jungian analysis that he came to terms with some of these issues. Because of a dream he still remembers from his early analysis, Hal now frames his father's situation in a more compassionate way.

"In the dream, my father was on a boat that kept plying its way between the U.S. and Europe," he said, looking around briefly to catch a glimpse of the deer wandering across the front lawns. "Each place he landed turned him away. He had to return from whence he came, only to have the story repeated over and over again. I think my father was a man without a country – a man who could ultimately never be comfortable in his own skin."

Sam Stone worked extremely hard. His efforts were, for Hal, responsible for the path he follows now. "Neither my brothers nor I would have had any possibility of doing the kinds of things we did had our parents not worked in the way they did," Hal said. "I knew many other people who worked hard, like my parents. They simply have my everlasting thanks. They worked terribly, terribly hard."

The late 1920's and early 1930's were times of tremendous industriousness in the bigger U.S. cities. Hal's father, and many like him, was at his business at 5 a.m. to do the physical labor. Hal still smiles with admiration for his father's strength, remembering the sight of him tossing around kegs of beer with ease. His father would supervise the morning shift, returning home in the afternoon. Ethel then took a bus to the business in the afternoon and worked until midnight three nights a week and on weekends with one of his father's partners.

"It was a very, very rough area," Hal said with that look of traveling to a distant place in his mind. "That they both survived was a miracle. The reason they did, I think, was because they dealt fairly with everyone ..." Then he paused, thoughtful. "...and, they were good friends with the police. They were surely protected by that."

Although Hal's mother worked in the family business, she was her husband's opposite in temperament and attitude. In part, this was likely due to that fact that in a time when women were not primarily in the workplace, Hal's mother was a "working woman." She was smart and effective – a businesswoman. Where Hal's father was all physicality and silent feeling, his mother was primarily mind and control.

"She was just very busy – and non-physical," Hal said. "She wasn't what we would call a touchy/feely person. It wasn't that she wouldn't give you a hug or something; she was just generally not a physically affectionate woman." As is the case in many families, generational experience differs. How our parents remember their parents is often very different from the grandchildren's relationship with the same people. It is the same with Hal's daughter Tamar. In a later conversation with me, she reminisced about her grandmother from a very different angle.

"I know my Dad had a very different experience when he was young, but my Grandma Stone was an amazing Jewish grandmother," Tamar said when we spoke over the phone. "She loved to prepare meals. I was young when she died, but I adored her, and felt loved by her. The best was when my brother and I spent the night. She would take us out to eat chopped liver!"

Left to right: Joseph Stone, age 70, Edward Stone, age 68, and Hal Stone, age 61.

Hal was the youngest of three boys born to the Stone family. His brother Joseph was eight years older than Hal. His middle brother Ed was six-and-a-half years older. It was clear early on that Joseph had his mother's primary interest. Although Hal acknowledges that his mother certainly loved his middle brother and himself, it was obvious who in the family was the favorite.

"Joe was definitely the power person in the family," Hal said softly. "He turned out to be a brilliant man … a true extrovert and a very hard act to follow for anyone who would have to come along after him. But I think Ed took the biggest hit in terms of comparison as we went through school."

A familiar theme ran through the brothers' history, the theme many siblings who follow older siblings through a school system both suffer and endure. Comparisons are inevitable. Roles divided around temperament and intellectual inclinations.

"I came into the family like the 'third brother' of a fairy tale," Hal said. "I was the 'magical child', the 'good child,' the 'special child' of the family …" he added beginning to laugh. "…who then had to spend a multitude of years in therapy to find his power base in the world!"

Like many brothers, Hal and Joe were complete opposites. In fact, his oldest brother was the opposite in every way of his father as well. But there was no real difficulty with Joe for Hal until Hal himself reached adolescence. "I was at the height of my inferiority and inadequacy," he said, wincing. "I saw Joe as too strong, too extroverted, too sexual … too everything, really. A good many people in the family didn't like him much, especially the women. He could be very teasing, judgmental and sarcastic. He alienated a lot of women that way."

Fortunately for Hal, his middle brother Ed took a more nurturing role with him. With his mother away so much, and Joe leading his own life, Hal was a child alone, left to his own devices. It helped Ed as much as Hal to have the connection that formed between them. Ed was simply there for Hal on a certain level.

"Of course, I've done a lot of work on these relationships over the years," Hal commented. "But after watching the unconscious at work for as long as I have, I understand you never know what you've really solved and what you haven't solved. I would never assume that I have everything tucked away in terms of my family." The reality of the psyche proves that Hal is quite right. These early relationship issues go on and on over time and touch deeper and deeper levels. Just as one thinks they might have it all tied up neatly, something will surface, and the story begins all over again.

"So, I feel quite clear with my family, but that in itself doesn't really mean much for anyone," Hal said, laughing again. "Tonight, after you leave, I could come up with a whole scenario about them and that time in my life, and I'll have to work through it again! It's unbelievable, the way this stuff works."

Indeed, the tenacity of some of these early issues is more than impressive. Hal and Sidra never fail to reiterate this fact in their various workshops and seminars. As recently as 2011, Hal addressed a group of students, advising them that they may as well accept this return to old issues as the process. "And even as I'm saying it," he said, "I hear a voice in me that begins to get upset about having to go back into something! I mean, what's the rule that says you're not supposed to go around the barn again? It reminds me that one part of me surrenders to the process, and another part of me is afraid. That's just how it is. Who knows how it's 'supposed' to be? Well, a lot of people think they know," he added. "But I think we don't really."[7]

Whenever a discussion of inner voices comes up, Hal is quick to point out the importance of continuing the work. As people know who have been in analysis and "finished," the analysis then continues in a different, "in house" form. In this case, he highlighted the importance of doing the work on one's Inner Critic.

"If you haven't resolved these Critic issues … not one hundred percent, but close, you're in trouble," he said. "If you still have an Inner Critic that chops you up for having to keep working on these old issues, it's very difficult to address the Higher Energies with authority later on. The Critic is the only system in the personality that can really cut the legs out from under you. When you have a strong Critic, it doesn't give you the right to demand anything in your life."

This is a good example of the creativity that characterizes the work the Stones embraced, even in the early days of formulating their ideas. The expression "embracing" one's Inner Critic points to their ability to hold everything equally and bring it to life. While this might echo Jung's work with the "shadow", Hal and Sidra brought to life what relationship to such an inner structure might feel and look like. It was revolutionary at a time when consciousness preferred another direction.

The morning sun began to warm the land and the office, and Hal's reverie revealed an image of a childhood painted in muted colors. In spite of the company of a number of housekeepers, and older siblings, Hal's main memory of his early life was that he was alone. He talked about developing a way of staying in fantasy a lot of the time. Although he no longer remembers how he managed that exactly, he looks back to it as a fairly evolved fantasy system.

"Later on," he said, "when I began my Jungian analysis, I did one of those family picture drawings. I used to draw a picture of a boat, and in it were a mother figure, a father figure and a child. It was only over the course of the analysis that the child became two children, and then three. I really was a solitary, visionary child in the beginning."

Hal credits his analysis with the realization that such a visionary child had the potential to become very disturbed. At a certain point, Hal reflected that it could have gone either way. Like Jung, if he hadn't taken the path that led him to working with that child and those visions, he might have turned down a very dangerous road.

"I realized during my analytic work that there are certain dangers inherent in living too much in that kind of reverie," he said. "I experienced it later as a kind of unhealthy introversion. I would be into myself, but really disconnected from anything else. In contrast to that would be a creative introversion, where one's energies go into oneself, but without losing one's relationship to the rest of the world."

As the morning's conversation went on, it was clear that Hal didn't receive the kind of caretaking that many children have. He and his brothers went through the three local schools in succession, so his orientation and support system began to look like a house divided. Like the stories of many siblings who follow one another through a school system, the teachers remembered and compared both Hal and Ed to their older brother Joe. According to Hal, Joe was a genius; a very bright and extroverted. He fit the profile of a "special son" on every level. Although the relationship carried with it a number of things to work out in his early analysis, Joe remained a father figure to Hal. With two father figures, one introverted and successful (Sam Stone) and one extroverted successful man (Joe), Hal carried two very opposite and powerfully conflicted influences into his early analytic work.

As his story unfolded before me, it wasn't hard to see that Detroit itself never offered Hal much in terms of spirit of place, or its spirit was incompatible with Hal's more sensitive nature. Perhaps the racial tensions and the talk of the war during the 1930's contributed to the kind of missing security and contentment that some landscapes provide. It was clearly a time of uncertainty and anxiety. By 1939, World War II had begun and U.S. participation in it was looking to be inevitable.

In response to the unsettling situation, Hal's parents began to collect extra stores of liquor, whatever they could afford. Like many businesses, practicing this kind of foresight was commonplace in response to the threatened wartime scarcity of supplies. By 1941 they had a good stock of liquor. But when a race riot broke out, looters broke into all the businesses in Detroit. Everything was taken.

"Yes," Hal said, "it was sad. Although my parents were on extraordinarily good terms with people in the old neighborhood, a riot is still a riot. That store of liquor was worth a great deal of money. Their business would have been worth several million dollars, if that hadn't happened."

Hal doubted that his parents would have ever left the Midwest had it not been for the riot. This early reflection perhaps speaks to an understanding of some larger forces at work. These might, in hindsight, have shown themselves very early in Hal's life, although at the time, the facts of the situation looked more like a loss than a gain.

As Jung advises in his autobiography, we can't really frame the events of a person's life in the context of being the best or worst of happenings. What looks like the boon today may, down the road, prove to be a disaster, and the reverse is also often true. Jungian analyst James Hollis would concur. In his 2013 book, *Hauntings,* he reflects on the meaning of a powerful dream he had, addressing a similar understanding.

"What I was forgetting was that the disparate parts of our busy world, which so easily can fall into disunity and neurosis, are also in service to profound currents that seek to shape and move us toward greater personal consciousness, on the one hand, and, on the other, the progressive surrender to participation in a cosmic consciousness." [8]

By the early 1940's, Hal was already enrolled at Wayne State University. His oldest brother was in the Navy and his middle brother was an Army officer. When the war ended, Sam and Ethel Stone's ties to their business had been broken by their loss. So, when his older brother Joe moved to California, Hal's mother wanted to go west as well. When Hal finished his semester at Wayne State, he followed.

One of the beautiful things about knowing how a story ends rests in the possibility of finding the theme of the page you're on linked firmly to the beginning. Hal's early life contains one of those threads, although it's unlikely he was even aware of it at the time. If he were to reflect on the material that takes his attention these days, the intervention and evidence of something larger, an Organizing Intelligence or Source Energy, guiding the path of our lives, I think he might see in the Detroit riots just such an event. While the riots were disappointing and financially disastrous for his parents, they precipitated a life-changing move into a new culture and identity for Hal.

"It was February of 1945," he said. "The war was still on. It was very difficult to get across the country at the time. Most travel then was by rail, and seats were very hard to get. When I finally got a seat, I remember arriving in Ogden, Utah, wearing my giant flaming red Detroit lumber jacket; the kind of jacket that would keep you warm in a hundred thousand degrees below zero!" he laughed, enjoying his own exaggeration. "I stepped out of the train, and it was hot! That was the beginning of my love affair with the West Coast. When I hit Hollywood, California it was ninety degrees. I loved it."

So, it began. No fanfare, no initiation … something as simple as a change in climate, but for Hal it was a life-changing moment. It was several weeks later that he embraced a new identity as well, because he had come to California using the name Harold, his given name. It was never a favorite.

39

"I was staying with my parents then," he said. "I was just seventeen. I was enrolling in UCLA. My father drove me to school because, as with some other milestones of adolescence, I hadn't yet learned to drive. We picked up a hitchhiker on the way, who introduced himself and asked me my name. I answered that my name was Harold, and he gave me one of those extroverted glad hands and said, 'Hi, Hal'. That was the beginning of my formal 'schizophrenia'. Although members of my family continued to call me Harold, I took on Hal for everything else. I'm very grateful to that hitchhiker, you can be sure. It began my path to things becoming more natural."

CHAPTER THREE

"The Best Things in Life Are Free"

Although Hal's sense of early identity did not come from his actual birthplace, his sense of belonging surely came alive once he found the West Coast. This idea about the spirit of place is significant for many people. For some, their original geography shapes them, binds them to an inescapable heritage. Others hide from their beginnings or idealize them like a lovely secret. As the initial interviews with the Stones continued, the remnants of their early histories surfaced like separate watercolors, the shapes and intensity varying by virtue of power, impact, and receptivity.

Questions of how deeply geographical roots attach in the psyche and how they operate over time have been the focus of many psychological investigations. Jung clearly recognized the importance and unavoidable impact of birthplace. Speaking of a heritage that springs from closeness to the mountains, Jung looks to the Swiss Alps as a telling example.

The great peaks of the Alps rise up menacingly close, the might of the earth visibly dwarfs the will of man; threateningly alive, it holds him fast in its hollows and forces its will upon him. Here, where nature is mightier than man, none escapes her influence; ....[9]

For me, an American Midwestern heritage has often seemed to slow me down. I'm not sure that's always been a bad thing. My curiosity has often propelled me with speed, rather than the wisdom of reflection. My Ohio conservatism, though stifling at times, has tempered my judgment when my passions would counsel me otherwise. There is a certain "groundedness" to my being that I think comes from the land I grew up on. My soul's contours were shaped and nurtured by the greens and gold of Ohio summers, the soft sounds of stillness in the stands of Scotch pines and firs that dotted the surrounds of my family's farm.

The most meaningful experiences of my childhood rested softly in this country setting. My parents had returned from the war to a farm, un-landscaped and filled with boulders and tree stumps. Much like America itself, who busied herself with clearing away of the images of the horrors of World War II, my parents slowly cleared the land I later called a weekend's haven. They put down roots, spread grass seed, and pruned an old apple orchard, tending to my infant sister in a century farmhouse standing in the shadow of an immense pine tree.

As time went on, that piece of land became the foundation for my psychological and emotional balance. I recognize its familiar peacefulness when my mind needs rest and my soul drops into its private basement. I fancy my muse still lives among those pines and thorn apple trees. I feel her close to me as I sit in front of this work, considering the lives of two people whose destiny it has been to seek and talk about consciousness.

The first interview with Sidra began somewhat spontaneously, as we decided to jump right in the evening of my first day there. Realizing the limitations of my length of stay, Sidra and I settled down at the dining room table of their home. While rubbing my fingers over the Oriental rug that lays over the tabletop like an elegant cloth, I began talking excitedly about the opportunity to hear her story. Although the Stones have taught Voice Dialogue together all over the world, on a personal level,

Sidra is a more reserved and private person when it comes to her history. She has always seemed to prefer sharing her story in small pieces, tending to stop in case she's repeating herself.

So, her "formal" interviews began with some shyness. Her natural style of expression is the opposite of Hal's genuine delight in telling anecdotes or dreams any time the occasion presents itself. As the daylight faded, Sidra sat at the end of the table, pushing the ever-present vase of fresh flowers to the back. She waited as I fussed with the computer. I could feel her nervousness about the interview. I watched her stand toe to toe with her unassuming nature as it argued with her intention to just talk about herself as I had requested. But it wasn't long before the pleasure of memory trumped her innate reluctance to take center stage. She got into it!

Unlike Hal, Sidra was in touch with and strongly influenced by her surroundings as a child. It seemed when consciousness passed over Brooklyn in 1937, Sidra was already alert and receiving. Curious, it seems, since the minute after she was born, Sidra took in everything … people, places, environment … and everything impacted her. To be born in Brooklyn in the 1930's sounded like the adventure of a lifetime, although she would say she feels fortunate to have lived in all the places she landed over the years. But her recall of the things that impacted her infant psyche is nothing short of remarkable.

"I actually have a few very strong sense memories from the beginning of my life," she said, more causally than what was coming deserved. "I have a very clear memory of being a newborn, carried on the arm of a black nurse in a white uniform. She was crossing a freezing cold, white tiled room. She was holding me away from her body on an outstretched arm."

Since Sidra had come down with impetigo in the nursery, she endured a three-week hospital stay for treatment, and was separated from her mother. It wasn't long before she was allowed to go home, and her horizons expanded out into Brooklyn proper. City life in the 1930's was filled with sights and sounds that seemed boundless. "The first conscious memory I have of Brooklyn," she said, "and this is a very 1930's memory, is one of lying in a baby carriage, looking out. My mother was sitting next to me, rocking the carriage and singing "The Best Things in Life Are Free." We were outside a brewery, and although I wouldn't have known that at the time, I can still remember the smell of hops brewing and beer."

Sidra Sue Levi, age 4, Brooklyn, N.Y.

Although she couldn't speak, Sidra entered the world with her other senses operating at full throttle. Herman and Belle Levi's little girl awakened to the smells and sounds of the city that surrounded and contained her as a baby. She was nurtured on every level. "In truth," she said, "the song was right. The best things in life were free to me then. All I had to do was breathe."

Brooklyn in the 1930's and '40's was an incredible place to be. Like much of the country at the time, the city was exploding with optimism and opportunity. As inflated or exaggerated as it might have been, "Brooklynites" of the time had the sense that the city was filled with people who would get their start there. There was great idealism, and it was contagious. "The neighborhood I grew up in was poor," Sidra said with an undisguised ferocity. "But it was a 'working poor.' The people were blue collar, employed, and hardworking. It permeated everything in the culture."

Sidra's father was a high school teacher, specializing in economics and American history. Her mother worked as well, which was unusual for the times. Belle Levi completed two years of college and worked as a secretary. "She was very bright," Sidra said. "She worked for a Japanese import firm. She wanted to learn Japanese to become a better secretary, but they wouldn't let her." I could feel the bristling of Sidra's feminist leanings when she added with sarcasm, "They wanted the 'girls' to speak English only. Then male executives could have a secret language. They were pretty upset when she began to pick up a few of the Japanese words."

Once married, Belle Levi had to stop working, as her employment would imply that her husband couldn't support the family. Of course, it was true that a teacher's salary in the 1940's was barely enough to meet the needs of the family, but the cultural attitude of covering it up would prevail for many years to come. So, Sidra and her younger sister, Linda, benefitted from their mother's presence in the home, a distinct developmental experience that was denied Hal at the same age.

"I don't remember a sense of despair about it, though," Sidra said, referring to her mother's departure from the work force. "I mean, we used to get these lovely silk kimonos from the 1910's and '20's in Japan. We used to play dress up in them when we were little girls. So, when my mother left the company, those stopped coming. Even though leaving the work force was sad for my mother, we didn't let it get to us. The American dream was simply a part of what we all lived. There was a broad cultural promise that 'you could move up from here'."

45

Sidra delivered these facts with the verve of an anthem. I felt the spirit of the times and the city in the room with us, even as the light faded into a thick, forest darkness. She became animated in some parts of her story, feeling again the atmosphere surrounding her youth. "I was raised with a kind of split," she said. "What I mean is that I came into life with a very optimistic way of looking at life, but I landed in a place that was tremendously challenged economically. Moreover, I wasn't raised in a neighborhood where you were supposed to be nice, like many little girls."

As the picture of life in Brooklyn became clear, Sidra's statement made increasing sense. Children were supposed to behave. That was a given. Additionally, as good education was available and free, there was no question the opportunity to make something of oneself was out there for anyone who went after it. But every picture has its shadow and Brooklyn had a big one.

"We weren't naïve," Sidra said. "Everybody knew that when it came to admission into the good schools, there were quotas for both black people and Jews. So, if you were going to get ahead, you needed to be tough. Compared to how I am today, I was very tough back then. I fought physically with my sister, and I loved to wrestle. It was excellent preparation for me."

Sidra's whole demeanor changed as she relived some of this rich New York history. She talked at length about lessons learned in the city. Some of the seeds of understanding the work she did later with Hal can be traced to early subway encounters growing up. For instance, she credits Brooklyn with teaching her to put an energetic wall around herself.

"If you were in the subways of Brooklyn in the 1940's and '50's," she said with an experienced look, "there were always people doing things they shouldn't be doing … exposing themselves or rubbing up against you weirdly … things like that. It was just a part of life. Once when I was older, I was on the subway and a man started rubbing up against me. I knew what he was up to. I was wearing high heels at the time," she said smiling. "I just took my stiletto heel, rested it on the top of his foot, and ground down with my entire weight!"

Sidra's enjoyment of this story and her solution to the problem was obvious. She was gleeful in her ability to take care of herself, even in high heels. Although Sidra credits her mother's inner strength as an early role model, it was the neighborhood that nurtured Sidra's feisty Aries nature. Evenings in good weather were spent playing a street game called Ring-a-levio.[10]

"For me," she said, "the game epitomized my Brooklyn childhood. It held the opposites. It was great fun … and there was war!" Sidra was getting into this story now - with all the energy of the actual game. "We would divide the entire neighborhood in half. One group would hide, while the other closed their eyes. Then when they opened their eyes, they became hunters and warriors who went after the hidden ones. They had to catch you, physically subdue you, drag you to 'jail', and tie you up!"

Sounds pretty archetypal, no? While the archetype played itself out in the European theatre with real military personnel, Sidra and her neighborhood buddies played out a parallel drama in the streets. Sidra described the specific neighborhood her family lived in as having much the same composition as the European front. Ridgewood during World War II was a totally German neighborhood, with a few Italian and Irish families. According to history of the time, they were all on the other side of the war in those days.

"We were Jewish," Sidra said, "so we had to assimilate. We were supposed integrate, be invisible, but always be tough. There was a church and school in our neighborhood named St. Martin of Tours. It was a religious school. They openly taught terrible things about Jews. My sister and I played with the boys of the school, because none of the little Catholic girls would play with us. We had one friend, whose father was Jewish, and her mother was Catholic. She went to the Catholic school and was being torn apart. She became a friend, but no one else from there had anything to do with us." The thought of Sidra being treated in such a disrespectful and racist way still squeezes my heart. Who she has become seems so distant from a past tainted with discrimination and intolerance. But then again, maybe it doesn't.

In an aside, Sidra talked about the tenacity of these old ideas and attitudes. In the year before these conversations, her sister Linda had returned to their old neighborhood of Ridgewood to visit a cemetery in the area. The Jewish cemetery, named Knollwood, was right next to a very old, non-denominational cemetery named The Cemetery of the Evergreens. Her sister fell into conversation with the custodian, talking about where she grew up. She had told him the block she had lived on, telling him she was going over to Knollwood. He said, "Oh. You don't want to go over there. That's the Jewish cemetery." When Linda replied that she was, in fact, Jewish, the man rejoined, "You couldn't be. There were no Jews on the block you grew up on!"

So, when Sidra talked about needing to be invisible and tough as a girl, she was quite serious. She and her sister needed to be careful, especially about matters of faith. "My mother knew the territory. She had been raised in Brooklyn by immigrant parents," Sidra said with a sense of pride. "It was she who went to school, learned English, and came back and taught her parents the language." Sidra's maternal grandmother was from Austria; her maternal grandfather was from Russia, near the

Polish/Russian border. Her father's parents were both from Germany, which is why they lived in a German neighborhood. Sidra stressed by repetition, that they were very, very German.

Having immigrated with the great wave of people who came to the United States before World War I, Sidra's paternal grandparents settled where things were likely to remain familiar. The Germanic influence matched the conflicting forces of the times, and Sidra picked up on it.

"My neighborhood rewarded the warrior," she said. "It rewarded the 'not nice,' rewarded a lot of energies we would say are 'disowned' today. I grew up comfortable and familiar with archetypal evil, as well as archetypal warrior energy. Archetypal darkness was a presence. You just knew it was there ... always lurking. You dealt with it as best you could."

Sidra was only four years old when Pearl Harbor was bombed, but she remembers the sight of her father sitting at the kitchen table with his head in his hands. Herman Levi was generally unflappable, but in that moment, when the news came out that the U.S. fleet had been destroyed, Sidra knew dread for the first time in her life. Her father sat silently at the table. She felt his sense of doom.

"And we children played it all out in the neighborhood: playing War, Cowboys and Indians, and Ring-a-levio," she said. "Our games were war games. It was in us then, and it's in us now. To pretend that it's not is the problem. I know it's in my very being."

The sheer physicality of the wartime Brooklyn came alive in the hours I listened to Sidra. The city's sociological and cultural impact became palpable as she filled in the spaces with the images and sense perceptions of a child. "There was

49

constant bustle," she said, looking off into the back garden as if Brooklyn's skyline was out there. "I grew up with the sounds of the city."

Horses and wagons crowded the Brooklyn streets in the 1940's, delivering everything from milk in glass bottles to coal that was shoveled into the cellars of the apartment buildings the Levis lived in. Everything had a rhythm and sound of its own, from the clip clopping of the horses' hooves on the pavement, to the crunching sound they made when parked with their feed bags on their muzzles. Shovelfuls of coal made the transition from wagon to basement to waiting furnaces in underground rooms. The scraping of the shovels and the rush of coal down chutes offered their own brand of rough and steady background music to life in the city.

Brooklyn at the time was all about commerce in the streets and specialty stores. Meat stores had sawdust on the floors. Butchers of the day would go into the back and come out with a half side of beef on their backs. Slamming it down on a huge wooden butcher's block, the work began with a saw and then a knife until the cut of meat ordered was ready.

"Of course," Sidra said. "It wasn't the same for everyone. Gentry existed at the time. It was defined not by income, but by longevity. There were, what we called *nouveau riche* settlements. There was a big difference in New York between *nouveau riche* and Old Money. To be sure, it was Old Money who decided who was gentry and who was not. The "A list" people, the ones we didn't even know about, were invisible. They were real 'society.'"

Sidra's years in Brooklyn spanned times before the invention of television. Saturday afternoon movies were the social and recreational activities of the day. An afternoon's performance would include two full-length features, a newsreel, and three or four short subjects like "Looney Tunes," or an inspirational piece about the war.

"We also had the choice of going to downtown Brooklyn or Manhattan to the movies," Sidra said. "They were the most amazing because they were shown in the huge, old theatres. The RKO Manhattan and the Radio City Music Hall had exquisite stages on which you could see a quarter ballet, the Rockettes, a male singer, then a female singer, one or two chorus numbers and a movie! I grew up hearing Tony Martin sing and watching Cyd Charisse dance."

Sidra was eight years old when the war ended in 1945 and was reading well by then. She could read the newspaper. She remembers when they opened the death camps. The knowledge came to her like a terrible storm that ruins a picnic. As the accounts of the Holocaust and reported deaths proliferated, young Sidra felt impacted in a direct and brutal way. "Although these aren't the words I would have used at the time," she said, "I sensed that the grown-ups around me didn't feel the full impact of these atrocities on the psyche and the soul. But I knew that children couldn't protect themselves by buffering themselves with words, thoughts, concepts or explanations. We knew that what had happened was unspeakable, and that the very act of putting it into words lessened the horror and impact of the events themselves. For children, the horror went right in."

CHAPTER FOUR

Countdown to Launch

While there is little to dispute about the importance of environment and geography when it comes to shaping the psyche, the people in our lives hold a place of prominence, equal to if not greater than, the accidents of geography that impact us as we grow. As Hal's story continued, and memory moved from the 1940's to the 1950's, I dropped into my own reminiscences about a decade in which I had but blurry experience.

I was still quite young, but I remember my mother's grey Plymouth sedan. It was shaped like a half circle with wheels. It had only two doors and my sister and I always sat in the back seat. It was just big enough. Everybody had their place; parents in the front, kids in the back. We sang songs, as a family, as we drove around town. My father taught us army songs from World War II. In my innocence, I laughed at them because my father made faces at us as he sang. We were happy. The world felt safe to me as the late 1940'sforties yielded to the '50's. The future was bright. But as we settled into Hal's office the second evening, the threads he picked up from the day before wove a very different tapestry. The atmosphere of the times he remembered had little to do with safety. He moved, not without pressure, toward a second and very significant set of decisions that became the building blocks of his career.

As Sam and Ethel Stone settled into life in California, Hal finished his college work and began a social life. My expectation was that his family's faith would have dictated some of their choices, as reactions to the Holocaust heightened everyone's awareness at the time, but this wasn't the case for Hal. His family wasn't observant, about which his parents had opposing reactions.

52

"My father had no guilt about it," Hal said. "I honestly don't think he even thought about religion. My mother, on the other hand, was a guilty non-observer. What that meant was that she wanted to keep a kosher home, but she projected all the 'no/no's' about that onto her sons. She had the idea she was making us suffer if she was strictly kosher."

So, Ethel Stone kept a kosher home, but if the family went out to breakfast, Hal's parents made sure that the boys had piles of bacon to compensate for her attempts at orthodoxy. Hal chuckled at the memory. But the humor of that particular conflict faded quickly as Hal's attention turned to genuine reflection on matters of faith. "I never had any serious Jewish education," he said. "Even for my Bar Mitzvah, I went to Temple and learned what to do, and so forth. But that was pretty much it. At Passover there was always a Seder, but little else."

The senior Stones had relatives who had also moved to southern California, and Hal became close friends with one of his younger cousins. His expression led me to believe his memories were fond ones when he spoke of their relationship as brotherly. He felt the closest to Herb Gelfand," and his older sister Audrey, and their parents, Helen and Julie. They were always warm and connected to Hal, like a surrogate family. It is sometimes the case that creative projects and people find benefactors or sponsors. This relationship with Herb became something like that for Hal.

"Herb was a genius in real estate," Hal said. "Together with his wife Beverly, they shared their success with me and became the most generous benefactors I could imagine." Many years in the future at this point in the story, when Hal started the Center for the Healing Arts in 1973, he found himself at his lowest imaginable point. He was working fulltime in his private practice, his marriage was coming to an end, and he was working out the financial settlement. He was in the midst of starting a major non-profit Educational and Research Center with very low funding. It was then that Herb and his wife approached Hal with a generous offer to help financially until things returned to normal. This was to become a role Herb seemed to take on behind the scenes in Hal's life. Even as recently as 2014, when Hal had a stroke, he was again feeling very close to the edge health-wise. Herb again insisted on offering financial help, even though he knew nothing about Hal's financial situation. This life-long connection remains of great value to him even now, like a "protective angel" behind the scenery of his life.

Angels aside, Hal would refer to himself as pretty atheistic back then, although he wouldn't have used that word. He had tried to make some connection to the faith of his ancestors, but nothing really worked for him until he got into the study of mystical Judaism.

"After I started my Jungian analysis, I had a very real religious experience," Hal said. "I felt the presence of powerful entities coming into me. It was amazing and that started me on a kind of search."[11] Hal paused for a moment during this reflection, running his hand through his hair. "The truth is I just wasn't very happy. All my life, I felt frozen and unfulfilled. I didn't really feel happiness until I started my analysis. I was only twenty-two years old. But somehow, from the very beginning, when the dreams started to come in, I had some kind of intuitive recognition, like 'What the hell is inside of me? This is unbelievable!'"

What Hal was most smitten by in those early years was the nature of the Intelligence of the dream process. Although he wouldn't have words for it for some time to come, he knew for certain there was something much larger at work there. This discovery, and his excitement around it, made it clear. Not only was this an awakening of the first order, it was clear that his amazement about it has never really gone away. Furthermore, Hal makes the easy connection of this event to his current ideas about the Intelligence of the universe that he now talks about with greater clarity. "Even back then," he said, "I had some understanding of an Organizing Intelligence that arranges dreams and organizes what comes next in a life. I was awestruck when that happened, and from the moment that started for me, I never felt alone again."

As an analyst myself, I can well imagine the impact of such experiences, and marvel that they came to someone as young as Hal was at the time. However unusual that might be, the difficulties he endured as a youth never bothered him again. Life naturally brought him challenge and sadness, but he had come to a recognition, an understanding of that ignition of something at such a deep level. It all happened for him on what he would describe as another level of being.

But before that, prior to this awakening, Hal's story rang like the sound of a lone chime. He seemed lost. He had begun college at the age of sixteen and had his bachelor's degree by nineteen. His older brother had become an attorney. That was a very important thing in the eyes of his mother. His middle brother had become an accountant, which was also approved of by Ethel Stone. But she longed for a son who was a doctor. The job fell to Hal.

His journey took a left turn at age nineteen, and he became a struggling pre-med student, emphasis on the word "struggling".

"Honest to God," he said, laughing with incredulity at his own experience, "I must have had angels working on my behalf. I didn't know what the hell I was doing, and I had no one to ask. I didn't even mind that my parents didn't advise me, because I knew they couldn't do it. My brothers couldn't help either because I lived in a very different world. I was like

Hal Stone, late twenties

the youngest brother in the fairytale who lived in the world of the dream, imagination, and fantasy. I just wasn't too great in the 'What-do-you-do-in-the-world part."

So, Hal did what he had to do. He jumped into pre-med only to discover very quickly how a course of study could bomb. He still laughs at how impossibly lost he felt. A change in career seemed a good plan, so Hal, still quite young for the importance of these decisions, looked toward teaching. His education courses went well and after making up for some unfortunate grades in the sciences, he landed a teaching credential. He even applied for an actual teaching job out in the desert.

"Fortunately, I got turned down," Hal said. "But I did get to do some practice teaching. I was lucky that the kids survived it, because I sure didn't know what I was doing." But what he lacked in knowledge, Hal made up for in relationship. He enjoyed the kids and tried a number of unorthodox things to engage their willingness to learn. Hal's supervising teacher noted that he didn't really know a lot about the subject of Science. But he also noted that Hal was very, very good with the kids.

But his ability to get along with and engage young minds wasn't sufficient inspiration to make him a teacher. So, he began to search in another direction. He had already acquired a BA in psychology and he turned his attention to graduate studies.

"I thought maybe I'd get a master's degree," he said, warming up to something that clearly still amazed him. "But you have to understand; I didn't even have a good functioning mind available to me yet. I had no idea what I was doing."

The picture was becoming alarmingly clear, at least alarming in the sense that his telling of the story was so infectious. I joined him in a shared anxiety about the end of the story, judging from its promise thus far. To complicate things further, Hal was the teaching assistant for three or four people in the psychology department, and responsible for the rent of his own apartment.

"So, there I was," he said, "working like crazy. I had a degree, and was pursuing graduate work, but I had learned nothing really. My studies had essentially no meaning for me whatsoever! I was the prime example of somebody who had a very strong mind that had nothing to do with who he was … absolutely nothing. I couldn't put my mind into gear for the pre-med stuff because it just didn't want to go there. Then it went to work for the other stuff, but that had nothing to do with me either. I remembered nothing."

The truth is, though, that Hal remains very grateful for that graduate school time, because first and foremost it gave him something to do. He had no idea what to do with himself, a condition I expect is not so unfamiliar even today when many college students are required to declare a major when they've barely figured out how to feed and clothe themselves without help. So, Hal consulted a psychology professor he'd been doing research for and things began to make sense. They talked about getting a master's degree, compared to a slightly longer exam process that would serve as a qualifying exam for the Ph.D. program. After they finished, the professor said to Hal, "You know, sometimes when I'm with you, I don't know if you're the brightest graduate student we have in the school, or the dumbest!"

With that send off, Hal faced his decision head on. The prospect of becoming a doctoral candidate was appealing, even though, believe it or not, he had no idea what it meant to be a psychologist. "I didn't know why I was doing what I was doing, but I was doing it," he said. So, it began. Hal set his sights on the PhD, and the course of his life changed accordingly. But he knew the answer to his professor's confusion. Hal was convinced he was the dumbest student, because he couldn't have talked about his mind as separate from who he was. But Hal knew his mind could do things he couldn't do on his own. He could put it to work … and work it did.

He had a mere four months to prepare for the exams. He was carrying a course load at school and working several other jobs. So, Hal went to his parents and asked to move home for a while to devote himself to full time study. "My parents were genuinely delighted to have me while I worked my tail off to prepare for the exams," he said. "It was the first time I'd ever applied myself in that way. I took the exams and passed them in 1951."

The 1950's for Hal were not the times of safety and normalcy I experienced in my Midwestern childhood. The Korean War had started in 1950, alerting the draft board to Hal's status. He'd gotten a number of deferments for military service, which once he entered graduate school, continued to keep him safe from the draft. But there was little that reassured him in those days. Passing the entrance exams was only the beginning of the hurdles he would have to jump as the race continued. Now that he was in the doctoral program, Hal was temporarily safe from the draft. Feeling some relief about that, he moved back into his apartment, only to meet another challenge. He found he was terrified of graduate school. It was then that Hal met a man named Bruno Klopfer, now considered one of the first Rorschach pioneers, and one of the first real clinicians hired by the school. But most of all, he was what Hal would call "a real human being."

As pressures mounted for everyone at the time, it seems the university did its best to increase them. Hal remembers all of the graduate students being called together. At their first meeting, they were informed that the program they were about to enter was so difficult, half of them would drop out by the end of the term. Then during the next year, another half would be weeded out. It's hard to imagine the rationale behind such misguided efforts at motivation. Like brutal and outdated management techniques, many of these threatening opening addresses have survived today, to which the stories of my physician friends testify. Competition was fierce then. I think little has changed even now.

But amid the threats, Bruno Klopfer stood up and said to the group, "If any of you have any issues or problems, please feel free to come to my office. I, or somebody I appoint, will spend time with you." To Hal, this was another moment of awakening, for it was the first time anyone had connected the idea of helping people to the context of what he had been studying.

"Remember," he said, "all the intense studying I was doing was not about Clinical Psychology. I had studied some clinical material to pass the exams. But that was it. I had to get three A's and a B in my coursework then or I'd have to wait another year. So, the pressure was really on. But when Bruno Kopfer said what he did, somewhere in me there was a spark ... a certain kind of knowing. Within six months of that meeting, six of us had begun a Jungian analysis."

As the pressure grew, Hal continued to sweat it out. By the time he made it to Bruno's office, he was in a full anxiety attack. He signed on with relief. "I then began my analysis with Jay Dunn and everything changed," he said. "It didn't matter anymore about graduate school lacking meaning for me. I was so grateful to have it. Whatever else escaped me, I realized that I was launched. It ceased to matter what I had to study at UCLA, or if it had meaning. I was satisfied in my analysis."

So, a small group of initiates formed. Marvin Spiegelman, Stan Green, Rob Stein, Harvey Mindess, and Hal Stone began analysis then and there. Bruno put the word out to the analytical society. Max Zeller and Jay Dunn, among others, were two of the analysts who volunteered their time to work with the students Bruno steered their way.

"It was in 1949 I began analysis with Jay Dunn," Hal said. "But then to have Max Zeller to work with was icing on the cake. He was such a lovely man. To have someone like him at UCLA, for someone like me, was simply a miracle. I met his lovely wife, Laura, as well. They invited us to their home for little seminars. It was wonderful."

Meanwhile, the draft loomed large, following Hal every step of the way. Then on the day of Yom Kippur in 1951, Hal received an induction notice from his draft board. His student deferment had been turned down.

"Now in those days," Hal said, "if you were drafted you went into the infantry and on to Korea. There was nothing funny about it. It was a bad war … a difficult war … and I was afraid. The hardest part at the time was that I had no one to talk to. I know that also had something to do with who I was then. But that's how it was."

One day, by design or divine intervention, Hal ended up perusing the UCLA bulletin board where all the notices were posted for courses, seminars and alternate learning opportunities. His eyes fell upon a single announcement amid the clutter, which read: "Senior Psychology Student Training Program. If you're a qualified graduate student at this institution, you can enter this program, and immediately be commissioned as a Second Lieutenant." Hal took one look at the induction notice in his hand, and one more look at the posting. He wrote down the number.

"Now, first of all," Hal said, "this meant money … $500-$600 a month, which was a fortune then! Better yet, I read on to find that they offered a one-year internship in Clinical Psychology, which didn't even exist at the university level. Clinical Psychology wasn't even a separate field yet anywhere else." Hal quickly made a personal call to the colonel in charge of the program in Washington, D.C. After explaining his difficulty and the urgency of his desire to join the army, the Colonel told him to get an application in the mail, and he would take care of this induction notice. This was in the fall of 1950. By February of 1951, Hal was at Letterman

Hospital in San Francisco, California, beginning his internship. Another year passed, and he had that internship in his back pocket as he returned to UCLA to finish his course work and dissertation.

At this point, the material he was learning was completely foreign to him. He still didn't feel like he knew what he was doing, but his mind was definitely engaged. This ability to let his mind lead the way when other aspects of his psyche were not strong yet, rests as the basis for a later understanding he would call the Primary Self system. He would later explain that Primary Selves allow people to adapt and survive relying on their strengths before the entire personality is in balance. So, Hal got his mind in gear and gave it gas. It was a tremendous effort, sometimes using his military leave to work on his studies. An internship under his belt and a lot of determination allowed Hal to finish up in thirteen months. "Ordinarily, a dissertation would take an extra year," he said. "But I needed to be done. So, when I wanted approval for something, I would go in my uniform." By then Hal was a First Lieutenant and the war was still on. It was a time when a man in military dress was one of the good guys. Hal would go to his committee with orders in hand, saying, "I have to report to Fort Bliss, Texas, to the Mental Hygiene Consultation Unit." If there was any resistance, he'd add, "They're waiting for me. I have to report in three weeks." Hal laughed talking about his good fortune. "They couldn't really mess with me like dissertation committees sometimes do: 'do this and do that and rewrite everything.' They just didn't do that. I got through the dissertation in a very short time. But to be sure," he said, "I worked my ass off."

With his PhD in hand, Hal was off and running. He was a functioning clinician, involved in interesting work. He loved his time in the military. He was in Fort Bliss for a year and a half. He talked about seeing hundreds, maybe thousands of people during that time. "I would see as many as ten to fifteen people a day at the

62

Mental Hygiene Clinic," he said. "Of course, I did evaluations then, not therapy." Most of the men he saw were troops who had served time in the Korean War. Hal spent sixteen months using the Rorschach test as an evaluating instrument. "We did ten-minute Rorschach tests then," he said. "Once I learned how to administer the test, I found I had a natural intuition I could trust more and more. There was no question I knew what I was doing. I felt at home in my work and I knew it."

Hal had married his first wife, Audrey Casman, (now Thea Saroyan) in 1951 while still in San Francisco. Two years into his time at Fort Bliss, their son Joshua was born. "Audrey was nineteen years old when we married," Hal said, "and I was twenty-three. We were quite young, and, in looking back, we were appropriately unconscious. My therapeutic work seemed to be about me and my process back then. I had no idea about relationship as teacher. That's just how it was in those days."

As he finished his work at Fort Bliss, some news came to Hal that was to extend his time in the army. "What I didn't know in the beginning," he said, "was that I had to go into the regular army after my clinical experience. I was so anxious when I signed up, I just couldn't take in that particular detail." Hal next spent an additional six months in San Antonio, Texas doing a regular Army basic training. He learned to shoot, read maps, get through obstacle courses … the works. Although it sounds incongruous given his intellectual leanings, Hal has always been an athlete and he enjoyed the training. This was followed by a two-year stretch at Madigan General Hospital in Tacoma, Washington during which Hal pursued an essentially full-time private practice while still in the military. He remembered it as a wonderful opportunity, even though he was still serving in the military.

By the spring of 1957, Hal's military service was coming to an end. Their son Joshua was three years old, and Hal and his first wife, then pregnant with their daughter Judith (now J. Tamar Stone) were preparing to return to civilian life in Los Angeles, California. From there, things really began to gel. Hal was on his way.

CHAPTER FIVE

The Ancestors –
You Gotta Love 'Em

I loved sitting in the afternoon light, listening to Hal's stories, imagining times rendered in different colors than the ones I recognized as his life. I liked the image of Hal in uniform and the gradual adjustment to his California self. I recognized the seeds of his future in his discovery of his unconscious. I could relate to it. For me, like Hal, it was like no other experience. But the experiences of history can't alone shape the man or the woman; and I think it's probable that we're all profoundly affected by the people with whom we grow up. Parents, siblings, aunts and uncles, cousins and best friends all contribute to our growth in ways we only later remember with fondness or forgiveness. I suppose my personality was formed in some ways around my sister's struggle with a handicap that left her weakened and resentful of my normality. I imprinted on her like a chick, and she was my first friend and my first enemy. How that might have pointed me toward the helping professions and a lifetime of encouraging others to take a running start toward their dreams, is a thought I entertain every now and then with a mild curiosity.

There were others, of course. It was my mother's sister, my beloved Aunt Julie, who nurtured my absolute fascination with and enjoyment of the outrageous; the kind of sidesplitting humor that only an energetic transfusion can offer between a loving adult and a child being let in on a secret. My great Aunt Brodie – every family has one – who drank beer and found dance partners at the stone quarry for lack of a proper dance floor, embarrassed and enraged my small town southern family. She still leaves me laughing in the halls of family history. These people are the stuff of character, offering us tolerance and empathy for the paths chosen that didn't really work out that well, and the ancestors in us who chose them.

We settled into Sidra's office at the other end of the house. She busied herself with building a fire as I settled into a seat near my computer. (I'm secretly convinced it can't function correctly unless I make small offerings of anxiety as I proceed in big projects on it.) The stories she told, and the family members who peopled them, show up in who she has become. The mix of influences and the play of opposites surely shaped her and laid a personal foundation of readiness for the work to come in her relationship with Hal. Once she began talking, I found myself relaxing into the tale, like a child at a story time library group. The details were rich and plentiful; the people colorful. I leaned back into my chair. My hands warmed around a cup of tea Sidra had insisted on making for me.

Although Sidra's environmental influences demanded that she toughen up on one front, there was also an element of great tenderness and softness to Sidra's childhood. This existed inside her home. Belle Levi created a space of safety and peace for her children. She made lovely doll clothes for her daughters and spent a lot of time with them. She taught them there was another side to wartime culture. And then, Sidra had additional education that most likely contributed to her later ability to stand between the opposites: the relationship she had with her grandparents. Although her grandfathers died fairly early in her life, she knew her grandmothers well, and they brought with them a lot of colorful and contrasting history.

Sidra's maternal grandfather's last name was Bolson, although one immigration document reads Berek Balshem. The family lore said that he was descended from the Baal Shem Tov,[12] the founder of a sect involved in ecstatic mystical Jewish explorations. "Whether or not that's true," Sidra said, "I don't really know. It could be one of those family legends. But what I know for certain is that my mother adored her father, who used to tell her wonderful Bible stories. And ... she heartily disapproved of her mother."

Her mother's side of the family lived in a part of Brooklyn that was foreign to Sidra. She described her grandparents as "very Eastern European Jewish people." They lived in the kind of neighborhood one could imagine from the movies of the period, filled with pushcarts and noise. Sidra's grandmother Flo spoke Yiddish and had come to this country at the age of twelve, lying that she was fourteen to get into the country. The journey to the New World was a rough one, and like many who made it through it once, Flo never went back to Europe. And according to Sidra, she never looked back either. Flo became one of those family members that some families have and prefer not to talk about ... except the latter in Sidra's case would be a shame. For Grandma Flo was wonderfully other. To keep her kind of colorful embarrassment a secret would be to rob the world of a fantastic character. "She was outrageous in every way," Sidra said. "She embarrassed everyone in the family. She was tall, very buxom, and grey-haired at age twenty. She dyed her hair a bright orangey-red. To add to the picture, she dressed in very striking, bold colors, had long blood-red fingernails ... and she gambled!"

As the stories went on, and Sidra assured me there were a million of them, it became clear that Grandma Flo was a woman ahead of her time. When she arrived in New York City she found lodging with an aunt who owned a flophouse in the lower East Side. Flophouses of the day were one of those creations spawned by poverty out of necessity; houses in which everyone slept in one room. And there was Flo ... blue-eyed, blonde at first, and buxom, as Sidra put it. When the uncles started going after her, her aunt married her off to Sidra's grandfather, the butcher on the corner who had fallen in love with her.

"Flo had three babies in a row before she figured out how they got there," Sidra said, laughing. "But once she figured that out, it never happened again. My mother, Belle, was the oldest, the responsible one, with two little sisters tagging after her." Sidra recreated her grandfather's butcher shop for me with wistful details. With a small garden in the back yard, there were always tomatoes, even in the middle of Brooklyn, and a bin filled with chicken feathers that Flo plucked to help her husband. But when work was over, Flo took off to the city, and left her husband with the children.

"In the early years," Sidra said, "Flo was a poker player. When she was older, she played the horses year-round. In the summer she stayed in New York, going to the harness races at Jamaica and Aqueduct. Then in the winter she'd go down to Hialeah. For the times, Flo's lifestyle was pretty unusual, but that's how it was with her. She was fascinating, really … incredibly outspoken, sexual, emotional … a real drama queen." Fortunately, Flo's husband adored her, so she had some leeway that other women of her time lacked. Furthermore, her interest in gambling wasn't just recreational. Flo was apparently good at it. She made a lot of money for the family.

During the Great Depression, Flo and her husband had a little apartment house in Brooklyn. "Nobody could pay rent, because nobody had money then," Sidra said. "So, my mother's two sisters, Dorothy and Rose, moved into the apartment house with their husbands. Rose went to work for *Sports Illustrated*. Dorothy took care of the house and fed the family. And Flo … well, she ran poker games on the whole ground floor of the apartment house. Then she collected a percentage of the pot. That's how they got through the toughest times while the Depression lasted."

Sidra's very German father disapproved of Flo's choices as much as her daughter Belle. Consequently, Sidra's and her sister's visits to their grandmother's house were infrequent and brief when they happened. "When we did go," Sidra said, "my father sat in the room and read the newspaper, in total disapproval. But we girls thought Flo was fascinating." The more Sidra described her, the more Flo took shape as one of the original entrepreneurs. When things were tight financially, Flo even set up a small cadre of seamstresses in the back of the house. Making dresses became another source of income during such difficult economic times.

"Honestly, I don't think Flo was afraid of anything," Sidra said. "She hung out in the speakeasies and gambling places of Manhattan early on, and never stopped. The story was that you never heard from Grandma Flo the week after her Social Security check arrived. Until the money was gone, she was just too busy gambling." Flo and her husband lived in a part of town that Sidra described as "kind of frightening." They had a two-bedroom apartment that looked dark and dirty, above a paint store. It was a very poor neighborhood. After Flo's husband died in 1945, she "took up" with a man named Izzy, who'd been renting a room from them. Sidra said she didn't think Flo had ever intended to marry Izzy. She was ultimately forced to though, when her daughter wouldn't allow him to come to her granddaughter's wedding unless Flo married him.

"So," Sidra said, laughing at the simplicity of an exceedingly non-romantic story, "they got married and Izzy came to the wedding. Izzy was as interesting as Grandma Flo in many ways. He spoke very little English, actually, but he was very funny. He was as dramatic as Grandma Flo and together ... talk about intense!" It seemed as if Sidra was showing me a movie, the telling of these stories was so real. I felt like I could see and hear the goings on of decades ago in the Levi family. "Grandma Flo and Izzy spoke Yiddish," she said. "My family ... not a word. Izzy would tell me jokes in Yiddish, and he laughed so hard, I laughed, too, even though I didn't understand anything he was saying! I never heard my mother speak Yiddish, save a few of those wonderful expressions that are so psychologically sensitive. Sadly, I've lost a lot of them now."

Izzy and Flo lived a long time, well into their nineties. Age seemed to diminish their juiciness not even a little. Well after Izzy and Flo had reached their respective eighties, Belle Levi apparently answered the phone one evening and it was Izzy, absolutely hysterical and sputtering in Yiddish. "It's your mother!" he screamed. "You've got to stop her! She's going to kill me! She's chasing me around the kitchen with a butcher's knife! Stop her! You've got to stop her!"

Sidra picked up the story, both of us laughing loudly now. "Then Grandma Flo got on the phone and said to my mother, 'Oh, don't worry. You know you've got the keep them on their toes. I'm not going to kill him. He's just been having an affair with some woman and I'm the laughing stock of Pitkin Avenue. I won't have it! I have to make him stop, that's all.' That was Grandma Flo!" Sidra said. "Never dull. But I was more proper then and embarrassed by her Yiddish speech and her outrageous appearance. She loved those brilliant colors ... always appearing in emerald green, fuchsia, or cobalt blue. Imagine that picture."

Not only could I imagine it, I loved doing so, always hoping these were only the early stories of her interview. Happily, they were. Flo stories rose to the surface of memory like bubbles in expensive champagne. In some of the anecdotes that trailed Flo's history the police were involved, a fact that seemed no surprise to anyone. By the time Grandma Flo had reached her mid-eighties, she was living in a high-rise senior apartment in Queens. Whatever one might imagine of life in past versions of retirement communities, there could be nothing close to how Flo sailed through her

70

maturity. "One night," Sidra said, picking up the thread, "the police came into her apartment and tore the phone off the wall. They told Grandma Flo she would have to stop taking book!" Undaunted, Flo wasn't out of business yet. It wasn't long before she contacted a local doctor for a letter to get her phone reinstalled.

"I'm an old lady," Sidra said, imitating her grandmother. "You're my doctor. You know I have a lot of things wrong with me. I need a phone in my apartment for an emergency. What if something happens to me," Sidra said, playing the "innocent" Flo with the skill of a veteran actress. Of course, Flo denied she had been making book, but this wasn't the only example of police involvement in the family history Sidra told so well. Not only did Flo make book, but she also became a taxi service for her contemporaries to go gambling at the racetrack.

Once the police stopped Flo for a minor traffic offense. "When the officer asked to see her license," Sidra said. "Flo slipped him some cash along with her license. He let her go. Everyone was upset about this incident. They thought Flo shouldn't be driving anymore, but she was adamant. 'How else will we get to the track,' Flo asked. 'So, I gave him a little money. You know how they are.'" Flo knew how the world worked then, alright. She used that knowledge to her advantage time and time again.

"I feel like I had a lot of her in me, even then," said Sidra. "I think I still have a certain amount of the irreverent, irrepressible quality that belongs to Grandma Flo. She always had a twinkle. She knew the absolute worst about people and laughed at it. I can do that, too. I have a very strong sense of black humor, which stood me in good stead later when I ran a California girls' home. I could find humor in things that would horrify others."

As delicious and powerful as Flo sounds, she wasn't the only influence in Sidra's colorful childhood. She had another grandmother, and this was Grandma Recha. If the term "opposites" needed an image, it would be Grandma Flo and Grandma Recha sitting side by side. Grandma Recha was Sidra's paternal grandmother. She was very German and very private. In contrast to Flo, Grandma Recha didn't really go out much at all. Today she would probably fit the criteria for agoraphobia. But actually, Sidra described her grandmother's condition as arrhythmia. She had fainted in the street one day, and when the doctor told her it could happen again, Recha never went out alone again. "She was just one of those people who needed a lot of control over her life," Sidra said. "She chose to live in a tiny little apartment, and believe me when I tell you, you could eat off the floor."

For all her eccentricities, Grandma Recha had some saving graces. For one, she was a wonderful storyteller. All of her stories began with the same setup: "When I was a little girl, I lived on the edge of the Black Forest with my three sisters and my mother and father." Then each story went on to develop its own adventure. "I wish I'd written those stories down," Sidra said. "They were simply wonderful. Her voice was so hypnotic. It just lulled you into a kind of trance state. It was beautiful and soothing." Nor were these Recha's only talents. Sidra talked about her grandmother's healing abilities, highlighting her healing touch and energy. "If you didn't feel well," Sidra said, "she would put a plaster[13] on you and lay her hand on top of it. You would just feel better by her touch and listening to her talk to you."

For Sidra, being in Grandma Recha's home was utterly peaceful. Much closer to her than to her Grandma Flo, Sidra spent a lot more time with her. Herman Levi was very attached to his mother and saw to it that she lived right around the corner from him. Sidra saw her every day. "She was a real cook and baker, too," Sidra said. "But she was what, today, we would call obsessive/compulsive. Being at

Grandma Recha's drove my sister crazy. It was too quiet and controlled. Worse, she made us wash our feet before getting into bed. We hadn't even been running barefoot! But we had to wash our feet, anyway."

For all her other issues, Recha was extremely frugal. Even during the hard times, she managed to save money. (She was the role model for a Primary self of Sidra's who is extremely well-known among Voice Dialogue enthusiasts who've heard her facilitation in teaching workshops. She's very, very frugal, clutching a tiny purse she opens only rarely. She came into being when Sidra was supporting herself and her children after her divorce.) Recha and her two other sisters eventually chipped in money to purchase a small farmhouse in upstate New York near the Catskill Mountains. The place was called Green Mount. It was a boarding house near the small town of Yulan. In the war years, people seeking refuge from the city would save their gas rationing coupons until they had enough saved for gas both ways. Then they would install themselves in Green Mount for a week or month at a time. Gathering supplies from the sole country store and one lone gas pump, New Yorkers from all walks of life retreated to the hills, where the demands of city life and the strife of the war fell away.

"It was sweet for me," Sidra said. "It gave me a taste for life in the country. We went up there every summer until 1946. But the truth is, my mother hated it there, and Grandma Flo ... never set foot on the place. She hated the country; even used to say that was the reason she left Austria ... to get away from the country. She loved city life. She never left it. At least my two grandmothers agreed on that, but very little else." Indeed, Sidra's grandmothers represented one of the foundational sets of opposites around which her personality was formed. Further, they generated the same dynamic with everyone. Sidra's mother worshipped Grandma Recha in the beginning. She was the epitome of the good wife and homemaker. It comes as no surprise that

Flo didn't concern herself with either of these roles. She didn't clean house, and didn't need to as her daughters, Belle Levi included, came regularly to do it for her.

"But Grandma Recha was a fantastic cook, as I said before," Sidra said, bringing her grandmother's energy into the room. "She made her husband 'look good'. You never actually saw her sit down to eat. She would just feed everybody. She had that strong German patriarch in her that I think I totally inherited … along with Grandma Flo's irrepressible rebel."

It took writing a book[14] to get herself out from under Recha's spell, but Sidra's understanding of it was clear … as clear as the old rules she so simply laid out for me. "Stand back and let your husband shine," Sidra said with some poorly concealed attitude. "Be quiet. You're a woman. You serve others. It's your job to keep everything flowing smoothly."

To hear these 1950's values coming from the Sidra I've known seemed incongruous, inciting me to object, or unnecessarily remind her of how differently she turned out. But there's little need of such reassurance. Sidra now lives a lesson learned and talks about herself with characteristic objectivity and compassion. "I lived those rules out to some degree in my first marriage," she said. "It was a time of the Inner Patriarch culturally as well as psychologically. Worse yet it included the devaluation of women by women. At first it came up in me in an attitude of superiority. I had a brain, a Ph.D., and I planned to use them both," she said, tilting her head back and forth for effect. "I had no interest in taking care of a man, a house, and children. I needed to find someone who would let me go to work and get on with a full life."

It's not hard to recognize Grandma Flo's energy in this manifesto that saw the light of day well ahead of the feminist movement. What feminism reacted to, Sidra

74

had already claimed. Like Grandma Flo, Sidra carried an energy that stood solidly in opposition to the cultural norm of her time. But she, too, was well ahead of the times for the 1950's. But what becomes clear in the telling, is that neither grandmother carried the day for long. Sidra's rich psychological inheritance honored all the gods or goddesses, so to speak, jumping into the fray on the other side when feminism made its debut. When the first feminist book came out, she didn't even read it. "The one I knew about directly was Betty Freidan's book, *The Feminine Mystique,*" she said. "It came out in 1963. Suddenly Grandma's Recha's sense of order and traditional roles welled up from deep within me. My first reaction to the book was 'Well, who's going to take care of the children?'" Sidra is quick to acknowledge that her grandmothers' influences were largely unconscious at the time. But that doesn't diminish her delight feeling into their energies when they are activated in the present - and her imitations of them … priceless.

"In reality, of course," she said, laughing about Flo and Recha, "they hated each other. There was a picture we used to have of the two of them at somebody's wedding. There were the two folks getting married in the middle, and the two grandmothers on opposite ends of the picture, looking like something really smelled bad in the room. The image still makes me laugh."

It made me laugh, too, while I appreciated anew the rich and fertile soil some of these relationships represent as seedbeds for the small souls planted in or near them. As the time went on, I regretted having to leave the sweetness of Sidra's emotional and colorful childhood. Moving on to other times and later years brought with it a nostalgia we both felt for the tenderness of early experiences and the juice that stays in them after all these years. But move on we had to, as did Sidra as life beckoned her to a still larger world.

CHAPTER SIX

Zurich and Back Again

It must be a sign of prosperity when one can talk about having *endured* an education. Or it could be a byproduct of luxury that many like myself spent four entire years being utterly lost while in college. Without direction or calling, I went on to graduate school for the simple reason that I didn't know what else to do. Moreover, I pursued a course of study that functionally prepared me to do very little in an extremely limited field. I could have been a French teacher. I'm not saying there's something wrong with that … just very far right of where I've ended up.

In this country, the gift of study is more commonplace and available than elsewhere. Although competition for spots in good American universities can be fierce, I've heard many stories like mine, tales of confusion and delayed focus, time indulged through the luxury of good fortune. What I understand from the perspective of three or four decades later, is learning itself is haunted by opportunity. Education's presence or absence marks the histories of individuals, influencing future choices and direction with silent and steady trajectories.

I didn't really awaken until the mid-1960's, but the rumblings of such could be clearly heard in the '50's. The alchemical mix and cook accomplished in my early youth, produced an explosion of curiosity and an insistent demand for change as I grew up. A new and dramatic attitude gelled into a consciousness that affected my life then like at no other time. I was on the move.

By the time I was pondering graduation from high school, college choices, and the impossibility of choosing a career path, the energy of unrest and intense awakening had already grabbed Hal Stone. He was well into his adulthood when he faced some of the most important urgings from his unconscious, leading him, as these choices often do, into directions that made little rational sense at the time. But the threads of interest laid out in the 1950's were durable, and my attention turned to Hal's early interest in and dedication to matters Jungian.

We settled into our chairs in his office as the sun turned the last of the evening sky to the color of a dusty rose. The flock of turkeys had left for the forest, the birds' characteristic clucking betraying their hiding places. The evening's small cadre of deer was already grazing quietly near the pond and under the apple trees. The weanlings had settled into the grasses while the does foraged nearby. A lone buck crossed the meadow in cadenced steps, slowly surveying his territory.

I had been looking forward to this session. I knew we would cover Hal's Jungian training and his time in Zurich. Although I was trying to develop my journalist's persona, the analyst in me is always a sucker for training stories. I couldn't wait. Hal leaned back in his usual style, his office swivel chair rocking him a little, allowing him to swing his body as his mind danced from memory to memory. I looked around the room, reconnecting to the soft couch, a warm throw, and the carved wooden dragon to my right. As darkness replaced the view through the windows, Hal smiled faintly. Cup of tea in hand, and the microphone light blinking its permission to begin, I let myself slip into Hal's story again, picking up the threads he'd left untied the morning before.

"So, I had been in analysis for about three years," he said, as if our conversation had been continuous since the day before. "I was getting to know the people in the Jungian group. They all sort of knew who I was, and many knew about my dream process, which was pretty astounding then. It was so clearly leading me in such an objective way. Not that it said, 'Do this'. But it was moving with strength and vigor. I knew to trust it. It was like coming home."

During every military leave, Hal had returned to Los Angeles to continue his analytic work with Jay Dunn. Hal was part of what he referred to as "a new wave of psychologists" and a very new group of analysands. At the time, traditional Jungian analysis dealt with second half of life issues. Yet there they were, a group of analysands in their twenties and thirties, seriously caught up in analytic work and with a new energy around it.

"Inevitably, of course, there were conflicts with senior analysts," Hal said. "I had my part in that. But really, I didn't care about those things. I was so excited about being in the process I had discovered. I wasn't at all interested in the politics of it. My own process was always primary for me."

By 1957, Hal had been discharged from military service as a Captain, and a licensed psychologist. He had changed analysts and begun working with Hilda Kirsch, exploring the possibility of training to become an analyst himself. As they were preparing to return to civilian life in Los Angeles, Thea became pregnant with their daughter, Judith (now J. Tamar Stone). Hal had already begun analytic training in Los Angeles when he heard about the grants to do a fellowship in Zurich. At that time, the Bollingen Foundation offered applicants a $4000 grant at the Jung Institut in Zurich to study for a period of three months. Although Hal was certain he wanted to go into analytic training, he had a wife with one young child and another on the way. His army salary sustained the family, but he had no real money and couldn't see how this would all play out. That's when the grant appeared on the horizon. The chance to study in Zurich was a wonderful opportunity he couldn't pass up.

"It meant leaving my wife alone while she was pregnant," he said. "It was quite selfish, really, but I felt in the long run, everybody would be a lot better off." So, he applied for the straight grant. After they evaluated him, they gave him the money. But finances were still very tight. The time in Switzerland pretty much used up the grant money. He still had to come back and even then, wouldn't have much to go on.

Although Hal might have been uncertain about how Switzerland might be, there were a number of things in place before his adventure found its legs. It is a common experience among analysands to develop a transference, or projected relationship onto their analyst's analyst. Hal was no exception. Since Hilda Kirsch's transference had been to Carl Meier, Hal followed suit and requested permission to analyze with him. Meier agreed to bi-weekly sessions. Many students at the time availed themselves of the opportunity to work with two analysts simultaneously, and Hal asked Marie Louise von-Franz to work with him as well. Everything seemed to be falling into place, so once again, Hal jumped in.

Naturally, he attended some of the courses at the Institut, but he soon lost interest. "I realized I simply wasn't in a place to take it in," he said. "I was caught in a conflict between my mind and my core process.[15] My mind had sent me there to study, and my core process refused to let me do so." I had to smile as Hal talked about sending a case of books ahead of his arrival. I remembered fondly packing an extra suitcase filled with books for training conferences as I studied for my Jungian fundamentals exams. I needed the security of being able to put my hands on the right volume, and Hal did likewise. But by the time things really got rolling, Hal found himself in his room, surrounded by books he couldn't read no matter how hard he tried.

"I mean, it was a joke!" he said. "I was suddenly a lost soul in a strange city. I didn't really know what to do. I finally ended up in the library at the Institut, looking for more books, because I couldn't read the ones I had!" Then, like an unexpected helper in a fairytale, a woman sitting at the desk in the library took one look at Hal and offered assistance. "She was very warm and caring," Hal said. "I explained to her that I was there on a grant for three months; that I had a case of books in my room waiting to be opened but I'd been blocked somehow from doing so. Worse, now I stood in a library full of books and I couldn't read them either!"

Indeed, Hal was stuck; and although his analysis was going well, it seemed to be the only thing he could do. His plan, of course, had been to include a great deal more. This kind-hearted woman told Hal that his situation was not uncommon for some who came to Zurich. "She understood that my mind wanted to get at it and learn it," Hal said, "but that sometimes it was necessary to start somewhere else." She explained that she was an art therapist and that her experience had been that when people allowed their imagination and creativity expression, it made a very big difference. She suggested that Hal try it out. This gracious woman turned out to be Annelia Jaffe, a well-known figure in Jungian history.[16]

Like many who are drawn to a Jungian analysis, Hal took to this kind of creative expression with real fervor. At first, he experimented with giant sheets of paper, trying different colors and paints. "I felt like I just went crazy," he said. "I was like a hot desert that had had no rain for many years. I think I scheduled appointments with her twice a week, in between my analysis. It was amazing."

As his story unfolded, the landscape of his memory changed as he reflected on his analytic experience in Zurich. The memories still held a lot of energy. Although

80

I was often ready with questions, I didn't have to ask them to keep him going. The story was all there.

"My analyses became very interesting, really," he said. "I had chosen Carl Meier because I was already connected to him through Hilda Kirsch, and others who spoke of him. I felt certain he would be able to carry my process. Marie Louise Von Franz was brilliant, as well. I loved her work with fairytales, expecting the work with her to be rich as well. But it was my head that chose her, and my heart that chose Meier. The result of those choices looked very different than I had expected before making them."

Hal described his work with Carl Meier as nearly perfect from the beginning. Meier allowed everything to come from the unconscious, without a lot of personal connection. But in hindsight, the down side of the relationship was that it contained very little linkage, or energy to connect them to each other personally; not enough what Jungians would call today *kinship libido*. Nonetheless, the work itself was important and meaningful to Hal.

The sessions with von Franz, however, were quite different. "They kind of dragged on," Hal said quietly. "She seemed preachy to me. It just wasn't working. She would talk for long periods of time, but it would seem like it had nothing to do with me. After about four sessions or so, I made up my mind that I would stop the analysis with her. What I planned to do was to go to her for the next session and tell her that although everything was going very well really, I had decided to stop working with her. You see, I wasn't going to tell the truth," Hal said with the look of someone enjoying telling on himself.

81

Like the foreshadowing in a fairytale, this dialogue smacked of drama to come, an expectation whose arrival I was not denied. As Hal set the stage for the next part of the story, I moved forward to the edge of my chair, anticipating the not-unknown-to-me consequence of choosing to lie to one's analyst.

"Now, von Franz lived a considerable distance from where I stayed," Hal said, capturing the mood and voice of the practiced storyteller he is. "It was a trip to get to her. So, on the morning of the fifth session, which was scheduled for 9:00 am, I woke up in plenty of time. I looked at the clocks … and I was in Switzerland … you know the clocks were right! So, I went out, found my roll and coffee, and headed to von Franz's house."

But the kicker was to come in the anteroom to his analyst's office. Hal arrived, took a seat, and waited. Hal continued to wait until it was clearly after the hour, when he sensed that something was wrong. Then his eyes fell on the little clock von Franz had on the table, displaying the time as after 10:00 am, not 9:00 am. Hal was stunned.

"I felt totally disoriented," he said. "I just had no idea what had happened. Then I realized that from the moment I had awakened in the morning, I had misread all the clocks. I had arrived for my analysis an hour late, missing my appointment. Von Franz was already working with someone else." Although uncertain about what he should do, Hal knew the training analysts would never let him sneak out of this one. He would have to man up to this. So, he knocked on von Franz's door. "She opened it, looking at me through a black cloud surrounding her," Hal said. "She was really angry." As he explained his misreading of the clocks and apologized, he offered her the fee for the day and rescheduled for the following week. Von Franz agreed and said that she was glad he was all right.

"You see," said Hal, "she didn't need the payment. When I went back, I shared everything. Afterward, she told me she had been unhappy from the beginning when she found out I was seeing Meier twice a week. She knew I was seeing her as a second choice and shared her feelings about that. She never had a chance to really be with me. We had a wonderful connection that hour," Hal said. "I told her that her work wasn't relevant to my life then; that someday it might be, but it wasn't then. The bridges to who I was were simply still missing."

As I sat with Hal in his office, it felt like I was in Zurich. I was completely caught up in the image of Marie Louise von Franz standing in the doorway. I could feel my resolve melting before the black cloud of anger surrounding her as if it had been me who had missed the session. Still a little uneasy, and more than a little impressed with Hal's courage and honesty, I was silent. Hal was not, fortunately. He showed me how the experience still yielded information as he looked at it through the lens of his maturity.

"What I think now is that the Organizing Intelligence really laid one on me," he said. "That missed meeting with von Franz was so profound. Think about it. For over a period of two or three hours, I completely misread every clock I passed and my own wristwatch! For something in the unconscious to have that kind of power over me, really impacted me. I've never forgotten to respect it since."

Although I was trying hard at the time to manage at least a semblance of objectivity, or at least partially so, my biographer/journalist/interviewer role became less defined. While there were certain things I wanted to know, it is sometimes more delightful to let someone tell their own story. Hal's recollections of this time and topic were richer than I could do justice to, and I knew it. So I waited for him to continue his personal musings.

"I didn't really have a transference to Jung," Hal said, kicking things off with a shocker for me as a card carrying Jungian devotee. Jumping to conclusions, as is my wont upon occasion, I couldn't believe someone who had the chance to meet Jung didn't immediately fall into a powerful transference with him. Hal didn't wait for me to gasp and went on. "But I had a transference to Jungian psychology. That said, I certainly wanted to see Jung when I was there. I'd written a 'nine thousand-page' letter to him before I got there, because I knew how hard it was to get an interview with him. He was already in his late seventies when I arrived. I was, of course, very excited when I learned I'd be able to meet him."

Hal continued, explaining, still unbelievably to me, that the most important thing about that visit with Jung was not meeting him in person. It was the dream Hal had had six weeks before he got to Europe. "It was one of the most significant dreams of my life," he said, and then began telling the dream as if he'd had it the night before.

"In the dream," he said, "I'm going to see Jung and my father shows up. I want him to go away but he's stuck to me like glue. I'm trying to get rid of him. I don't want him there. But he's sitting next to me like this is nothing. Then Jung walks in the room. He looks at me and says nothing. Then he looks at my father and they rush into each other's arms and embrace in this wild embrace, as if they hadn't seen each other for centuries! Then they start talking in Yiddish together and walk into Jung's consulting room! That was the end of the dream," he said, still feeling the impact of the experience.

I was mindful of Hal's statement about lacking a real transference to Jung, and even he had to admit that such a dream might indicate just the opposite. Of course, it's impossible to study Jung at depth and not have some kind of transference to the man. But usually, as Hal pointed out, in a transference there's a personal dimension in the relationship to the actual person. Hal felt little of that. But the transference with Jung was deep in Hal's unconscious. As the dream pointed out, the work in the realm of the father had already begun with Jung before Hal landed on Swiss soil.

"Of course, analytical psychology has given me enormous gifts," Hal said, again more to himself than to me. But then he began to smile, reliving a scene he was clearly watching on a private screen. "When I finally did meet Jung, I had a lot of questions, you know. Many of them I've talked about before. He was very funny, you know. Among other things, he did ask me why I was there. I said to him, 'Well, I just wanted to meet with you. I'm working with Meier, which is going extremely well. I just wanted to see you,' I said again. That was when Jung took up his pipe and began loading it. He sat very close to people, knee to knee. So, he leaned forward into me with this big pixie face of his, and he said, 'Well, then, take a good look.' It was very funny. It's a good memory," Hal said and then fell silent.

In a living experience of "six degrees of separation" all I could hear next was the humming of the cooling fan in my computer. I was grateful for the pause. Still caught in my own vicarious experience of Hal's meeting, I sat there frozen to my seat. I could imagine being knee to knee with Carl Jung, and now enjoyed being knee to knee with someone who'd had a session with Jung. As time goes on, there are fewer and fewer of those people. I admit it. Personal Jung stories delight me beyond all good sense. Even better, Hal wasn't finished, and continued with some nostalgia.

He mused about the connections he felt with Hilda Kirsch and Carl Meier, and other analysts with whom he had very good relationships. "It just didn't happen for me with Jung," Hal said. "I could feel it when I was with him. I mean, I was this young guy; just a kid compared to Jung. I was thirty years old in 1957, and he was

85

seventy-nine. But another factor was that I'm just not a very mental person; at least not mental in the way Jung was. I have a mind that functions well, but I'm not a Thinking Type. I'm much more of an Intuitive/Feeling Type."

Although I might have some romantic notions about my introduction to Jungian work and my own analyses, Hal shared little of my dreamy notions and wasn't hesitant to be plainly honest about his connections to Jungian work. "To be honest," Hal said, "with the exception of *Memories, Dreams and Reflections,* and *Two Essays in Analytical Psychology,* a lot of what I read, even in training, bored me. For that matter, a lot of the Jungian writing today strikes me in much the same way unless I feel some energetic connection to it … and it's that energy that's reflected in the way the material comes across. Unless something speaks to my heart, my soul in some way, I just don't have interest in it."

Of course, this struggle with differing typologies is both frustrating and commonplace, and in some way pertains to feelings of being with one's tribe or not, as Hal points out. But it's rare these days for Hal to draw such definite lines. So, he was quick to add more inclusive thoughts to his experience. "I don't mean this as a judgment," he said. "A big part of the world comes from that organizational place of the mind and loves it. I just find that it limits me. Jung was a genius. He had an amazing mind. But he wasn't energetically connected in the way I understand it today. Even at the age of 30, that's how I was operating, except I wouldn't have articulated it that way at the time. Back then, I just felt inferior."

It's hard not to appreciate this kind of honesty from a man who could easily rest on the importance of his accomplishments in the field of mental health and personal growth.[17] His humility and openness about his process has always endeared him to me, but it generates admiration as well. True to this self-observation, Hal proved his point by finishing this part of his story with his reactions to Jung's death in 1961.

Hal had just gotten his analytic diploma in Los Angeles when he learned of Jung's death. He wrote to von Franz because the only thing he could think of was how sad she must have been. "She was the only one I wrote to," Hal said. "When we had that final meeting, we really touched. We made a connection from such an honest place. I received a lovely letter back from her, a very sweet thank-you letter from the heart." Hal understood that had he continued to work with her at the time, it wouldn't have gone well. But it's clear that it ended well.

Hal mused for a while longer, noting that when he left Zurich, he didn't really stay in touch with anyone, including Meier, who was a very strong personality, according to Hal. But the analysis was less on a personal level. "My unconscious responded extraordinarily well to him and at a very deep level," Hal said. "But he really had very little to say. He did say that my unconscious was doing the work, which is, on one level, a very good analysis. A lot happened in that time. Don't forget that. But I didn't make a personal connection with him. Nor did he do anything to support a personal connection."

In part I could understand this feeling. Those fellowships lasted only a few months, not offering the time or opportunity to develop a personal connection. As an analyst myself, I know it's possible to do a good piece of deep work with someone if things align well in the unconscious. But it's a relationship clearly defined by structure. Additionally, Hal was young by analytic standards of the day. Relationships characteristic of longer-term work have a different texture than the analysis Hal talked about with Meier.

"But I didn't feel badly about it," he said, in a tone that hinted we were coming to the end of the story. "It just didn't happen. Years later, I was asked to write a chapter about Meier for a book about him; an anthology that was put together for one of his birthdays." Most of the senior people in L.A. at the time had worked with Jung. So, Hal wrote a chapter for them, and then later heard from Meier, who mentioned he had not heard from Hal since his time there. "I think that's just the downside of working in that way, only engaging the unconscious without attending to the relationship. I can't work that way anymore, although I used to for a time after my training."

True to form, however, Hal's unconscious dealt with the ending of his work with Meier in a beautiful way, that allowed him to experience the effectiveness of their work together. "In my final dream in Switzerland," Hal said, "Meier and I were standing on a mountain overlooking Zurich. It was sunset, and we shared this with a sense of sadness and timelessness. I understood it was sunset in Zurich on a much deeper level. It was a perfect dream, one that brought to a close, a remarkable three months in Zurich. I was ready to return home, begin my own practice, and enter into my own analytic training."

Hal looks back on his time in Zurich, describing it as "staggering." Although short, his analysis there felt complete, and propelled him in a new direction with an energy and drive he would need, as his reentry was a rough one. He was a new therapist who didn't have a practice to return to. He had applied for admission to the analytical training program in L.A. before he went to Zurich, and once accepted, things really heated up.

"I didn't come up against the issue of length of time of analysis until much later," he said, "when I felt I didn't want to be in analysis anymore, and I still had hours to make up. But after returning from Zurich I knew I was expected to be in analysis, so I was. I also had to find work, and right away."

A familiar picture was forming in my mind as Hal went on to describe working at a psychiatric clinic in Long Beach, California, three days a week. Then he found another job through an Episcopal priest named Morton Kelsey, who called him to Monrovia, CA one day a week. Then there was his work at a Jewish Community Center near home one evening a week. He had two other days to fit in private clients. In a breathless and vicarious kind of *participation mystique*, I winced at the rigors of life in training. I never forget the kind of energy and commitment that one has to rally for this kind of training. I never forget the costs either.

"I had all this going on," Hal said, beginning to smile now. "By December … I had pneumonia! But once my practice filled up, it stayed that way. My life went on like that from 1957 to 1961, when I earned my diploma as a Jungian analyst."

The country darkness had swallowed the house and grounds by the time I turned off my computer after that evening's conversation. I packed up my things and walked to the apartment that welcomed me with a stove fireplace and a simple kitchen. I had had to learn a significant piece of technology to do these interviews, which strained my virtually non-existent sensation function to its limits each night as I nervously transferred the day's "Garageband" recordings to the small army of thumb drives I'd brought with me. I'm not a techie type. This was stressful. But, to say it was worth it so understates the experience, I almost can't say it … but I will. It was indeed worth it.

CHAPTER SEVEN

For the Love of Learning

For some of us, education becomes a hiding place. From my earliest days in school and later during periods of unrest or indecision, I have to admit to a certain affinity with Hal's experience. College gave me something to do. Moreover, I've never been the kind of thinker whose passions led me down ten thousand paths, each one richer than the next. There's a utilitarian attitude to my scholarship, like Hal's. It simply wasn't until I discovered Jung in my forties that I understood the joy real scholarship yields.

Sidra, on the other hand, had a love affair with learning almost instantly. She has the kind of mind that can lock onto anything and digest it with gusto. Hers is one of those stories about a rare seedling simply born in full bloom, with a capacity to renew itself before anything passed her by. Her recall of her studies from high school on into college and graduate school is nothing short of amazing. As we sat together in her office, I let my eyes wander to the shelves of her bookcase, recognizing volumes in a couple of languages. There's no shortage of variety either. From drama to poetry to great thinkers, her bookshelves boast collections and titles from the classics to modern literature. Sidra rattled off titles like she was reading an old Rolodex filled with the names of treasured friends, whose relevance in her mind was still fresh.

As we spoke that evening, Sidra would suddenly pop up out of her chair, rush to the bookshelf, and snatch a book to show me, as if touching it would transfer some of the delight she felt in remembering its contents. To be honest, I think it did. As

one of the last of a dying breed, those who pursued a liberal arts education in the 1960's, I remembered a shared feeling when she talked about these volumes' influence on a fledgling psyche ... at least fledgling in my case. In Sidra's psyche, I think they were grist for a mill that was instantly open for business.

Frustratingly for Sidra, when it came to school, she met the brick wall of misogyny when her talents outstripped the culture of the times. "Girls just don't get math" may have been a dictum that barred the door to Advanced Placement Algebra, but it didn't stop her passing the boys up anyway with an attitude of "I'll show you!" In fact, that attitude lasted throughout her entire co-ed education because the standards were so different for women ... "and unfair!" Sidra added with a little fire of her own.

Sidra's parents, however, were thankfully more progressive than their times. It was a given that both Sidra and her sister Linda would go to college. Sidra was only sixteen when she graduated from high school, so her mother and father didn't want her to go out of town. That meant that if she was going to college, it would have to

Sidra, age 15, Banff, Alberta, Canada

be close or she wouldn't be going at all. That left Barnard or Brooklyn College as choices. "You can bet I worried until I was accepted at Barnard," she said, smiling.

Then the fun really began, or at least that's an impression easy to form of Sidra's undergraduate experience. Resting solidly on literatures and thought of the mid-twentieth century philosophers and writers, Sidra identifies two main principles that guided her thinking from the age of 16 to 20, when she graduated from Barnard.

"Those threads would be the concept of *entelechy*[18] and *élan vitale*[19]. Those two ideas really spoke to me," Sidra saidd. "Entelechy was first used by Aristotle. Later, the physicist and philosopher Leibniz[20] talked about it. I studied both of them and their work fascinated me. They are similar ideas in that they touch on a self-actualizing force from within that propels life and growth in a way that makes *actual* an individual's unrealized potential." As Sidra warmed to the explanation, she obviously enjoyed the images she found to clarify the ideas of her favorite thinkers. "For instance," she said, "it would be the force or energy from within that would move a caterpillar to build a cocoon and become a butterfly. In some ways, it fits beautifully with Hal's idea of the *blueprint* of the soul. *Élan vitale* would be the energy that transforms that blueprint into a reality."[21]

It's as startling to me now as it was when I did the actual interviews, how divergent Hal's and Sidra's paths seem at their beginnings. Hal's early moorings attached somewhere in the fog of his dream world. But Sidra was grounded, inquisitive and energetic from the start. Yet, the divergent threads they followed led them to what seem like an inevitably similar destination. No matter how purist my notions might be around how one comes to incorporate Jungian thought, I couldn't ignore the Jungian flavor of Sidra's early reflections.

92

She did a lot of reading about man in society when studying at Barnard. "We were given a very strong sense of what the collective was; that it's not always good to go along with it," she said. "We learned you had to be an individual; that was important for us especially as women." Of course, she was talking about education in the mid-1950's. Sidra graduated in 1957. "I'm describing something that was extraordinarily counter-cultural for the time," she said. "It was still proper and intellectually sound. We were simply getting an education like the men." An inherent distrust of the collective, honoring the individual path, and valuing the feminine are all cornerstones of Jungian thought. Yet in Sidra's reminiscence, they surface without exposure to Jung, as a simple acknowledgement of a college curriculum. But its influence stood her in good stead for a future of "hovering" in the tension of the opposites.

In September of 1957, just after graduating from Barnard, Sidra married her much-loved and admired college sweetheart, Jim Winkelman. He was as similar to Sidra then as Hal was to be different years later. The newlyweds spent their first summer travelling in post-war Europe, following a tradition of direct experience education that Sidra's parents had started as far back as the 1940's. Because her father had the summers off, the family took off by car to French Canada one summer, and to Florida the next. One such summer trek took them all the way across the country. They went to all of the national parks, from Brooklyn to Los Angeles. "I swore I would never live in L.A." Sidra said. "The two cities just didn't like each other. One time when we were parked in L.A., someone walking by actually spit on our license plate."

Offering a list of projections worthy of a textbook, Sidra recounted with some enjoyment the critiques of anti-intellectualism and Hollywood *craziness* Brooklynites lobbed at their Californian cousins. The irony that Sidra ended up settling there herself for nearly twenty years was not lost on her. "There were two places I said I'd never live in: Baltimore or Los Angeles," she said. "Then, I lived in both of them! So, there you go. I tell my children, 'Never say never.'"

Naturally, it's tempting for me to frame the wisdom of that phrase in Jungian terms of integrating the shadow, or the Aware Ego Process of embracing the opposites. As Jung said,

"The psychological rule says that when an inner situation is not made conscious, it happens outside, as fate. That is to say, when the individual remains undivided and does not become conscious of his inner contradictions, the world must perforce act out the conflict and be torn into opposite halves."[22]

Sidra laughed at those sweeping statements of youth, her bold declarations about what she would never do. Pastimes in fantasies such as these hold a deliciousness that never seems to fade, even in hindsight. People rarely share them without smiling. Sidra was no exception.

Because her husband was finishing his third year of medical school at Johns Hopkins, Sidra went to the University of Maryland in Baltimore for her Ph.D. in psychology. She had a five-year plan. She landed on psychology because she reasoned she could do it full or part-time when she decided to have children. "Also," she added, "I thought that just living life would likely make me better at it … and at eighteen, I thought I'd never be too old to practice. I would just know more."

But much like Hal's experience, Sidra was faced with the same deficit in the field at the time. There was nothing going on in psychology but psychoanalysis and testing. There was no dynamic therapy at the time. But if anything was going on, it was happening at the Veteran's Administration. They were training psychologists at

94

the VA, a discovery Sidra still feels fortunate to have made. They provided her with ample financial and training resources. Although it's hard to believe today, there were no women in the field at that time. Sidra was the only one in her year to make it all the way through.

It was a time of difficulty and uncertainty for everyone, but there was a particularly dark refrain that played in the background for many Jewish Americans: "What if Germany wins the war?" Sidra was no excused from posing the question herself, and the uncertainty behind that question fueled a number of her subsequent decisions. Having always been drawn to stories of girls lost in the forest and surviving on their own in her youth, Sidra identified with making her own way in spite of difficulties and challenges that threatened to stop her. She gave herself a time window to get her PhD, and she did it.

"I wanted children, then, not really because I so much wanted to be a mother," Sidra said. "But I didn't want to miss the experience." She and her husband had a five-year plan. Children were part of it. I knew how to make it work. I had such access to my mind then," she said. "At age seventy-four, of course, I've lost some of that now."

Sidra got her PhD, a license to practice and had two children by the time she was twenty-eight. Although she waited another seven years to have her third daughter, there wasn't even a hiccup in the plan. She was working part time as a psychotherapist when she became pregnant with her last child. Sidra had actually begun her professional training studying Experimental Psychology at Barnard in the mid-1950's. There just weren't many options then, even into the 1960's. Psychology of the day was still desperately trying to be recognized as a science. So, if one wanted to go on in the field, it had to be in Experimental Psychology or in Research. Fortunately, Sidra became fascinated by the idea that one could learn how to understand and manipulate behavior. It was a fit from the start.

She also drew from an unusual opportunity from her Barnard days in which she had been exposed to an unusual blend of theories. In a seminar with a young instructor who had been in psychoanalysis for years, and who had a keen interest in Skinnerian Psychology, she was exposed to deep discussions of anxiety and neurosis … not the standard fare for the day.

"So, my plan was to become a therapist before there was therapy," she said. "In line with operant conditioning,[23] I began to ask questions about the people I saw, about what was being rewarded or punished. Also, why was a certain trait or behavior developing? I rested my thinking on the foundations of psychoanalysis, basic ideas about the unconscious, dreams, defense mechanisms, and then of course, the projective tests." These early students were to be V.A. trainees. They administered the tests of the day – the Intelligence Tests, the Thematic Apperception Tests, the Rorschach, the Draw A Person Test, and the Tell A Story Test. Then they would write them up, score them, and bring them into supervision with the licensed psychologists of the day.

Sidra continued to work at the V.A. until she finished graduate school. While working on her dissertation, she talked about hitting that discriminatory wall again, thinking that "the powers that be" were trying to slow her down. "I admit I fell into a little paranoia then," she said. "I didn't realize the professors were just overworked. I thought the delay in reviewing my work was because they didn't want a woman to finish before all the men. I kept telling them, 'Just tell me what you need, and I'll do it.' But things continued to be slower than suited me."

Sidra was referring to a time before computers were commonplace. She had to complete a statistical analysis of covariance that measured about four feet by four feet in dimension, filling in each square by hand. What computers there were existed in ten-by-ten-rooms with card sorts and were rarely available to graduate students and their projects.

"So, I just did it myself," she said. "You know, the rest of that story is kind of fun, because I ended up completing that analysis, the work spread out on the ground at a nudist camp. I laid a big chart on the grass and filled in the little squares completely in the nude! Well, everybody else was nude, too," she said, responding to my look of some surprise. "That was one of the rules. You had to take off your clothes. Actually, you'd have felt pretty self-conscious wearing clothes in a nudist camp."

The camp itself was well hidden behind a stand of trees, so travelers, even those of today, would have no way of knowing what went on behind those pines. I reflected on my naivety as I imagined what seemed a fairly popular activity despite my notions of those conservative times in this country. The way Sidra described the camp sounded like a perfect image of the American culture of the 1950's, at least, all the rules would fit with the '50's (Well, okay. One would have to overlook the fact that everyone was naked.) But at the time, there was a lot of respect shown for the institution of marriage, and married women. "Men knew they were supposed to keep their hands off," she said. "It was still a time in the culture when women could flirt and not mean much by it. That was a lot of fun. But those days are long gone, I fear."

By 1960, the couple moved to Washington D.C. While her husband did a stint at the National Institute of Health, Sidra began an internship at the D.C. Bureau of Mental Health, where she was one of only three women on staff. This period began

Sidra's early foray into a feminism that was well ahead of its time. She remembered the publication of *The King Must Die* and its place on the New York Times Best Seller list. It stood as a singular consciousness-raiser for her from then on. When she returned to New York in 1962, she began a much-coveted job at the Veterans Administration. There was only one other woman there. Her name was Marianne Beran. She was Viennese and already in her seventies, and Sidra thought she'd already had some Freudian training.

"I'm afraid, as I look back on it, I didn't take her as seriously as I might have," Sidra said. "– at least in part because she was a woman. I regret the lost opportunity now. I'll never know what gifts she might have brought to me. But there was no sense of solidarity among women then. I was much closer to the men. On the other hand, I resisted joining the New York psychoanalytic community of the day. I intuitively felt it was not safe for women; that it inhibited them from developing naturally."

So, Sidra continued to follow her own path, so to speak, receiving her license as a psychologist in New York State in 1963. It was later in that same year that she gave birth to her first daughter, Elizabeth. This opened a whole new world.

"Aside from the awesome experience of having born a child," she said, "– a real live human being – I felt the first inkling of the amazing power inherent in being a woman. I could be a 'doctor,' have a job and respect, AND have a baby."

There was no such thing then as maternity leave, so Sidra took accumulated sick time of three months off. Then she went back to work full-time over her mother's strong objections. "I didn't breast feed either," she said. "Science of the day had created formula that was "superior" to breast milk, and everyone bottle fed their babies, unless you lived in a third world country. Of course, that's a notion that has now seen it's day."

By 1963 Sidra had her first direct encounter with the then new feminism. Betty Freidan published *The Feminine Mystique*, which became the talk of the playground among mothers who had never worked. But Sidra's patriarchal attitude questioned these early stirrings, and she worried privately, and in direct opposition to feminism's cause, "who would take care of the children?" When some questionable events happened with a home care worker who watched Sidra's young daughter, Sidra summarily quit her job and became one of those stay-at-home moms without hesitation.

"I felt perfectly comfortable leaving work and dropping the entire financial responsibility of supporting the family on my husband!" she said. "Up until that week, I had been the principal wage earner. Even so, as a woman of that time, I felt that the basic financial responsibility lay with my husband. I left it up to him to figure out where to get money. And he did." But when Sidra received her last paycheck, complete with the pension she had opted to liquidate, she felt totally stripped of power. "I sat on the side of my bed and cried," she said. But the consequences were not hers alone. She reflected years later on the burden her decision, fueled by her own strong Inner Patriarch, suddenly foisted upon her husband

By 1964, Sidra had given birth to her second daughter, Claudia. Life changed significantly for her then. Sidra enjoyed the best of both worlds for a while. As a woman, she was not "required" to work. So, she could relish the joys of being a stay-at-home mother during the day. At the same time, she stepped into a man's world two nights a week in her role as a psychotherapist. New York women of her day were sophisticated and educated. They dressed and acted like the professionals they were.

In fact, Sidra confessed that they were fairly smug about it as well. But such attitudes were to undergo some major renovation in a few short years to come and change things did.

As was the dictum of the day, Sidra followed her husband's career once more and found herself in Los Angeles in 1967 during the "summer of love". Once there, she began to hear about consciousness-raising groups and feminism, but she initially had little interest or involvement in them.

"I had my career already," Sidra said, "and my children. I felt special, and honestly, a little bit better than most women – particularly in L.A. where they weren't as sophisticated as New Yorkers," she added with an exaggerated expression that mocked her own snobbishness. "Furthermore, I was from Barnard and Brooklyn. Of course, I was to come to understand that absolutely no one cared about that in California," she said. "L.A. was so foreign, I think I'd have been more at home in London or Paris at the time. But I came to love L.A. It wasn't long before I realized I was really free."

Sidra replaced those heels and hose that were everyday dress in New York, with a bikini and bare feet, even at the market. Her incredible hair was already sprinkled with silver, hanging loose and flowing now, released from the shorter styles and chignon. It was she this time who became the focus of tourists' cameras as she stood in line with other California clad women at the grocer's. In a role reversal she wouldn't have expected, she became the object of a scrutiny she gave to natives of the countries she had visited abroad.

On one such trip, perhaps foreshadowing her West Coast transformation, Sidra met her first personal consciousness awakening, head on, so to speak, while traveling in Honduras in 1968 with her husband and friends.[24] The two couples travelled from Guatemala City to Copan to see some Mayan ruins. It speaks to how the world has changed to realize that the four of them set out in a Land Rover alone, without a guide, to travel poorly paved and then dirt roads with only loosely accurate travel directions. The world was indeed different then, and Sidra was always looking up places to see and then saying, "Let's go!" And off they went. Longer than expected drives and the absence of border patrol landed the group facing a river without a ford and the realization that they would have to leave their vehicle on one side and canoe to the other and continue on foot. Paying a boy to watch the Land Rover, they jumped in the dugout canoe while others waded beside them, reaching the other side to be offered even more vague directions and the promise of "horse-like" animals to ride the rest of the way. Again, with the relentless optimism of the 1960's, the four trudged on to look for a house and barn somewhere an hour or more down a road they'd never been on before … and it was getting dark.

At last a few buildings in sight, the little group found someone in charge. They were directed to the barn across the road where they would sleep until morning when they could continue on the waiting animals. "Of course, even though we were very hungry," Sidra said, "we were afraid to eat anything there. So, we opted for some clean-looking bottled beer and some bananas we'd packed. We curled up after that under some grain sacks on which was printed 'Gift from the People of the USA.'"

As the images formed in my mind, I tried to calculate exactly how many beers it would take for me to abandon my car in a foreign country, walk in the dark to an unknown destination, sleep in a barn overnight to retrieve animals the next morning that were unidentifiable even in daylight. It came to me that I probably couldn't drink as many beers as it would take for me to pull that off. Of course, the bananas were a nice touch, but even with bananas it's unlikely. In any case, the small troupe mounted

101

the creatures the next day and rode for a couple more hours until they reached the town of Copan. The stage was set. The world was slowly developing a different texture for Sidra.

As it happened, there was no other way to get to the small town than the journey she described. Copan is located in the Cordillera Mountains. The altitude alone would contribute to the otherworldly feel of the trip, not to mention that the "road" they followed was nothing more than a path worn in the dirt by the feet of the animals and residents who travelled it. The beauty of the jungle stood out with an intensity that gave the scene a quality of unreality. "The colors were so intense," Sidra said. "I'd never seen anything like it. Poinsettia trees grew as high as the ceiling in my house. Orchid trees, which I'd never seen before, were in full bloom and the colors were exquisite. I was feeling like a million dollars!"

It was the second day of the local festival when the four travelers arrived. None of them had eaten since the beer and banana feast twenty-four hours before, so Sidra felt a little light-headed anyway. Undaunted, they rode in on their wobbly mounts with the flair of John Wayne to greet a village filled with bodies lying around in varying states of drunkenness or disarray. People were scattered along the sides of the road, their feet in it and their heads propped up on the sides, their gazes focused on other planes of consciousness perhaps discovered during the festivities of the night before. They proceeded to a small two-story hotel near the ruins. They dismounted and took their things to the door of the hotel, where the one Spanish-speaking traveler went in to secure their rooms. That accomplished, the group moved across a small courtyard to stone steps leading to the second-floor rooms that were to be theirs for their stay.

"I started up the stairs," Sidra said, "and the next thing I knew, or the next thing I felt, was the earth pulling at me; pulling me down and then, nothing. I remembered getting to the top of the stairs, looking across the sun-dappled stone floor, but my friends told me I went totally stiff and fell forward without even trying to break my fall. I hit the edge of the step below and in front of me, splitting my chin open and breaking my jaw. The next thing I saw was a view from the ceiling. I looked down on myself lying in a bed in the opposite corner of a strange room."

Her companions were hovering over her, saying there were no vital signs; that Sidra simply wasn't there anymore. She could see they were upset, reflecting wryly that there were two physicians and ER nurse in the group, so they should know when to get upset. In the meantime, Sidra was fully into another plane of consciousness.

"I was caught up in an incredible feeling of being a point of consciousness," she said. "I felt the entire universe extending outward; I mean, there was just no separation. It was still me, but I had no edges. I was in absolute bliss. Everything was light. I was trying to say to them that I was fine, really fine; that I'd never felt this wonderful! It was really exquisite." But the pull of responsibilities and the trappings of this world proved stronger than the delight Sidra discovered in the ethers above her own body. She understood that her husband and children needed her. That awareness literally pulled Sidra back to the world.

"I felt myself come down through a damp, mucous-like thing," she said, "and enter my body again through the top of my head. I can still remember the feeling of coming in and having to squish down to fit into my body. I felt the constriction of the physical world, the relinquishment of the joy, the feeling of absolute peace and bliss. As I came to, I was really crying. My companions didn't realize I was crying about the loss of that magnificent expansion."

103

The rest of the story is a study in great difficulty and discomfort. Finding quick transportation out of the remote region to acceptable medical care was a feat that must have been aided by the gods of courage and good fortune. A Honduran army plane had brought visitors to the festival and they took Sidra and her husband to another in Tegucigalpa, where she found a compassionate nurse who spoke English. Her chin finally stitched, Sidra and her husband awaited boarding the last plane home when she had what she would call at the time a spiritual awakening. She understood that not only had she had a near-death experience, but that there was something larger at work in her life; other forces that functioned beyond her mind and resourcefulness.

"I realized that it wasn't our cleverness that got us out of this," she said. "I understood that there was something else that had been protecting us through this one; protecting me. Further, there had been something else pulling me down when I fell. There was something going on with the earth itself and I was part of it." Although Sidra wouldn't necessarily refer to this as "spiritual" today, the result of this experience was that it led her to more mystical studies. The world of the mystery opened, and she became interested in the unseen dimensions of life. She credits this event with preparing her for what she was to discover following Hal's lead into the inner realms years later.

While Sidra was on her way to an identity she'd always sensed in herself, she had not yet begun to live out in the world. In a perspective reversal of her own, Sidra digested her experience and moved from the pragmatic to the mysterious with the enthusiasm of a lover, and never looked back.

104

CHAPTER EIGHT

The Jungian Years

It's a pleasant if inadequate fantasy for me that Jungian training set the stage for my life. In fact, that any one thing launched me into my maturity would be an oversimplified version of the truth. Nonetheless, I am grateful for the journey my analytic path has yielded. It has enriched my perspective, opened my consciousness, and offered me endless questions to continue to ponder. It is, of course, Jung's idea that the dialogue with the unconscious opens more doors before us than it closes after, especially when our studies or analyses are complete; and for me, that's the beauty of it. With this reflection in mind, I was still curious about Hal's relationship to his Jungian work after his stay in Zurich. There were more years of study and analysis before he received his diploma. I wanted to know the details. Hal was, as always, willing to tell me.

One evening we met in the dining room of their house. The sky had already begun to change its color behind the back windows that open to Sidra's garden. As we settled into our chairs and put the finishing touches on our tea, Hal began an impromptu "conversation" with the microphone I carefully attached to my computer. Significant anxiety about my technical skills for this project was my constant companion. Logistics dictated that I'd best get these interviews recorded faithfully and then backed up, (a term that by itself frightened me), or the opportunity would be lost. Pressuring myself to do things perfectly never works well, but I was caught up in it. I had explained the procedure and the equipment to both Hal and Sidra, who listened with the patience of experienced therapists as I neurotically described the equipment as if it were alive. I explained, to the delight and interest of no one present, that the mic arrived with the name "Blue," although it was the size and shape of a softball, with a brand name of "The Snowball."

Although I gave a passing nod to the idea that "a ball named Blue" sounded like a bad country western song at best, Hal picked up the dialogue as I hooked things up with the tenacious nervousness of someone with little confidence in her IT skills. With the exception of working with a dream, Hal might be at his best when finding spontaneous humor in an opportune moment. Addressing the mic, he said, "So, good evening, Blue. It's good to see you again. How are you feeling this evening? Quiet? Yes, I can see that."

Although I try to have the focus of a neurosurgeon when plugging the right plugs into the right holes in my computer, I started to laugh, instantly undone by Hal's playful energy. My armor thus compromised, Hal, enjoying the moment, again addressed the mic. "I hope you're getting some time to yourself, Blue" he continued with an irresistible grin. "You know, you have to speak up to Dianne. A fellow like you might be ignored, and given the duties you have thus far performed, I would be concerned if your other needs weren't being met. Your accommodations are to your liking over there at the apartment? Oh, that's good. Well, let me know if there's anything that comes up for you while you're here." Blue kept his silence. Hal's playfulness was so contagious, I could not keep mine. I began to laugh and relax.

As the light escaped with the sunset and darkness crept over the house, the dining room turned a cozy gold color under the evening lights. The next part of the story seemed to take a deep breath, along with me after I stopped laughing, and Hal began telling me about his Los Angeles life and his years as a Jungian analyst. It was the late 1950's and early '60's. The West Coast was exploding with energy and a focus on consciousness. New ideas and perspectives on healing and awareness proliferated.

106

Hal was in the thick of it, at first as an analyst and teacher, working with adults, adolescents, children and families.

"From the early days on I had a broader base than some analysts," he said. "But I didn't focus on couples' work. It terrified me because I had no framework for it. I just didn't do it. I was in good company, I think. Many Jungians shy away from working with couples. As surprising as it sounds now, it never occurred to me that transformation had anything to do with relationship."

So, Hal enjoyed a full and varied practice in Westwood, CA from the early 1960's through the 1970's. Complete with three sand trays for sand play work[25] and a large collection of figures and miniatures of all descriptions to illustrate unconscious figures and landscapes, his office seemed the reflection of a contented analyst. His collegial relationships such as the one he had with Edith Sullwold, a child therapist whose office was across the hall from Hal's suite, were rich and much valued. It was a happy time for him.

Then in 1963 there was a kind of side effect to all this stability. The psychologists in the United States decided they wanted to create the equivalent of a residency program in psychiatry. So, they developed The American Board of Examiners in Professional Psychology, the ABEPP. After a psychologist had been in private practice for a period of time, he or she could apply for examination and go through a very demanding and extensive process, ending with another clinical certification. Given Hal's relationship with his graduate studies and his already enjoyable practice, it would seem that such a certification would actually add very little to his resume, and even less to his interest in further scholarship. But like many of us who heed those inner voices when they counsel us, Hal was engaged in conversation with an inner voice of his own.

107

"In those days, I listened to that inner voice," he said, "sometimes wisely and sometimes from an 'unthinking son'. These voices would come into my awareness and I would get into bonding patterns[26] with them. It's like going into a room full of people who are listening to someone channeling. They are all sons and daughters to the channeled energy, no matter what it says. It's unbelievable but whatever it says is so. It causes a lot of mischief."

Like many of us who attend to such experiences before we really understand them, Hal interpreted them through the lens he had at the time. Unsure of the source, he at first thought the voice emanated from an otherworldly energy. He had gone through periods of reading extensively in spiritual literature, but eventually tapered off in disappointment. Hal sat looking out the back windows as if he could see through the darkness.

"My yearning for God felt so extreme then," he said, "that if I read someone's book in which they had some kind of a *samadi* experience or Big Bang, I yearned for it so deeply it totally destabilized me. I had to stop reading that kind of material because it just threw me for a loop."

This time though, Hal's inner voice directed him toward the very thing he was inclined to avoid: the ABEPP certification. Hal was informed by this inner counselor that he was going to be on the cutting edge of things, and the more goodies he had, the more traditional requirements, the more authority he would have in promoting the things he would want to promote later on.

"It seemed to make sense," Hal said, "except I had no clear idea of what the voice was referring to. But I went ahead with it." Then the dance began, the kind of dance anyone with graduate credentials knows well. First the written exam, followed by the orals, and then the certificate is awarded. But life predictably interferes with our most carefully conceived plans. Just as Hal prepared for his Orals, his father died, and things had to be postponed for half a year.

The most significant aspect of these exams for Hal was that he made up his mind he was going to be completely honest about any issue that was brought up to him in them, either in the written or the oral parts of the examination process. "It's too easy to become a psychological prostitute," Hal said. "You simply give people what they want to hear. I had done it many times in my educational career. The exam process was difficult, but I stayed honest and clear;" and he passed, on his own terms. But Hal always acknowledged that having that certification certainly helped later on when he was establishing the Center for the Healing Arts, when he needed all the properness he could get. Hal would subsequently serve on these boards, but he became increasingly immersed in his own creative projects and turned his focus in other directions.

By the mid-1960's, Hal began to feel some dissatisfaction with his life. His first marriage was not going the way he wanted, although had you asked him directly if he was happy, he certainly would have said yes.

"You see," Hal said, "when you're in a relationship in an unconscious way, you don't really know how the relationship is going. You can be completely unaware that you're in a relationship that isn't working for you. But f you counted the number of peanut butter and jelly sandwiches you ate at midnight, it might give you a clue that somewhere in there is a truth you can't face. It's a kind of entrapment that's engineered by the psyche. So, I just experienced it as a sense of unhappiness. I knew I wasn't fulfilled. But the analytic work gave me such richness, I didn't address things directly for quite a long time."

Hal had continued his analysis with Hilda Kirsch, and as is characteristic of Jungian analysis, these problems were dealt with under the rubric of "going deeper into yourself and that will heal a lot of things." He followed that advice for years until 1963, when he hit a wall.

"I began asking myself when I was going to feel like a grown up. I was in my forties, then, and looking at the personae of the psychoanalysts. They looked and felt like men. But I did not. I just felt young."

It was about that time that Hal had a break in his analysis, and termination followed quickly thereafter. Hal described Hilda Kirsch as a blessing in his life. But in those days, little was known about the transference in analysis and its effect upon the work.

"Of course, I knew *the word* transference," Hal said. "I had studied *the word*. But I really knew nothing about the experience because I knew nothing about bonding patterns yet. So, I broke the relationship with my analyst. I wish I could have done it differently," he said, musing. Then he added with a grin, "But if my mother had been a bus, she would have had wheels, you know? I did it the way I did it."

This rupture resulted in a new freedom, which Hal needed. He felt his analyst's influence was one that encouraged his placidity. What followed must have been a true *enantiodromia*. Hal discovered his feisty side and beyond. He began to argue with the authorities. During the same period of time, an opportunity at Berkley in San Francisco came to Hal through some acquaintances and collegial relationships. Hal had been spending time in Northern California. He felt an affinity with the San Francisco Jungian crowd. So, although he realized the southern group had saved his life, he was a young man catching the scent of the world.

Then in 1967, Hal met John Pearson, who was then director of extension programs for University of California Berkeley. They hit it off immediately. John was a gifted photographer at the time and had a free spirit quality. He and Hal began to talk about doing some new extension weekend programs. During this same period, Hal had attended a professional program of Jungian analysts. He was particularly struck by James Yandell's presentation about the music of Bob Dylan.

"It was fantastic," Hal said. "Jim played the music and talked about the music from an analytical standpoint. It was pure genius! And he did it in that typical Yandell way … very off-handed, as if he wasn't really doing anything at all."

Hal spoke to John Pearson right away, suggesting that Jim Yandell become part of the team. The planning began immediately. Between the years 1967 and 1969, these three men put together seven weekend programs. They averaged between five and seven hundred participants for each one. Hal was a strong teacher but talking to these kinds of audiences was a new experience. It was here that he learned what vulnerability was really about.

Hal generally started the Friday night presentations. One difficulty though on Fridays was that people were generally tired from a week's work and a rushed dinner. The room was filled with discomfort and fatigue. "The first time I stepped out in front of them I came within a millimeter of fainting," Hal said. "Although I was a strong teacher, I wasn't at all in touch with my vulnerability about talking to a group that size. Remember, I was talking to hundreds of people at a time. I knew very little about the child within me then, although it's common knowledge today. I discovered in a very real way how frightened that child was. From then on, I had a stool placed next to the lectern, so I could sit down. That took care of it for me."

The subjects of these programs covered a variety of Jungian and consciousness topics. Dreams, fantasy, and myth were all well represented, including the dreams of artists, clients, visionary material, and literature. Music and movement were a big part of these programs as well. "We all felt this was an explosion," Hal said. "We felt we were part of a revolution. That's what it felt like … and we were in the middle of it."

But not everyone in Hal's circle was as excited about this expansion of Hal's and his colleagues. The older L.A. analysts weren't very happy about what was going on. They weren't quiet about it either. They felt Hal was leaving the intimate chamber in which analysis occurs. "And I was!" Hal said. "I mean, in my private practice I still saw people one on one. But these programs constituted a brave new world … and it was a very big world out there."

I well know how much work it is for me to prepare a single presentation. So, the idea of appearing before huge crowds on a regular basis, say, seven or so times in a two-year period, was very impressive. And even the list of participating analysts touted names such as Joe Wheelright, Joe Henderson, and John Perry. Many of the northern group of analysts, meaning the San Francisco group, participated in these events, as well as artists of all disciplines. In a reflection that smacked of the 1960's, Hal referred to this as a real "happening" of the time. The excitement was contagious and carried some of this second generation of analysts beyond the comfort zones of the older, Zurich trained practitioners, earning them the nickname of the "Bad boys of the Institute." Observers of the time now reflect that it was more a case of "generational differences"[27] than any real objections to the work. It was simply an extraordinarily creative time.

As one would expect, these events made Hal Stone quite well known. But he had a certain intuition about his role in all of this. "I had a certain reputation by this time," he said. "One might have said my stars certainly shone. But I had the sense that it wasn't really the time for my sun to fully shine. I understood then that it was my job to initiate the suns of other people."

Given the amount of professional expansion that seemed to be supporting Hal's personal process, it's hard to imagine he had time for a life outside of his work. He had a wife and two young children, to whom he was devoted in many of the "traditional ways." But there had to be difficult choices at times, or what might appear as divided loyalties. I wondered both privately and publicly how he managed.

A wise analyst once told me if I wanted to know the true nature of a man, to ask his children how he was at home. So, in the case of Hal Stone, that's what I did. I met with J. Tamar Stone on several occasions, asking her to reminisce about growing up in these exciting times and her life with Hal and Audrey Stone. Tamar is a petite woman, with wonderful curly hair and a fantastic smile. She described the 1970's as a great time to be growing up in California. Tamar's description of life with her father was rich with detail and tenderness. If Hal was focused on his professional life, it seems he was able to shed his analyst persona and simply enjoy his children.

"As a father, Dad was a combination of things to us when we were small," she said. "On one hand, he had a very strong impersonal attitude ... very mental. Then, he would drop that, and simply play with my brother and I."

Tamar then painted the picture of herself as little girl. She would listen for the sound of Hal's car. He came home every night for dinner. In that sense, they had a traditional kind of family. So, when she heard the sound of his car, she would run and get his pipe and slippers. "If I could catch him before he got to his office," she said, "he would come into our world, and play with my brother and me. He actually got down on the floor and played Solitaire with us. My brother Joshua was very competitive, and Dad played seriously with us. It was great."

Hal also watched TV with his children; shows like *Man from Uncle* and *Star Trek*. "Those were "our" shows," Tamar said. "We had a whole language and experience with him around these things. But if we missed him at the door, he went into his office, that was it. He was in there working for the night, except for dinner." This one exception stands out: family dinners were a magical event. Tamar smiled remembering happy memories of dinnertime. The Stones didn't talk about sports or politics. Tamar's mother was as interested in things both Jungian and spiritual as her husband. So, one can only imagine the richness of dinner table conversation. "We talked about dreams, or myths and fairytales. We were raised on that stuff and I loved it."

Then, as if she had landed on another delightful landscape of her past, Tamar asked if I remembered Sara Lee cakes from that time. I admit stifling the urge to sing "Nobody doesn't like Sara Lee" as proof. "Remember the pound cakes?" she said, laughing a little like her father does when he enjoys something funny he's going to say before he says it. "Everybody would have had a piece of cake, and then my mom would look at the remaining cake and say, 'You know, that doesn't look straight. Let me even that out.' Then Dad would look at the cake and say 'Nope. It still doesn't look straight. I'll just even that out a little' and he would take another slice. Pretty soon the whole cake was gone!"

Tamar slipped easily into the pleasure of a rich past, telling me of her mother's interest in Native American art and culture. They took family vacations out

114

into "Indian Country" before it was politically incorrect to call it that. New Mexico, Arizona and Colorado, where Tamar now lives, were all places of wonder and education as a family while Tamar and Joshua were still young.

"We went to Native American rituals and dances," she said, "bought their art and other goods. We stayed in low-end hotels, with vibrating beds … a high point for Joshua and me, to be sure," she said, immediately evoking the image of something every kid has to try at least once and never forgets. Memories of kids laughing at a jiggling mattress, the fun fading and then the wish that the quarter's worth would run out, came back to me in an instant. We both laughed.

In quieter reflection, Tamar describes her parents' marriage as a young marriage. Hal met his first wife when she was only thirteen and he was a little past eighteen. Their families knew each other from Michigan. They were Jewish. They all lived in L.A. "It was a relationship of comfort and familiarity," Tamar said, "like brother and sister. They got married as soon as my mother was eighteen. Then the other part of their connection was that they shared an interest in Jung and dreams. They jointly enjoyed the workings of the psyche."

When the children came along, they grew up surrounded by the richness of their parents' fascinations. Their youthful psyches flourished in myth and fairytale. Hal read the *Red, Yellow, and Blue Fairy Tale Books*[28] to his son and daughter, not ignoring, to be sure, the worlds of ancient Greece whose myths came alive in the telling. Tamar and Joshua were very close as siblings and friends. But Tamar's connection to her father was different than her closeness to her brother. Even early on it seemed her destiny was to be an intimate part of her father's life work.

115

"By the time I was eight or nine, I had a total crush on my Dad," she said. "I just became a groupie. I shadowed him whenever I could. Wherever he went, I went. Whoever he talked to, I talked to or listened. I even met Anais Nin, if you can believe that. He did the ordinary things, too. He came to talk to my high school class. I even went with him to Humanistic Psychology conferences, where I was exposed to the whole exciting world of Berkley at the time. Really, growing up around my father at that time was just amazing."

Hal's son Joshua was less attached to his father's process. But he and his sister were still very close, maintaining a deep love and affinity for one another. Although he was very much into sports, Tamar was part of his group, too. "When I wasn't tailing Dad," she said, "I hung out with Joshua and his friends. I just wanted to be where the energy was, to be embraced by it.".

The archetypal world is always more available to children, all children. They simply live closer to the unconscious than adults. But to be raised and nurtured in what was surely an archetypal atmosphere in the Stone home must have increased the intensity exponentially. Add to that the energy of expansion in California during the 1960's and '70's. Tamar and Joshua Stone's world must have been nothing short of electric. And yet, memory offers the ordinary things of childhood … how was discipline handled and by whom?

"Honestly," Tamar said, "I was never punished; partly because I was just so good. I was a huge Pleaser. I just did everything to make things pleasant." One time when I was about fifteen years old, my Dad knocked on the door of my room and asked to talk to me. I said okay as we sat down on the floor together. He said to me, 'You know, you're just so good. I want you to do something bad. Why don't you smoke pot or something?'" Tamar laughed broadly, adding a wry reflection. "Of course, even if I had, it would have been laced with a father's permission."

On Hal's professional front, however, things were anything but traditional. The years between 1966 and 1971 could be characterized by an intense activity and growth that contained the seeds for the Center for the Healing Arts. With them, holistic medicine was to come to the West Coast. Enjoying close affiliations with both the San Francisco group and maintaining connection with the southern group, Hal began a process of personal expansion that changed his life dramatically.

It was during this time that Hal met a psychoanalyst named Ernie White. Although he was reluctant to call him a maverick, Hal acknowledged that White had his own mind. The two men hit it off very powerfully and began working with each other. Every Monday evening from 6pm to midnight, they would meet, get a bite to eat, and then spend two hours apiece analyzing each other. Hal took the psychoanalytic place on the couch on the couch, and then introduced White to Jungian work. It was a gold mine of experience. Hal got to areas of work that his analysis had not touched.

Then a third man joined Hal and Ernie White, a psychologist named Phil Odorberg. The three men became a very close group. By sharing their individual perspectives, they expanded their theoretical bases. Then when Hal met Sidra, there was an explosion in his life. His friends became concerned.

"Not at first, really," Hal said. "But when it began to look like it might be getting serious, they tried to slow me down. They were afraid for me. They feared I was going too far, too fast ... and I was!"

Like Sidra, Hal saw their respective differences as protection against overturning their lives in a very big way. They just didn't feel they were meant for each other. "But it was only when I very first met her that that was the case," Hal added. "It disappeared very quickly. Furthermore, Sidra was not a client. She's just not the client type. But she did want to learn symbolic visualization."[29]

Hal's familiarity with the process came naturally for him, tapping into his childhood propensity for fantasy, now useful professionally. When it came to visualization, he was simply on home ground. At the time, he had just finished a 3-hour lecture and experiential piece on symbolic visualization for 400 people at UCLA. He took all of them on a symbolic visualization *trip*. The result was that Hal became very well known for the work. But when it came to teaching Sidra, he found himself in an entirely different landscape.

"Most people close their eyes and wait for an image to appear, or can be directed to do so," Hal said. "But Sidra closed her eyes and she'd be deep in ancient Greece! I mean, Christ Almighty! It was a huge shock when she started like this. I'd done a lot of work in this, but Sidra was simply another story. So, we really met each other very deep down. But I never expected that we would end up together. It was unthinkable that I would leave my marriage. Sidra felt much the same."

The process between them, however, seemed to have other plans. Struggle though they might have, their connection remained life changing. Neither of them could ignore what was driving them. Nor could they fit it into familiar territory. Nonetheless, the experience was so demanding and intense, neither Hal nor Sidra could or would let go of it.

"Now, you have to understand," Hal said. "I'm not a heroic man. But I became like a lion about the process between Sidra and me. I had found something in connection with her that was changing my life, and no one, but no one was going to take that away from me. If you asked me at the time if I planned to marry her, I wouldn't have looked that far ahead. It was all about the process then."

Like many people whose task it has been to contribute to consciousness in a larger way, Hal's and Sidra's understanding of the process that carried them has had its own evolution. In the beginning, Hal acknowledged that he didn't have a clue about what was happening. In the language of Voice Dialogue today, one would say his Primary Self Systems were falling apart.

"I spent so much time crying. I mean I cried in front of my family at home, my friends … it was just a breakdown of the entire way I had organized and run my life. But I knew it was right. Of course, dream material began coming through at the same time. Sidra and I were sharing all of that as well, but it wasn't enough to hold the whole process."

That's where Voice Dialogue came into such important play at the time. It gave Hal and Sidra a way to literally work with every feeling they experienced, as they experienced it. During what they now recognize as a real fragmentation of their identities, they found a method to contain it, or at least make it manageable.

"Of course, the dream process was great," Hal said. "We had that from the beginning. But it couldn't possibly do the job alone because of the disintegration of the Primary Self Systems. We were all over the place! We would repeatedly say 'Let me talk to the person who wants to feel all together.' Suddenly it all felt contained … manageable. Honestly, it was almost a joke how much Voice Dialogue we did in those early years. Every place we went, all the time we spent together ... all of it was spent facilitating each other, talking to selves."

Then they turned their attention to the dream process, watching it change around the Voice Dialogue work. As they became clearer and clearer about the opposites within them, Hal told me the dreams shifted. They began to get a sense that 'somebody' out there liked their process. "It" was agreeing with them, cooperating.

Talking with both Hal and Sidra separately actually makes it unclear sometimes who was leading this powerful process. Of course, there were times when Hal introduced material, resting on his Jungian background as a jumping off point. Then Sidra brought him out into the world; Hal brought the unconscious to Sidra. Often, he brought something out that had always resonated with her in another way. Then it simply wasn't long before they were in union around the process.

It's not hard to imagine that life for Hal and Sidra, and those around them, was far from settled during the beginnings of their relationship. Understanding what that meant was very elusive. There was such disruption to their senses of themselves, which objectively, makes more sense now than it did then. There is no answer to a call to a new consciousness that doesn't disturb the *status quo*. But with a frank and genuine honesty, Hal and Sidra are the first to dispel the fantasy that this love story was not without cost. There was difficulty and sorrow for others that had to be borne by Hal and Sidra. They don't shirk from the truth of that, even if in their parents' hearts, they hated the thought of it.

For Hal at the time, the outer picture of his first marriage and family life looked if not traditional, rich and filled with color and texture that earned them the title of "the coolest home" among his children's friends. But as is true for all completely positive situations, there is always a shadow. The love story that swept Hal and Sidra inescapably onto such a new and dramatic path, was not without pain, a fact Hal and Sidra acknowledge with the sadness of parents who have caused their children harm. Tamar explained why.

"I was fifteen when my brother and I found out that Dad was in love with Sidra," Tamar said as our interview drew to a close. "It simply rocked our world. We had no idea there was instability in my parents' marriage, at least not consciously. Unconsciously, I think I'm still healing. My brother was in college in San Diego and after my father moved out, I inherited my mother's *dark night of the soul*. It was very painful for us all."

Although the ensuing transition was filled with difficulty for everyone, Tamar said she was never really angry. The change was presented to her as a situation that was simply happening. She didn't question it. But these events in all of our histories carry deep feelings that surface in a simple telling of the story, and Tamar's voice was often charged with sadness.

"My father told me, and my mother told my brother," she said. "The hardest part was that at first we weren't allowed to tell anyone. My grandparents were coming for dinner that night! We just sat there with all this difficult news and no place to discharge it. Then it became more complicated when I met Sidra and her daughters. I started staying with them and my Dad sometimes. After that, it was harder on my mother, because I simply liked Sidra and her kids."

While this might look like the closing of one story, it heralds the beginning of another. New ways of handling the world were forming for Hal and Sidra to manage the depth and breadth of the transitions to come. Like the country they lived

121

in and the energy surrounding it, the tides of consciousness and culture were changing. Many struggled between the opposites of staying put or jumping on board and hanging on. Hal Stone and Sidra Winkelman jumped for it.

CHAPTER NINE

When in Doubt, Adapt

By the time Sidra and I sat down to pick up the remaining East Coast threads of her life and connect them to the West Coast, I had come into a comfortable relationship with my new technology. The microphone Hal affectionately called "Blue" sat unsupervised on a cane bottom stool near Sidra, while I sat in modest comfort in a chair to her right. Sidra was ready to talk about the leap she took when she and her husband hit the West Coast. Nothing, and I mean nothing, could have prepared Sidra for the challenge she met coming to L.A. When her husband heard of a job as clinical director of a California lab, he, too, jumped for it. Then the excitement began.

The winter weather in New York in 1967 had been miserable. They arrived in California that January to interview, and the sun was out, and everything was in bloom. The contrast was powerfully seductive. Although they'd been very happy New Yorkers, and loved their years of travel, by the end of the interview, they couldn't wait to move to California.

"The sun was shining brightly on the hotel pool that day, inviting me out for a swim in the middle of winter! I mean, I was still in black or grey dresses and a single strand of pearls! I was totally mental and very proper … a real New Yorker. I knew what I was supposed to read, what I was supposed to think. I knew which plays to see and what I was supposed to think about them. It was the one thing I was completely secure in. Further, since I had gone to Barnard, it immediately put me in a certain category of New Yorkers."

123

But that which had prepared Sidra for life on the streets of New York was next to useless in California. Los Angeles was seemingly filled with her disowned selves, the ones her education and upbringing had guarded against. But that's where the rub began. They made the move to L.A. in July of 1967 during the "Summer of Love". The transformation of Sidra's Primary Self System was both dramatic and inevitable. She was immediately put in a position of having to hold the tension of the opposites. On the one hand, she was absolutely free. All kinds of things that had not been socially sanctioned in New York were allowed in L.A. On the other hand, who Sidra was didn't matter. The persona she had carefully constructed in the East, didn't count at all on the West Coast. "Suddenly, I lost my ace," Sidra said. "I had absolutely no 'street creds.'"

Although things seemed grim enough socially, it was even harder for Sidra to break into the psychological community. They seemed completely uninterested in the work she'd done at the VA and The New York Psychoanalytic Institute. Adaptations loomed large on all fronts.

"It seemed like nobody out here cared about the things I valued," she said. "I had to make a decision. So, I adapted by loving it. I hit the ground running, or swimming or driving out into the desert. I embraced it all and it embraced me. In the end, I felt like a woman who had just been released from prison."

In the fall of 1967, Sidra joined a group psychotherapy practice where she had her first exposure to a very different kind of work than she'd been doing back east. Gestalt therapy was just finding its stride. Fritz Perls was at Esalen[30] introducing a confrontational style of group therapy that took Sidra by surprise.

"I was introduced to it by someone who had studied with him," she said. "He was in full beard and all about 'Perlsian rebellion.' It was so refreshing, and very, very different. I never saw him do 'empty chair' work, but his interventions in group were both startlingly confrontational and famous."

Finding her place professionally continued to be a concern until Sidra took a job as Psychological Consultant to a residential treatment center for adolescent girls. This was Hamburger Home, a Social Services funded program, and an agency of United Way and The Jewish Federation. Most of the girls were placements who were either on probation or from neglectful or abusive situations. Hamburger Home focused on older adolescents - a difficult population. When Sidra was first there, it wasn't a very cohesive or coherent place. But she ran groups, did psychological testing with the girls, and made presentations to the Board of Directors. It was then that Sidra met a woman named Selma Heringman – a soul sister twenty years her senior and Chairman of the Board. The two women simply fell in love with each other around the work they did there. Sidra thought of them as a "marvelous team." Selma and Sidra were instrumental in making the necessary therapeutic changes in the program, and their friendship fostered some life changes for Sidra as well.

Characteristically, Sidra's version of the story leading her to Hal Stone's door is as different and interesting as Hal's, and worth backing up a little in time to hear it. Sidra had loved the work with "her girls", but by early 1972, she had lost her position at Hamburger Home due to budget cuts. With the help of Selma, she was rehired several months later, but in the interim, Sidra worked The Marriage Guidance Institute as a very part time therapist. By chance, the director of the practice gave Sidra an article by Roberto Assagioli.[31] Sidra became fascinated with this new dimension of working with the psyche. Then when she heard about the guided imagery work Hal Stone was doing, she definitely wanted to meet him. "At that

125

point," she said, "it had nothing to do with a relationship. I thought maybe Hal would be a referral source. I wanted to impress him, not seduce him for God's sake!" When she met him in person, her stance was confirmed. There was no chance of romance here. "He was completely not interested in me," she said. "I could tell. I wasn't his type. Moreover, he wasn't my type. It was just a non-issue."

So, Sidra began doing guided imagery with Hal, answering a deep question that had been stirring in her since early 1967. While talking with her co-therapist in the Gestalt group practice she had joined, she had a spontaneous vision that began a period of deep reflection, changing the rational ground of her being.

"I don't know what to call it exactly," she said. "Something broke through my ordinary consciousness. I saw myself on the bank of an Incan river having a picnic. Then suddenly I was in the midst of a raging river. Floodwaters carried whole trees and rocks downriver. Suddenly a huge tree, roots up, floated up behind me. It caught me up in the crook of its main trunk, protecting me from all the debris and turbulence. I hung on for dear life. I ended up in a part of the river that flowed gently. When I came to shore, I stepped out into a lovely valley whose air smelled like the best bread in the whole world."

Something new was clearly afoot, and her rational way of understanding the world was under siege. Sidra began to put together experiences in which she had tapped into something larger than the intellect alone could conceive of or explain … and she instinctively understood that it meant something. While her consciousness moved slowly but steadily to a different landscape, she and her husband were still confronted by a new and fast-moving culture. California was awash with change; the sexual revolution was in full swing and consciousness expanded like an explosion.

126

Although her deep connection to Grandma Flo allowed her to watch much of this with a steadied eye, the energy was contagious.

"I was so busy watching that my husband didn't cheat on me, I forgot to watch myself," she said. "The truth is, I eventually wasn't good at either."

"Breakthroughs" multiplied and Sidra's interest in them went in many directions before she sought further education about them. Like many of us who step away from the norm, Sidra first explored these new worlds with friends. "My friend, Jackie Lustgarten, did something she called *cave tripping*," Sidra said. That's how it all started. Sidra was interested, too, so they jumped in. "It was actually similar to Jung's active imagination," she said. "We'd start in places in our minds, and then usually go into a cave, and follow the pathways to see what was going to happen next ... like a real exploration but in our minds."

Sidra's friend was also interested in Tarot cards, and they had already explored their numerology. When they determined that Sidra's numerology added up to the Empress card, they were ready to embark on a "trip". Sidra held the card and closed her eyes. "I was going to see my Empress," Sidra said, "and I found her! She was a dark-skinned naked woman sitting cross-legged with black and white colors painted on her like I was to see later in photographs of tribes in New Guinea or somewhere. And in-between her crossed legs she held a skull with the top cut off. She was scooping out the brains and eating them."

As powerful as this vision was, Sidra watched it all with that particular brand of curiosity that came from her Barnard training, and came out on the other side as fascinated as she'd been before closing her eyes. "I knew she was something I'd been

127

looking for in myself", she said. "That was my first foray into it. It was an exploration into myself. That's why I went to Hal in the first place ... to learn more about this."

When Sidra tells her version of their first meeting, it's not hard at all to see why Hal might have been impressed, to put it mildly. The story is worth telling from her side. For even for Sidra, where this would lead and what would have to be dealt with was very unclear early on. Hal had been doing a lot of visualization work at the time. Sidra then heard about Hal through another friend, Jean Holroyd, PhD. She was the director of psychology interns at UCLA. Jean had seen Hal lead a large group of people through a powerful experience of guided imagery. Even though she had already been doing some of this with a friend, Sidra's interest was pricked. "I wanted in on this," she said, "so I made the appointment."

Their meeting began in the usual way. Hal was very reassuring as he instructed her to lie down on the couch. He told her not to worry if no images came to her at first, implying that not everyone could think of a place or landscape their first time. But no sooner than he had directed her to close her eyes, Sidra was off into the deep interior of her own psyche.

"I was looking out over a vast valley covered with trees," she said. "Then in front of me was a cave. I could see a flat space inside and a four by eight-foot stone altar with cold ashes on it. I walked into the cave and made a fire on the altar. I was barefoot and wearing a white robe. I can still feel the earth under my feet when I remember it. I looked around and saw three or four small rooms that had been hollowed out in the cave walls."

The rooms were filled with foreign objects. The first room had Mayan pottery in it, and little statues. Then in the second room, she found an ornate candelabra. As

128

she left the rooms and started down a path nearby, the path narrowed and kept going down. Dark stonewalls flanked the path, which continued to descend until it ended in another room that was huge, with a lake on the floor of it. Sidra could see white sand on the bottom as she stepped into the water. The minute Sidra did so, she was pulled down through the sandy bottom and dropped onto another narrow path walled by stone. It led to a rough-hewn room with a rounded ceiling, some fifteen feet above her head. There was a woman in a white robe standing in the room. As Sidra looked at her face, she could see beneath the robe, seeing that her skin had been shredded. She seemed to be a priestess of some kind.

"Although she was welcoming me, I was horrified by her shredded skin," Sidra said. "She pointed to a mound of dirt to her left. It was maybe four or five feet long and rounded up to about two feet high. She motioned for me to kneel beside it and I laid my head down on it. As my ear touched the ground, I could feel the heartbeat of the earth. My whole being started beating with it. The next thing I knew I had been thrown back out on top of the ground again. That was my first visualization with Hal."

Now, as an analyst, I know if I'd been Hal Stone at the time, I'd have been blown to the back of my chair, by the energy and tension such a vision would have created in the room and between us. Of course, Sidra, who'd typically deliver such a story in the most nonchalant of attitudes, would drift off into her memory, saying quietly that that was how she and Hal had met, adding as an aside to me, "More tea for you, dear?" But nonchalance couldn't hold such an experience for long, and even Sidra had to acknowledge that when she came out of the visualization, she wondered if she'd read one too many *National Geographics*.

129

"But that was me, of course," she said. "I was sitting with a Jungian analyst whose rational mind was strong and well trained. But I was unimpressed with this group ... generally felt Hal was not my type. So, I bristled at his first remark about not worrying if I couldn't come up with anything. After that visualization experience, I thought, 'Guess I showed you, buddy! You thought I couldn't do a visualization? How about *that*!'"

But there was more. People don't walk in those levels of the psyche and return unphased. For Sidra, it was unbelievable. "I just felt incredibly moved," she said. "It was more real than real. I felt touched in my entire being." Neither Hal nor Sidra heard the closing of an invisible door behind them as they were launched into a process neither of them would want to or be able to escape.

The youngest of Sidra's daughters, Recha, had been born in 1971. She wasn't yet a year old when Sidra met Hal. Of course, the meeting wasn't significant in a way that would impact her family. Sidra had no intention of getting involved with Hal Stone. But the next few years were filled with an expansion of consciousness destined to cause disruption everywhere. It is generally true that no transformation is possible in consciousness unless it happens in the unconscious first. For Sidra, the breaking through of visions continued, telling of deep currents of movement beneath her awareness. In the context of people whose lives revolve around a relationship with the unconscious, such events fall into the category of the expected; material on which to reflect. But for Sidra at the time, they stood as foreign events in a psyche formed around a whole other set of ideas. Yet, their appearance resonated with Sidra at a deep level, like opening a door and meeting oneself. She had always known it was there.

What part Hal was to play in this story was still vague until a final dream installed a new truth into Sidra's psychological machinery. "I have always loved turtles," she said. "So, I had an amazing visualization that I was holding on to a turtle, diving down, down, down into the ocean. Everything was empty. I was doing my own exploration. I was feeling very, very good, and when I reached the bottom of the ocean, there was Hal, sitting on a big, throne-like seat. I couldn't get away. I grudgingly realized after the dream that I couldn't go to those depths without him." After only a few sessions, Hal and Sidra became colleagues and worked with each other on their own material. Sidra began to record her dreams and the fascination built. The readings about magic and mystery of her youth connected with the expansion in her study with Hal. The effect was explosive.

As I followed the details of the Stones' respective histories, their introductions to the unconscious, it was impossible to ignore the recurrent acknowledgement of my own journey to the same realms. While I had always had a very active and vivid dream life, even as a child, I had no container for it. Most were dismissed as foolishness by the adults around me, and I joined in the merriment of ignorance as I laughed my way into maturity. But much like Sidra, chance offered me a friendship with a well-meaning therapist interested in dreams, which led me to a deep and powerful Jungian analysis of my own. A vista opened before me with the power of a tidal wave, pulling me into years of reverie, deep emotion, and connection to a humanity I had only read about.

I once dreamed I had been allowed entrance into a special museum. It was built in the shape of a great sphere. The floors of the museum were made of glass, the edges of which were etched with strange images and complex plant life. I walked to the center of the building and when I looked down, I could see all of life through the ages. The images led my gaze to the bottom of a spiral, around which ran dogs and children and beings I couldn't recognize. This dream became a focal point of the mystery that was to unfold for me as I moved into analytic work, its mystery carrying me to heights and depths whose existence I'd intuited but avoided as too much to handle. With my analyst, I jumped in and never looked back. It has turned out to be the best decision I've ever made.

Sidra clearly felt as I did. "It was magic ..." she said, "simply magic. I never thought of it as spiritual, although I did love the idea of individuation. I felt like it contained in a word what I'd been trying to do all along. I could share this with Hal. He was the first person I could really open up to. I had read Herman Hesse's *Steppenwolfe* in the 1950's. I felt like I could finally enter the 'Magic Theatre.'"

Sidra's stage at this point had Hal on it, and he had the words for a process she'd kept to herself for many years. She was on fire with the energy of discovery. Love, it seemed, was inevitable. But what to do with that was another problem. Like Hal, there were others in Sidra's life who would be affected by what was happening between them. Although at first it seemed nothing would change with this new kind of education, it became clear there was a major overall happening within Sidra, and old roles and values were strained to their limit. Something had to give.

"When I say I was let out of jail as these experiences came to me, I mean I was really liberated," she said. "Active imagination, meeting Hal, exposure to gestalt therapy and the opening of feelings all contributed to the explosions I underwent in my inner world. It was like moving from a black and white world into a world of color, texture, and dimension. I was delving into formerly forbidden areas, like the archetypal world, liminal and imaginal spaces. I was stunned by what I found there and excited. Like Hal, I just couldn't let it go."

But the cost of this massive opening was to come due, because Sidra couldn't go back to her rational and sensible existence. While on the surface her marriage looked perfect, high achieving, respectful, and loving, it no longer held a place for Sidra to continue her process. Although the psychological transition took over two years, when it was over Sidra and her husband separated. It was summer in 1974 when she and her husband separated. Divorce was not far off. "It broke my heart to cause such suffering," she said. "But by this time, I was unable to turn back." But even at

that time there was no clear picture of where the relationship with Hal would lead. They – and their lives – were so different.

Of course, Sidra tried to normalize things, exploring her new freedom with interesting and fun things to do with her daughters. But when it came to Hal, the girls held firm. They didn't want to meet or see him in "their house". Eventually, of course, they relented.

Sidra, 1975, Santorini, Greece

"I remember the first time I brought Hal home," Sidra said. "We were sitting in the living room with the door to the hallway open. My two older daughters were in the back, with their friend Kendra. They were still angry with me, but they were curious. So, first we heard a commotion and then through the doorway appeared a single arm. Then it disappeared. Then a single leg sneaked out, waving in the doorway. Then it disappeared. It was like a short striptease act with a lot of giggles.

Then Kendra came out, pretending to be Claudia, and said, 'Hello, Hal.' Then the other girls followed and that broke the ice."

There was a long period of adjustment following this performance, as well as the introduction of loyalty issues for the girls. Two of them left for periods of time to go and live with their father. But Hal and Sidra were lucky in a number of ways many divorcing and divorced parents are not. In the first place, Sidra's daughters loved Hal's children. "Tamar was a fit from the beginning," Sidra said. "My daughters adored her." All five of the new family's children lived with Hal and Sidra at some point and built deep and loving relationships with each other and their respective new stepparents.

In the second place, Sidra's daughters simply couldn't ignore Hal. Word has it he was, well, irresistible. So, when the dust settled, Hal became a new kind of father figure. He was the kind that allowed a little girl to pretend to be a puppy in order to get up in his lap, so he could pet her head. By the junior high school years, he was the kind of dad who wrote an excuse to the teacher saying, "Please excuse my stepdaughter for being late to school. She could not get past the fire-breathing dragon at the end of our driveway this morning."

"Although I believe in it, of course, my children never went into therapy over this," Sidra said. "I simply folded them into my life and work and then we PLAYED. I built a chicken coup right next to the fancy swimming pool and put in a garden in the front yard. Claudia had to feed the chickens and gather the eggs. I got a waterbed for Elizabeth during that time and a potter's wheel for Claudia. Hal even suggested Claudia and Elizabeth begin riding lessons, which they did for a very long time. They loved it."

134

So, while Sidra regretted "robbing them of their innocence" in some ways, she didn't only open the door to a new world for herself. It went for everybody. To begin, there was a basic difference in Hal's and Sidra's styles of parenting. For the girls, it was a shock. Elizabeth, Claudia, and Recha had grown up in an inclusive environment. Where their parents went, the girls went.

Hal, 1975, Santorini, Greece

"Some of my happiest memories are of our trips together as a family when the girls were young," Sidra added, "especially the five-week trip through Greece when Elizabeth and Claudia were both under two years of age." But Hal had a strong belief in the adults holding the power in the family. It was a transition for everyone, as was the idea of parents having alone time. Hal and Sidra travelled for fun. It was a significant transition for Sidra and her daughters, as was the idea of parents having alone time. "But in the beginning, Hal and I traveled quite a bit and did so as a couple, not as a family," Sidra said. "Finally, one of my daughters let me know on no uncertain terms, that we had had enough honeymoons!"

Hal's daughter Tamar had her own reactions to the new family arrangement. "What strikes me about those early years," Tamar said candidly, "was how clearly and intentionally my Dad and Sidra modeled a new template for relationship. This was a huge change for me. When I wanted something, my Dad would tell me he would talk to Sidra and get back to me. I was in shock! But he reminded me that he was in a primary relationship with Sidra, and that meant that they made their decisions together. It was a new way of life for all of us." This new template so stressed the importance of time alone for the adults, it could even mean going to a hotel for the night to spend time together.

"It's a sweet memory for me, the time I lived with my Dad and Sidra, Claudia and Recha," Sidra always modeled a relationship that stressed time to themselves and how important it was." Then Tamar began to laugh. "They sometimes even told us they were going to bed early and took the boom box into the bedroom with them," she said. "Of course, we all knew what they were doing. They were going to retire to have sex. We laughed a lot about it."

It's well documented that blended families are often plagued with high tension and difficult adjustment. The gift in this case was the constant effort toward consciousness. In many ways, Tamar became the intermediary for the two families, suggesting to Sidra's daughters that they all try something different than being angry with their parents. "Of course, it helped," she said, "that we liked each other very much."

But there was much that kept Tamar near her brother's side as well. "He lived an emotionally and spiritually difficult life," she said. As early as age twenty-one, Joshua hit a wall that sent his father down to his college in San Diego to bring him up north, to live with Hal in the apartment he leased at the time. It rebalanced Joshua for a time. He pursued graduate studies in academic psychology, married and became deeply involved in disseminating esoteric spiritual studies.

"He studied with many well-known spiritual teachers of the day, such as Paul Solomon and Alice Baily, and he became a scholar and author on the teachings of the Ascended Masters," Tamar said. "He even M.C.'d for Buddhist teacher Wesak," she said. "He eventually settled in Mt. Shasta and founded a school with Gloria Excelsias, called the I Am University. He was known globally as a guru of esoteric consciousness and wrote many books about it. My brother was a force of nature."

It's hard to imagine a psyche of this type functioning in the ordinary world, but Joshua Stone never lost touch completely his sister. "Later, when Joshua was thirty-one, he hit another terrible low," Tamar said. "His second relationship had gone badly. He didn't feel he could make it through. Even though we're Jewish, I went with him to every church in L.A. We got down on our knees together and prayed for his survival. It was very scary," she said. "He made it. But those times cost him dearly, I think."

The dimensions of change and growth at this time tested everyone. Sidra made the transition from an all-inclusive mother to making her relationship with Hal primary. In an effort to avoid making his daughter the replacement for connection as his marriage began to fail, and aware of how unfair such a role would be for Tamar, Hal chose to disconnect energetically, offering her an abandonment wound as the better of two difficult choices. But that, like so many other things, was about to change for Hal.

"Dad and Sidra had gone to New York City," Tamar said. "I'd been diagnosed with Rheumatoid Arthritis and was getting multiple injections for joint swelling. I was in so much pain at dinner, I broke down in tears in front of my Dad and Sidra. My Dad woke up to me at that moment in a way he hadn't before, through the heart." Her voice cracked as she relived the moment; the moment when Hal once again really saw his daughter. "It was like falling in love. My Dad became directly re-involved in my life in that moment. He's never stopped."

The changes continued on every front, for everybody. The word transition doesn't come close to expressing the inner and outer remodeling of life that Hal and Sidra and everyone around them encountered. But remodeled was how it was going to be. From interior design to political persuasion, Sidra turned the dial on her life from conservative to liberal, her limits seeming invisible. There was simply no going back.

In a dream she had after her first visualization, she saw herself walking out of a building. As she did so, the door blended back into the wall of the building. The building was perfectly round and smooth again. She stepped out into a perfectly tilled garden, with green bushes and rich fertile turf. She knew she would be exploring another house.

"Of course," she said, "the personal/psychological door had closed behind me as well. Moreover, I was in a position to leave my marriage. I had an income and opportunity. Although I hated hurting the children, I was never ambivalent about making the move. The hard part was that I brought someone into their lives that was so "other." In time, they became very close to Hal. But at the time, the idea of marriage was an impossibility."

Besides, even when conditions changed, there was plenty of reason to wonder if it was a good idea.

138

CHAPTER TEN

The Love Story

The suggestion that the universe seemed ambivalent about Hal and Sidra's nuptials would be an understatement as the date approached. For although there's no question theirs is a love story, the events leading up to their marriage would easily make one wonder if destiny had had a clear plan in mind. Their decision seemed riddled with false starts, warnings, and obstacles that seemed impossible to ignore. Yet, the love between them proved unstoppable, dragging along with it, a host of shadows. When the decision to marry was firm, Hal and Sidra commissioned their wedding rings from a jeweler of Gypsy descent. Like in a tale Sidra's grandmother would have told at the edge of the Black Forest, the dark jeweler came, took their measurements, and went away.

After knowing each other for five years and working together creatively on Voice Dialogue and the Psychology of Selves, Hal and Sidra were very much looking forward to getting married. Years had passed before taking this final step. In the meantime, they had also waited a long time to hear from the gypsy jeweler. Finally, there was word.

"We thought she'd come to us saying 'Here they are. You are a blessed couple,'" Sidra said. "Instead she greeted us with concern and doubt. 'I don't know what's going on' she said. 'I've never had this happen, but these rings fell apart three times!'" With a warning to the couple not to leave the house, or travel, the gypsy left the rings and left the house, suggesting that 'someone' was after them.

While some love stories begin with romantic episodes of the universe seeming to come together in support of a relationship, Hal and Sidra's plans look like that other kind of love story. There were no stars aligning, no being swept up by something beautiful and wondrous, even numinous. No one in their immediate circles gave this union much hope. The psychics, astrologers, and some friends who counted themselves in Hal Stone's circle all thought he and Sidra were completely incompatible. Predictions that nothing would come of this love affair surfaced both in front of and behind closed doors. Paradoxically, others' certainty of their relationship's failure seemed to free Hal and Sidra to explore their connection's outer limits; and explore they did. When their passion for the work they were exploring and for each other eventually won out, and they finally decided to wed, the universe reacted. Hal and Sidra were inundated with synchronicities and unexplainable happenings.

Sidra was still working at Hamburger Home when one day she received a dozen yellow roses. Since she had told Hal those were her favorites, she assumed they were from him. But he had sent nothing to her at work. Then Sidra began to hear things her coworkers had been keeping secret from her. Reminiscent of the Gypsy jeweler, they intuited that something or someone was threatening her. One friend independently dedicated a two-day fast to Sidra because she'd felt something malevolent in the space around her. Following the incident with the wedding rings, one of the hens that Sidra kept died, with an egg half way out of her. Although this should have seemed mysterious enough, the discovery of a dead, five-foot long King snake under Sidra's bedroom window topped things off. Even the most skeptical of us would pause at such a list, images all suggesting foreboding and doom. Perhaps if they had happened to just anyone, this would have been a union interrupted, and much of what has come to the world in the form of the psycho/spiritual practice of

Voice Dialogue, would have faded into the recesses of unfinished projects. But Hal and Sidra trusted what they felt and didn't let go.

For Hal, the surrender to what he at first referred to as the Intelligence of the universe, and to relationship, simply go hand in hand. "If people just chose one side or the other," he said, "it turns out differently." That's what the love story demanded of him from the beginning: surrender to both.

"At first, it was clear that we were surrendering to what was happening between us, this incredible process," he said, "without knowing whether we were going to marry or not. I think that was harder for Sidra, although later I think she got what I meant. I simply loved her to pieces. And yet, I had the wherewithal to also say, 'It's this process between us. This is what counts. We can't lose this.'" It seemed then natural they would wait to see what happened with their connection. It ended up being one of the reasons they remained separate for a while.

"There's always that thing in us, human beings I mean, that wants to close the gap," Hal said. "We want to close the space between the people we love and us. It's the incest archetype.[32] It wants fusion. It wants the other person to make it safe inside the relationship. Then you can hide in there, both of you. When that happens, you sort of lose yourself. You can't make choices about what belongs to you or doesn't belong to you."

So, this love story, running like a program in the background, was frequently put on hold in service of something larger that Hal and Sidra sensed, but couldn't define at the time. Maybe this sense was an inkling of the Source Energy looking for expression, as Hal would articulate it today, maybe not. But he and Sidra had a clear realization that they had to do their own work first. Their respective marriages had taught them how to go about things in service of that fusion type relationship. They felt like experts in the field. But the demands of this new process were something very different. For the first year and a half, they were simply forced to do their own work because they were, in fact, still married to other people, with families to concern themselves with.

"Whatever illusions one might have about the glories of love and the rightness of fit, the work carried all the trappings of several archetypal patterns," Hal said. "What comes with those kinds of opportunities is a lot of psychologically radioactive dust that gets kicked up and needs clearing away."

I'm reminded of the discomfort I feel when I hear criticism of Jung or Freud for boundary transgressions that today would be unthinkable. While it goes without saying that dual relationship are prohibited in modern times, these judgments ignore the reality that these men were pioneers, the first workers in a nuclear plant that was the unconscious. They had no protective gear because they didn't at first know they needed it. Pioneers go first not really knowing what will come to them, but they go anyway. Unforeseen trouble comes with the job. Like all explorers of psychology of the time, Freud and Jung used themselves as the experiment and drew their conclusions from that. There was no other resource.

Voice Dialogue's beginnings show a similar pattern in that Hal and Sidra were using themselves as models for the process. Hal talked openly about the early stages of the work, which involved a lot of dialoguing with the different selves for several years, not knowing where the relationship was going, if anywhere.

"We weren't thinking about sorting out *our* marriage because we were both married to other people," Hal said. "But here was the situation. We had fallen in love with each other. We had begun a process in our relationship that was like nothing we had ever imagined. The level of change we experienced doing the work with each other was gigantic, yet we still weren't together as a couple. When we separated from our respective marriages, we still lived apart. We spent more time together, of course, but still it was the process between us that held us. It wasn't until 1975, after three and a half years of knowing each other, that we began to feel we were going to be together as a married couple."

Hal and Sidra marry, 1977, California

So, in spite of all the predictions and omens to the contrary, Hal and Sidra married and then, according to each of them, the fun really began. Marriage brought up a whole new set of issues. Much to Hal's and Sidra's dismay, they were in the same situations with each other they'd been in with their former mates, sometimes calling each other by their former spouses' first names! One can only imagine the confusion and difficulty. It was only after they married that the usefulness of Voice Dialogue in the relationship aspect of the process became visible.

143

"I started to diagram these interactions between us," Hal said. "And I kind of pulled Sidra in, I think. We began this three-month period where I got pretty crazy with it. What I mean is I was diagramming every interaction we had. I was absolutely fascinated by it all. It came from a place in me that was absolutely committed to the process between us. I just wasn't going to lose it. I had such determination. When anyone came along in Sidra's life, who threatened to disrupt our connection, it really brought out a lion in me. I called it 'proactive' then, but I was on to something. I simply wasn't letting it go."

What Hal was talking about here was "crazy" in a good way. Jung suggests that fascination with something -- be it process, person, or problem-- connects us to the numinous. It takes us over in a unique and powerful way. In this situation, Hal and Sidra became the experiment, for or with something larger behind them. Embedded in their evolving relationship were the seeds for the work they were to bring forward as Voice Dialogue and the Psychology of Selves, a body of work that has had its own evolution. Their parallel processes remain the center of the work … and the seat of their inspiration.

THE SELVES

When I was a child, the best part of my week was going out to the farm with my father. He allowed me a great deal of freedom, unlike my mother, whose attention was often drawn to warding off the disasters that might befall me if she weren't scanning the horizon for predators, tornados or the earth simply opening up and swallowing me whole. But on the weekends, I wandered the farm at first near my father, experimenting with different identities.

While he worked at clearing brush or mowing, I would return to his side and instruct him how to address me in the character I was trying out for the afternoon. These ranged from a train engineer to a cowboy to a circus clown with sloppy clothes. Indeed, I was a tomboy, and my father named each of my identities, from Cowboy Jane to Engineer Small to Droopy Bottoms. I delighted in all of them, and in him, for playing along and taking me seriously. There was no shortage of playmates for me then. I had my pick close at hand.

It's possible that time in my life prepared me for a career in things creative and psychological, as well as the need for many years of personal analysis. But my point here isn't to pathologize something as innate as a child's natural flexibility around fantasy and identity, or experimentation with it while their little ego forms. My point is to suggest that these experiences, which I now know are an integral part of human development, play a central role in the Stone's early understanding of Voice Dialogue. Moreover, they don't end with puberty.

What I love about Voice Dialogue is its naturalness and utter availability. Experiencing the selves resonates with us because it's available in the psyche from our beginnings. The demands of adaptation and socialization can create walls without openings; we lose touch with our innate abilities to transform ourselves by accessing our inner figures or judge them as aberrant and disturbing. But Hal and Sidra refused that brand of limitation. Leaving pathology in their dust, they followed their paths as witnesses to their own process, taking seriously everything that came to them about it.

So, like most of the tenants of Voice Dialogue, the concept of the existence of selves springs naturally from experience. If this doesn't spring from childhood, as did for me, it seems inevitable for most people as the demands of adaptation require

145

different attitudes and behavior in the socialization process. In fact, our culture insists on the development of different aspects, or "sub-personalities", if we're to make it on our own in the world and live in community. But when this adaptation breaks down, and no longer serves us by maintaining our relationships and providing us with what we enjoy, then the problems begin. We often become identified with a particular self for periods of time. But one such self can't cover all the bases as we mature, and the demands of living become more complicated. What happens next is the interesting part.

The Psychology of Selves isn't just about selves discovered in the psyche and talking to them, although in part that's how things began. I start with the Selves because Voice Dialogue with them was the original component Hal and Sidra recognized as basic to how people interact with one another. They had a heightened sensitivity to the connection they enjoyed in each other, and the moment it changed, they seemed to ask the right questions. Initially, Sidra felt enriched learning all this new stuff. Even as their respective primary operating systems began to fall apart, they struggled to be open and appreciate what was going on. There was general chaos at the level of feeling and understanding, even if they knew they are moving in the right direction. They attended to their dreams, sharing them and trying to work with them. But eventually they understood that it simply wasn't enough.

"That's why we began Voice Dialogue," Hal said. "We engaged in it whenever we could. It gave us a chance to literally work with every feeling that came up as our Primary Self Systems disintegrated." So, a way of dealing with all this fell into place with the simple request, "Let me talk to the person in you who wants to feel all together." Suddenly, the process found a container. When one self was identified, its opposite appeared as well. Then, always attentive to the dream process, Hal and Sidra began to get a sense of higher energies supporting their process.

The idea of dialoguing with inner figures stands in illustrious company and stems from Hal's Jungian background. As early as the late 1800's, Pierre Janet began using automatic writing, "to bring to light sub-personalities and [enable] dialogue with them." The goal of such practices was, at the time, to reintegrate the personality of severely mentally ill patients and to explore the constitution of the subliminal in human psychology.[33]

In his later years, Jung deepened his appreciation of the reality of the psyche and its cast of inner characters.

"The essential thing is to differentiate oneself from these unconscious contents by personifying them, and at the same time to bring them into relationship with consciousness. That is the technique for stripping them of their power. It is not too difficult to personify them, as they always possess a certain degree of autonomy, a separate identity of their own. Their autonomy is a most difficult thing to reconcile oneself to, and yet the very fact that the unconscious presents itself in this way gives us the best means of handling it." [34]

While there is clear precedent for this type of exploration, it was by no means being done actively in the1970's when Hal began developing his work. Of course, Jungian analysis was becoming known and contained within it the practice of active imagination, an internal dialogue with dream figures that analysands usually engage in near the end of their analytic work. Hal had been one of the "young Turks" in the work of formal analysis. But this kind of active dialogue in the process of relationship was unexplored and unheard of. In fact, this is one of the places where the nuts and bolts of Voice Dialogue and the Psychology of Selves meet and mingle with the current Psychology of Relationship. The birth of these twin studies seemed midwifed by the energy of love and the Stones' need to weather the incumbent storm of transformation simultaneously. Jungian theory seemed insufficient, even with the

147

powerful dream process Hal and Sidra shared. Their process needed relationship to survive.

On the first evening of the interviews in 2011, Sidra had been rummaging around in her bookshelf and came in carrying a slight volume by Miguel Serrano. She had located the place where Jung actually talked about relationship from his perspective. Serrano had given Jung a signed translation he'd published called *The Visits of the Queen of Sheba*. When they met next, Jung reflected on it and subsequently, on relationship in general.

'Your story about the Queen of Sheba is more like a poem than an ordinary tale,' he said. 'The affair of the King and the Queen of Sheba seems to contain everything; it has a truly noumenal quality…'

'But if you ever meet the Queen of Sheba in the flesh, beware of marrying her. The Queen of Sheba is only for a magic kind of love, never for matrimony. If you were to marry her, you would both be destroyed, and your soul would disintegrate…

'In my long psychiatric experience, I have never come across a marriage that was entirely self-sufficient. … Moreover, a marriage, which is devoted entirely to mutual understanding, is bad for the development of the individual personality; it is a descent to the lowest common denominator, which is something like the collective stupidity of the masses. Inevitably one or the other will begin to penetrate the mysteries.

'… Basically speaking, man is polygamous. The people of the Mussulmen Empire knew that very well. Nevertheless, marrying several women at the same time is a primitive solution, and would be rather expensive today,' [Jung finished laughing.][35]

Hal and Sidra finished with some excited energy between them, causing Hal to start a sentence Sidra finished. "You see," Hal said. "It's very interesting because this shows the difference in …"

"His approach to marriage and relationship and ours," Sidra finished up. But Hal wasn't done. He added, "If relationship is the path, versus it's not possible to do [with one person] then relationship as a path doesn't exist. It can't exist. If individuation is the path, and this is a very deep issue, then many a woman gets crucified on that cross. The man sees his path and the woman is an interference."

So, essentially, each of us, according to the Psychology of Selves, is made up of a group of individual selves, or sub-personalities, that manage our lives for us as we interact with the outside world. There are a number of groups of selves, designated for specific jobs, starting with the Power Selves, whose job it is to protect our vulnerability as we face the largeness of the world. These selves get us what we want and need and run interference against anything or anyone who would deprive us of that.

Like Jungian complexes with archetypal cores, there is a group of selves whose dominance defines how we handle the vicissitudes of our lives. In the early days of the work, these groups seemed common to all human beings, and Primary Selves seemed more generalized. Later work revealed that selves are actually more individualized, but it was not always that way.

Like archetypal elements in the psyche which contain positive and negative valences, these selves have opposites that are unknown or disowned because they represent what we don't like or identify with in our personality. This is reminiscent of the Jungian shadow qualities that we project onto others rather than acknowledge

149

them as our own. These then became the Disowned Selves in the Stones' work. When they would discover a new self, they immediately wanted to explore it.

"So, we might have been driving someplace," Hal said, "talking about a self. Then one of us would say, 'Could you talk to mine next?' So, I might be driving, and Sidra would be talking to the two sides of the self in question." Then he paused, smiling at a memory he wasn't probably going to share. "Although it's really better if the person driving does the facilitation."

I let myself imagine driving along, being facilitated by my passenger. Then I imagined the possibility of discovering a self of mine who doesn't know how to drive, or hates traffic and escalates, or a self who needs a nap. The problems seemed endless. I instantly agreed with his recommendation. But his point was that in the beginning, facilitations as such were not always formal; but they were rich in their contribution to the whole.

"We covered a huge amount of material," Hal said. "I wasn't yet really introducing this out in the world. At the time, I just didn't get the larger implications of it. I simply didn't understand how big it was. The Aware Ego Process that we talk about so easily today wasn't clarified yet. When that began to come through, and I got a sense of what was happening for clients who took to this work, I realized we had a tiger by the tail."

This is the scaffolding on which the Stone's work was built. But the key piece here rests not on what the selves are, although Hal and Sidra spent years identifying and teaching how to find the selves that make us tick. The key to the work's success and value is how these selves operate energetically. Energy is inextricably linked to every aspect of the Psychology of Selves and remains inseparable from any discussion of the work.

Now things get juicy.

CHAPTER ELEVEN

The Work

In a nutshell - okay, a very large nutshell - Voice Dialogue as a psycho/spiritual process came into being during this rich and turbulent decade of the 1970's. For the Stones, there seemed to be discovery upon discovery. As I've said earlier, the Psychology of Selves found its roots in a culture expanding as quickly as the Stones' understanding of what was happening between them. Their traditional, and familiar, inner figures - as well as their opposites - became active, autonomous, and articulate members of internal and external conversation. An incredible period of learning and forward thinking ensued while they struggled with appreciating what they had bumped into. The Selves were just the beginning. Moreover, and perhaps consequently, Hal's and Sidra's professional and personal lives made earth-shaking shifts as well.

Although Hal's dissatisfaction with the Jungian community in L.A. had been growing since the late 1960's, things didn't really gel for him until 1970. Like many big changes in understanding, there remained significant resistance to deal with.

"There was a two-year period during which I got really nasty," Hal said candidly. "I was fighting and arguing all the time. Then there came a moment at a Certifying Board meeting when someone presented a beautiful dream of an analytic candidate. To me, it seemed to point to the end of analysis. I thought, 'Congratulations! You did it!' The presenting analyst held a completely opposite view, supporting the idea that this was the beginning of an analysis that would last another five years! The wrongness of this hit me hard. I lost control. Unable to take in the breadth and depth of this moment all at once, I moved from the good son toward the opposite archetype: the rupture and repercussions were massive."

Hal recognized the intensity of this quickly, and knew he needed to get away. Against all precedent, as he and his wife had one child and she was pregnant with J. Tamar, he called a travel agent and booked passage on the SS France. During the last week of the return trip, Hal happened to see the Zeffrelli film *Romeo and Juliet*. He began to cry and kept crying for the next five days.

"I realized I had been shutting down my feelings for a long time," Hal said. "It was an enormous effort. When the anger had started earlier, it was freeing, even cleansing." Hal returned to the group meeting after his trip and started to share what had happened to him. "Someone started jawing at me," he said, "but I wasn't angry anymore. That's the moment I understood something profound. I realized that this had been my tribe at one time, but it wasn't my tribe anymore. I had caused enough mischief. I had no intention of raising any kind of fuss. I would finish out my term, install a new President for the group, and not look back. No big announcement. It was just over."

In the next two years, Hal was introduced to some key people who were to support and direct him toward his next project. Edith Sullwald, a colleague and Jungian psychotherapist who worked with children, came to Hal, telling him of a psychic she wanted him to see. As Hal wasn't then inclined to consult psychics, he hesitated, asking what was so important. Edith responded that she had seen George Osteen, and again insisted Hal do the same. He made an appointment.

"I sat down," Hal said, "and he looked me in the eye. He said, 'Your life is going to change completely and quickly. You're going to be starting a teaching and

153

research center. I can't see it all, but it will be very large, involving a lot of people. You have no idea how big this thing will be.' When he said that, it was like he burst my brain open. I saw the whole thing. I knew it was true. I understood I was the right person to do it, and that I was going to do it."

Edith Sullwald became Hal's co-director as The Center for the Healing Arts came into being. This heralded a new period of growth and exploration for Hal. The dial on his path clicked one space to the right, narrowing his focus for the next near decade. The Center opened in 1973, bringing the West Coast an introduction to holistic approaches to healing. It became, in fact, as big as George Osteen had predicted.

It was a major undertaking. Hal was divorced from his first wife by this time, making child support payments, and maintaining a private practice. The operation of the Center alone was a big job and its scope was only expanding. Programs drew audiences of five to six hundred people, which continued for quite a long period of time. "Those programs filled consciousness holes at the time," he said. "When they stopped working, which they did eventually, they had done their job."

It was clear listening to Hal reflecting on this time that he didn't think he could have created and run the Center without his relationship with Sidra. But her involvement wasn't hands on at the time. Although Hal leaned into their relationship for support and grounding, Sidra stayed separate from the actual Center.

"This was very intentional on my part," Sidra said, "and a saving grace. Frankly, I think it was one of the things that kept things working between us. The Center was a huge operation. I was an anchor on the outside."

Although Hal's description of the Center contained some details of the times and the feel of the place, the breadth of the accomplishment pales in comparison to the expansion of consciousness for Hal on which it rested. He was galloping across the consciousness of the time and burning to teach it as he went. People involved in the early days of Voice Dialogue's creation, like Voice Dialogue facilitator Marsha Sheldon, would remember the times with enduring appreciation.

"Hal gathered all these amazing people at the Center for the Healing Arts. He invited the Simontons, Joseph Campbell, Robert Bly, and Ram Dass to come and teach about consciousness and healing. Then on Fridays, Hal created what he called a *Guinea Pig Group*. He would try out all these new, cutting edge techniques on us. It was great ... a real risk-taking group. He started teaching Voice Dialogue there. Then we all became staff for later workshops."[36]

In the tradition of many innovative psychologists and psychiatrists, not the least of whom were Freud and Jung, Hal also developed his work and subsequent teachers from the people who had worked with him. The development of the method has as clear an evolution as Hal and Sidra's personal processes. Its origins rest on the small groups Hal ran, or offered in various venues in the area with a small but growing staff. Although his process continued to deepen with Sidra, his actual teaching of Voice Dialogue was not a major part of the Center's offerings.

In the 1970's, the Center for the Healing Arts worked with a lot of cancer patients. Hal required everyone to have a consulting oncologist in their treatment team, but there was a group of very innovative people around as well. They consulted and created new attitudes and treatments. David Bressler, M.D. founded the UCLA Pain Center Clinic, introducing acupuncture, hypnotherapy, and other alternative modalities to help with pain management. The work of the Simontons was also ground breaking in their work with cancer patients.[37] William Brugh Joy brought energy work to the mix, clearing energetic fields and moving energy in the body.[38] Jaqueline McCandless, M.D. brought new attitudes and study to bear on autism during that time as well.[39] She was joined by Jack Zimmerman, Ph.D., a spiritual teacher responsible for bringing the Ojai Council process to the Center, best known as working in a circle and passing the talking stick.[40]

Hal and the Center for the Healing Arts were on the cutting edge of new age ideas and therapies. It was a union of the worlds of psychology and spirituality. It was definitely a time of merger and transformation. To label this time driven by enthusiasm would hardly do it justice. Hal was expanding and taking the world around him with him. Talking with Hal's daughter J. Tamar made the time come even more alive, as she recalled watching it all happen.

"My Dad was giving it all. It was the culmination of a part of him that was generous and visionary, giving on a cultural level. It was simply revolutionary at the time. It became a template for our family, giving in this way. The only words to describe it are expansive and creative. It was incredible."[41]

All the while, the process between Hal and Sidra grew and strengthened. As she supported his imagination and growth at the Center for the Healing Arts, Hal shared his drive for innovation in his work with Sidra, who had become the Executive Director of Hamburger Home in 1972.

"What Hal gave me," Sidra said, "was the idea that you could be creative in working with people. I had the girls at Hamburger Home doing yoga, poetry, creative writing and art." Considering that the place was in such rough shape when Sidra started there, this was a real departure from a dying traditional approach. For her, these were golden years of excitement, expansion, and innovation.

Hamburger Home was a residential treatment center for adolescent girls in varying degrees of trouble. Unable to adapt or conform to the standards of the day, they usually arrived at the behest of the court system and stayed until their treatment or maturity sent them on. Although they attended classes at Hollywood High School, Sidra had her hands full in the beginning. Not only had she inherited a dispirited staff and seven unruly girls, Sidra had to recreate the entire program.

"At first, I was constantly running to talk to the principal about one or another of my girls," she said. "They were always getting into trouble. They were truant and sometimes caught smoking dope in the halls. They were always being kept after school. So, I had two teachers and a school program installed right at the Home. Then all they had to do was go upstairs to go to school."

It's not hard to recognize the beginnings of a joint understanding of what Hal and Sidra now call the *psychic fingerprint*. Even back then Sidra held that everybody has something unique to contribute. It became her *modus operandi*, right down to allowing each girl to decorate her own room. It wasn't long before Hamburger Home was a haven for girls who needed therapy, education and a chance to rediscover or reinvent themselves. Sidra made it so inviting the residents didn't want to be discharged.

She was still raising her three children in these years and integrated her daughters into the running of the agency. They often accompanied their mother on field trips with residents of Hamburger Home and had no idea the kids in treatment were any different from any other kids.

"Sometimes I took them all out into the desert," Sidra said, "into the Devil's Punchbowl. They all took their cameras from Photography class, but I soon realized the inner-city kids were afraid to get out of the car. Here were these very tough, street kids, clinging to each other because they thought there were ghosts and wild animals around them. It took some time before they relaxed enough to just walk around and take some pictures. I was a process of understanding for us all."

By the late 1970's, and again in answer to urgings independent of one another, Hal and Sidra began to tire of administrative responsibilities. Sidra wearied of the paperwork and bureaucracy of running the Home. In a synchronicity that still never fails to surprise them, Hal resigned from the Board of the Center for the Healing Arts without knowing that Sidra had simultaneously stepped down as Executive Director of Hamburger Home. Listening to the persistent calls they heard to change direction, they again turned toward each other.

Their marriage in 1977 had set so many things in motion, sorting out the results took time. Hal's energy was shifting. The responsibility and demands at the Center had weighed heavily. Although he felt the field clearing and energy work he did was his home, Hal again looked into a future of that kind of work and just couldn't see it. He closed his office on San Vicente Boulevard in Los Angeles. He and Sidra began a joint practice while Hal created the first teaching modality of Voice Dialogue in the form of seminars in the backyard of Sidra's Sherman Oaks home. They both stepped into a period of enormous change. As the dust settled, their archetypal identities began the inevitable pull to embrace what the other person carried for them. Ever an observant and willing participant in the journey, J. Tamar remembers this shift in family life with obvious enjoyment.

"It's hard to list all the ways my life changed with the "ingredient" Sidra. We had been in introverted family, but I saw my father enter the real world. He had always embodied the Archetypal Mind. But Sidra brought in the Archetypal Body, the earth element. For my Dad, the world then became his oyster."[42]

Sidra's impetus encouraged travel. She expanded their lives out into the world, making the richness of her Sherman Oaks gardens a declaration/expression of herself. She simply had a big appetite for life, for food, especially dessert. Her children knew that the meal was only a vehicle to get to dessert. In fact, she was known to say, "Let's skip the meal and go for ice cream." Still in touch with the child who enjoyed this, J. Tamar laughed telling me about it.

"That was Sidra - never wedded to form or tradition. She stopped coloring her hair when she was still young. She called grey, silver and wore it with pride. She's like the archetypal feminine: her hair, her dress, her energy. I couldn't ask for a better stepmother, friend, colleague, or mentor.[43]

It seems that Hal and Sidra continue to represent more than the individual archetypes they have lived out. They represent an archetype together as well. Their relationship has contained both the masculine and feminine archetypal journeys: Sidra with her writing of *The Shadow King*, the world and appetites, and Hal, moving from the upper, impersonal realms in his head, to connecting with his heart, being tender, loving and sweet. They have changed and expanded each other.

Taking their respective urgings seriously, Hal began teaching what he was learning in his own process. He moved his tutorials to the gardens behind their Sherman Oaks house and began teaching small groups of interested people the ways of Voice Dialogue and what was still at the time, called the Psychology of Selves.

159

I've always secretly envied the folks who were there at the beginning. The stories shared about those days in the backyard bubble with delight and hilarity. Not only was exploration and imagination the *zeitgeist* of California's psychological community in the 1970's, it became the cornerstone of a consciousness movement that took the country by storm in a single decade. Those fortunate enough to jump in when invited, talk about the early days with a wistful smile and ready laugh; like this memory from an early participant Martha Lou Wolff, PhD:

"In the beginning, things were fairly structured in terms of training. Hal taught three times a week for three weeks. But there was tremendous creativity and encouragement to try new things. One day when it rained in Sherman Oaks, we went into the living room. Hal had the inspiration to play different kinds of music and instructed us to be the self that fit with the music. He did the same thing using different animals. Then he would ask us to tell the person next to us a secret we'd never told anyone, just to have us experience the liberation from releasing it. We even did gibberish communication. It was absolutely delicious."[44]

Stories like these abound among those who qualify as the "old guard" of the Voice Dialogue community … and they're worth hearing. One facilitator observed that one could look back at those days, like listing the comedians who got their start on the Johnny Carson Show. Many of the early participants in the garden have gone on to create training events and Voice Dialogue Institutes on their own. As time passes, those present at the beginning also recognize the beginning threads of the Stones' current understanding of consciousness. J. Tamar adds to the description an important reflection.

"From my point of view, the seeds of recognition of the Organizing Intelligence or now Source energy, were sown in that garden at Sherman Oaks, as well as in the Summer Kamps and Intensives at Thera that came later. They were like the Salons of Socrates and Plato. An experience had been had!"[45]

From the rich beds in Sidra's gardens, Hal tended the flowering of a new understanding, complete with a physical education aspect in the form of Aikido sessions with a master, Larry Novick. While Hal worked toward a black belt of his own, he began to make connections between the martial art and the process of energetics in the work of Voice Dialogue. Larry talked with me extensively about this time in the work's development.

"One day in the early 1980's," he said, "Hal was on the freeway when he had a sense that he was about to be in an accident. Then someone suddenly cut him off. Because he'd been alerted energetically, he avoided what would have been a very bad accident. Hal credited that heightened sensitivity to his practice of Aikido."[46]

Hal and Aikido Master Larry Novick, 1993. Hal's final test for his black belt at Summer Kamp.

The parallels between Voice Dialogue as a consciousness process and the work of Aikido are many. The kind of energetic sensibility Hal recognized on the freeway seems only the beginning of a list of qualities the two bodies of work share. Lines between the two intersect on several important levels, and for me, resonate with Jung's understanding of the analytic process as well.

"When one does Aikido," Larry elaborated in another conversation, "it initiates someone into a process of conscious response or choice, versus an unconscious reaction to vulnerability. Like the Primary Selves jump in to protect our vulnerability in Voice Dialogue, Aikido is the same thing, embodied. People learn to distrust natural reactions, taking time to consider other options. It results in having compassion for the moment at hand, rather than sheer survival."[47]

On one level, these conversations with Larry added another dimension to my understanding of the Psychology of Selves' breadth and depth. There appears to be a commonality of metaphor between Jung, Aikido and Voice Dialogue. As does the complex, so does the Primary Self System, as does the practice of Aikido. Now if you're like me this begins to get exciting because I'm beginning to make some connections. I can tell you that it was exciting for Hal's former teacher, and for Hal, who eventually earned his black belt in Aikido. So, I sat back and listened. There's nothing quite as engaging as listening to someone talk about their passion, and when Hal and Sidra, or Larry Novick, or Dianne Braden, I guess, start connecting the dots, the images become exceedingly engaging.

On another level, Larry helped me understand that the actual facilitation of the selves, which was the major part of the early work in Voice Dialogue, also had a corollary in the martial art he practices. When teaching people Aikido, the lesson is one of tying energies together. People learn to connect with energies, track them, and then let them express themselves. If I hadn't used the word Aikido, it would be hard to know I wasn't talking about Voice Dialogue facilitation.[48] In fact, I could just as easily be talking about activating and depotentiating complexes in a Jungian analysis. Further, each discipline had the somewhat humble beginnings of students grouping around a teacher in informal settings. Jung gathered colleagues and analysands to discuss and teach his work, much like training seminars do today. Aikido began for Hal as another way to get into his body and connect with a feeling/energetic life neglected in his early training. The combination of these rests at the foundation of the work he introduced.

Meanwhile, Sidra was working at her private practice and observing this explosive discovery and balancing of energy. Ever the Brooklynite who needed proof, she was more cautious about bringing the work into her practice. Even though she

163

and Hal continued to dedicate much of their time exploring their relationship and using it as the model for their discoveries with each other, Sidra was slower to bring the results into her work with clients.

The concept of energetics took hold while Hal was still at the Center for the Healing Arts, but Sidra chose a more conservative approach. Hal's work with William Brugh Joy taught him about the chakras and rebalancing them. This evolved for Hal into doing energy clearing. Although Sidra continued to do visualizations and Voice Dialogue in her private practice, she wasn't lacking curiosity about the energy work.

"So, at the time," Sidra said, "Hal was getting more interested in energy clearing, working with the chakras, and working with other peoples' energy fields. He was very enthusiastic about it. In those days, we could be in a museum and Hal would be in touch with the energy of the statues, or paintings ... even the artifacts."

Slowly, Sidra began to try it on. Although her practice was more stylized then, "when no one was looking," she would begin to talk about energies. Then a voice would come in for her, speaking for a part of her that was simply shocked she'd strayed so far from her original training. It wasn't until she and Hal travelled to Montreal, Quebec that Sidra's experience changed her direction.

"In those days, we worked with a lot of spiritually-oriented people," she said. "I was actually doing energy work then, too. We were gathered in a large hall of a church, calling on the larger energies, and I had a feeling I was in touch with the Archangel Michael."

The amount of courage it took to step into these uncharted waters is staggering for me, even as I write about it now. Although the Stones stand in good and revered company in this tradition of just putting it out there, it is still flat out scary when I think of being the first ones to teach energetic work in front of a group of people. When I reflected as much to Sidra, she jumped in quickly.

"Indeed, it took a tremendous amount of courage to do it. Hal had that kind of courage," she said. "I did not. I thought at first, 'Oh God. I hope nobody hears me!' As I said, even in therapy there was a part of me that stood in disbelief that I was saying these new things. I needed proof. I wanted to see it happen."

In her own direct way, Sidra began to actively try to move energy. Remembering the feeling of clearing energy fields, she would pull her energy up, up, up as she sat with a client. When she saw the person's arm literally rise up in the air without her having asked them to do so, she was finally convinced. She had her proof. But she intuitively knew the same would be necessary out in the world. They needed something concrete to seal the package. The same stream that fed the work for Hal with Larry Novick, appeared for Sidra in her own experiences of Aikido at Esalen Institute.

"Esalen was a pretty world-shaking place in the 1970's," she said. "I had avoided getting into that popular mindset of waiting for earth-shattering experiences. If you didn't have one, people thought there was something wrong with you. There was an Aikido workshop offered with George Leonard and I signed up while Hal took a workshop for runners. He was a big runner then."

What happened for Sidra during that weekend was formative. From the "energy rolls" of the martial art, to the "pushing exercises" and "strong arm tests" the two streams came together. Hal and Larry Novick continued after Sidra stopped, but she holds the experience as central to her acceptance of the energetic work that supports and characterizes the Psychology of Selves and the Aware Ego Process.

165

"I loved the energy of the work, and the metaphors," she said. "The idea of being centered was so 'Aware Ego-ish' before there was really a formal Aware Ego Process in our work. Also, the idea of projecting energy and controlling your energetic field was amazing. It all just spoke to me and went in very, very deep. It was incredibly useful when we went out to teach. I could start feeling how to expand my energetic field rather than collapsing it, which would have been my natural way."

It wasn't long before an energetic vocabulary was established between Hal and Sidra. It was a part of their interaction with each other and a way they came to see the Selves - as uniquely energetic. Just when the temptation arises to glorify their wisdom and creativity, Sidra reminds me that it came out of living their lives.

"We picked up a little here, a little there, put it in a pot, cooked it, and waited to see what came out," Sidra said. "It was a part of how we were together … like saying something when your attention drifts instead of keeping it to yourself. Or, we would acknowledge it when we felt energetic linkage to one another, or the lack thereof."

From the initial recognition of Selves to the experience of their energies, the Stones talked, worked, and lived their concepts. The early energetic exercises differed from those Hal and Sidra do today. There were still traces of chakra work and running energies, blending them, and running them out through different chakras. They also did three-way linkage exercises, in which two people linked into each other and then one dropped the linkage and linked in with the other person. These were ripe for reactions and people clearly feeling the shifts in energy.

"We haven't done those in many, many years," Sidra said. "It takes a long time. In truth, it was more my exercise than Hal's anyway. We didn't even call it linkage then. That came along much later, in the 2000's. We were fascinated with what we found in each other. By the late 1970's, both the bonding patterns and the consciousness model were in place, though not in as expanded a form as we now understand them. But the energy work was the real beginning."

Thus, the foundation was built for a body of work that has continued to expand and deepen for the last forty years. Brick by experiential brick, the Stones constructed the energetic foundation on which to rest their future work. From there, they looked to understand the path onto which they had seemingly been thrown. That understanding was an adventure in itself. At every turn, there seemed to be another surprise.

CHAPTER TWELVE

The Work

ENERGETICS AND BONDING PATTERNS

There are times when the energetic connection that people have with one another is more palpable than others. It's one of the perks of being human, this kind of invisible linkage to another being that yields such a feeling of belonging. It is one of those things I sometimes don't recognize until I'm losing it, or it's gone all together. This is not a sad thing. Goodbyes aren't always permanent. Connections, of the valuable kind, can be reestablished if tended to and, repaired, if need be. Or, energetic connections can simply be rediscovered and enjoyed all the more for their history and the sweetness of memory.

When I was in my forties, the wisdom of the spheres brought me to a kind and strong analyst. I sat before him for a while, not really knowing what to do, or why I was there specifically, until the energetic connection was established. Jungians call it transference; spiritual pundits call it devotion and a number of other things. What I understand about this experience now is that it's the energetic linkage that is fundamental to a good analytic relationship. This is also a central component of the Stone's work that impacted me right away.

In the late 1980's, I busied myself driving to Pittsburgh for my analytic appointments, a two-hour trip each way. I would do this faithfully for the subsequent eight years. I would sit in the waiting room listening to pretty awful music and wait for my analyst to open the door. I felt the usual uneasiness, that mix of excitement and dread, in case I hadn't had a dream to explore. In essence, it was none of those things that seemed as daunting on the front side of my appointments, as what I faced leaving. What I realized when the hour was over, was that I had been so well held and attended to, I was filled with an energy both wonderful and terrible. I knew as I started my car, it would be another week before I felt loved like that again. That's energetic linkage.

I was fortunate. I found a good analyst and stuck with him until I felt connected. Not immune to loss and disappointment, I found a place to take my pain. Our work together healed my heart of wounds I'd assumed were untouchable. Not all analyses go like that, offering that positive feeling. Further, some are thought lacking if the opposite isn't true at least in some stages. But for me, this first experience turned my energetic dial to a new intensity. It was exactly what I needed. I was well served in those hours with him and the long drives were a part of the linkage, during which I was spared the critique that so often plagues my receptivity. I just let it happen.

This early experience of real energetic connection ultimately prepared me for long and deep relationships with subsequent analysts, and importantly for this book, with Hal and Sidra, based on the same feeling, ramped up by a million gigahertz. (I learned to exaggerate from Hal. It's contagious.) As mentioned in the early chapters, walking into their offices for my first sessions, I recognized the real thing and never backed away.

While a one-on-one experience has always been my introverted preference in working with almost anyone, the Stones became well-known for their ability to work with groups, large and small. Their success lies in their ability to make energetic connection, and doing so with Sidra in a group setting, while different from Hal, bears its own place in the narrative of the work. To say that her energy is feminine is

169

naturally true, but not in the least is that to say it is weaker. It's more like a different flavor of a special ice cream or a different vintage of a fine wine - so worth tasting.

While my first energetic encounter with Sidra was as impactful as the one with Hal, I want to talk about a different one, THE one that speaks to the nature of their energetic work with people in any setting. Their intense interest in this would eventually lead them to group experiences called Intensives. At one such event, an experience with Sidra gave me a first-hand lesson in how it works. So, although this is a leap ahead of the chronological narrative of their lives I will continue to tell, lean back. Join me in this one snapshot.

So, for starters, I need to say that I don't see auras. I've always envied folks who do, though. I think about all the trouble I'd have avoided if forewarned by such a subtle and helpful gift on the front side of developing a relationship. Bright colors are definitely out ... certain softer shades of specific hue are good omens ... and some varieties of everyday earth colors are recommended. I stagger to think of how damn quickly I'd have extricated myself from some really awful experiences if I'd had just had a hint that there was trouble coming by a quick flash of someone's aura. Unfortunately, it has just never been my thing. But in 2002, that would change.

I was living in Washington State then. I had decided to attend one of the Stones' group seminars called Intensives, which regularly offered teaching and group experience of the Psychology of the Aware Ego Process. I lazily thought about not having to deal with the West Coast time change that had often plagued my visits with the Stones. A nice group experience would be just the thing; an antidote to my usual introversion.

No matter when you come to see her, Sidra greets you like you're a missing child who has just found its way home. Her delight in everyone she cares about is both obvious and sincere. I hadn't seen the Stones since my graduation from analytic training, and I looked forward to seeing them again in a different forum I thought would be deeply personal and demanding of my reluctance to let people in close. Although I hadn't lived in the Pacific Northwest long, I had already adopted that independent stance that moving and starting over gives one. I walked into a group of people I didn't know, thinking that it would be wonderful to watch Hal and Sidra teach without the drama that had often unfolded around me when I worked with them alone.

So, I let myself stand between my introvert and extrovert, settling into a comfortable impersonal kind of self, observing and engaging superficially, taking it all in. There was a wonderful international mix of people attending. The feel of the room was alive with a variety of accents and syntaxes. The morning passed with a group dream session, in which one person shared a dream and Hal worked with them on it while others observed. This led to questions, followed by the participants splitting off for individual sessions. Others gathered in the living room with Sidra for a group session. I was the participant to be worked with in a Voice Dialogue facilitation while the group observed.

Although there were others in the room, once Sidra turned her attention and energy toward me, I found that my impersonal independence failed me immediately. Some people in the world seem to simply radiate love and compassion. Sidra Stone is one of those. The minute she connected energetically, I felt my heart swing open like the gates of heaven. I was full out open in front of a room full of strangers. The awkwardness of this appalled me, since public vulnerability had never been on my bucket list. I had no intention of opening that door. But I was way late in coming to that thought ... like when you wish you'd have worn a life jacket as you're slipping over the falls.

So, there we were, Sidra in this incredible openhearted attitude and extraordinary bond, asking me what I'd like to work on. For a fleeting moment, I realized what I was feeling was so amazing, so comforting, it both embarrassed me and held me like a young girl who didn't really know what working on something meant. I squeaked out a question anyway, one that I had, in fact, been thinking about in my quiet moments. It was an experience I had about a year after I moved to the West Coast.

I had been in Port Townsend about eighteen months when the opportunity had come to me to lease a piece of land, with the intention--and yes, I know this was a little crazy--of building my own house. I had no training, or carpentry skills, or resources. This might have been a tip off I was caught in something not entirely rational; not to mention that I owned a posthole digger, one hammer and no power tools. But I was convinced this was my destiny. I began by putting up a fence, one posthole at a time--by myself--creating a boundary around the orchard and field that was now my sole responsibility.

The Olympic Peninsula, on which Port Townsend rests, was once covered by migrating glaciers that broke off great pieces of the rocky cliffs that meet the ocean on its three sides. Powerful rivers picked up these big chunks of stone, rolling them miles south to the ocean. The force of the waters wore down the pieces of rock, smoothing them into mid-sized sand and granite bowling-ball-like objects, lying buried under a foot or so of soil on my property.

172

I know this not because I am a passionate student of geology. I know it because about twelve inches down into a two-foot post hole, my aching hands would reverberate with the shock of hitting one of said stones, full force. The stones won the day, every time. After I checked to see that my teeth had survived the shock, I would have to try a few more times to loosen the intruder into my intention. Then I would need to lay myself out flat on the ground, reaching down the hole to get my fingers around the offending rock.

It occurred to me one day, laying prostrate at the edge of the field: I was in a unique relationship with this land. It was changing the way I walked on the earth. I lay there, relaxed, breathing, feeling supported by the ground. With my arm down the hole up to my shoulder, I felt in connection with what I thought was the earth's heartbeat. This experience was so moving, I didn't really know what to do with it, until that Sunday morning when Sidra asked what I'd like to work on. So, I told her, about the feeling, the sound, and my understanding, wondering if any of it was real. I had begun to cry.

Now, the situation was entirely different for Sidra. She was suddenly aware that she was in the role of teacher to a room full of students interested in Voice Dialogue. On another level, she was also in very deep energetic connection with me. There were simply no words for it. So, she just held it. She started to say she was aware that this was a teaching group, and that this demonstration was turning out to be of a different kind than planned. But when she looked around, every person in the room had fallen asleep. I looked around, too. I was shocked to see people leaning against walls and pillows. They were stretched out on the floor, completely unconscious.

173

Sidra stayed with me in what she and Hal would call "being" energy, until I began to see something behind her I knew instantly hadn't been there before. Behind and around her I saw a rose-colored aura, a circle of warm light shimmering around her outline. Always curious, but softly resistant to strange things that come my way, I determined I was hallucinating because I hadn't been drinking enough water. I hoped it was a change in barometric pressure, a fluke—anything--until I really noticed the color. It was beautiful.

There it was, surrounding her while she stayed in the most incredibly loving energetic connection with me. I had no idea what time it was, or how long we'd been together. In the stillness of the room I felt my energy reach out and connect to Sidra, who I believe could enchant the devil if she thought he needed love ... and he probably does.

So, in the end, I still don't see auras, except Sidra's. Whenever I visit now or have worked with her in the past, in her quiet little room with the fireplace crackling, we sit in connection first, like an energetic welcome. I see the rose-colored aura behind her, leading me gently back into a now familiar experience of energetic connection like none other.

BONDING PATTERNS

If one were to Google Voice Dialogue International, (and I recommend it), one would find an up-to-date website complete with a clear Glossary of Terms in the form of commonly asked questions about the Stones' work, written by the Stones themselves. There are also articles and books written about the work by others, a listing of Voice Dialogue facilitators and their locations of practice, and then a bookstore filled with books, CD's and downloadable mp3's created and recorded by

Hal and Sidra talking in depth about the work they do. Therefore, I'm not inclined to restate their definitions because I won't do a better job. This is the case for dealing with bonding patterns as well, which is my immediate focus. As a Jungian, I direct you to the parental complexes for a familiar, to me at least, antecedent.

From a Jungian perspective, a Bonding Pattern is a form of the parental complexes that define human relationships. While Bonding Patterns are similarly designed in that one person in any given relationship can become the child, requiring the other to step into the role of the parent with positive and negative valences, from a Voice Dialogue perspective the important element is less the role one plays, but the energy with which one does so. Bonding Patterns become the basic element of education in relationship situations, often dramatically spotlighting the Primary Self Systems in the respective personalities.

All that said, my interest here is cut from another piece of cloth than concrete facts about the work. I want, essentially, to focus on the experience of bonding patterns. What makes the work live and available in ways other depth approaches sometimes miss, or drag out, or strangle in an effort to reach the rich underworld caverns of the psyche? Not to disparage other methods or paths. As I've shown, the Stone's work rests solidly on Jungian and cognitive/behavioral foundations. It also contributes something significant to consciousness work. But it's the experience of the work that "sells" it. I want to explore why that is. How do Bonding Patterns work? How did the Stones figure that out? How do they stack up against an understanding of Parental Complexes? Finally, what does the Psychology of the Aware Ego process tell us to do with all this?

Like most psychological "methods," the Stones' work evolved in that unreasonable and non-rational way, defying order and delivery in a neat theoretical

175

package. Hal said to me recently, "Learning comes out of life. We did things. We tried things, and we learned." Like the early pioneers of depth psychology, the work came out of an attitude like that. Hal and Sidra used their relationship and put that experience to the test. Bonding Patterns are the cornerstone of that experiment.

That's how it opened up for me in the early days of working with them. I was partway through analytic training on the east side of the world, and I arrived on the west coast to "see" about the work. In an unconscious bonding pattern with practically everyone I knew, I complained to the Stones that I was *just off* somewhere; that I seemed to end up in the same place every time, in the same kind of relationship. By virtue of years of analysis and personal growth work, I now *understood* what there was about me that influenced this, and yet my insights didn't seem to bear fruit I enjoyed. It occurred to me more than once, that such understanding was a psychological mile or two away from *being able to do a damn thing about it*. I was a mile or two beyond frustrated, as well.

This is where the bonding pattern comes in. Like the unconscious parental complexes that plague our lives even if we're lucky enough to find a kind and patient analyst to enlighten us about them, the nature of the bonding pattern is that it is also derived from the parent/child relationship, and it's unconscious. For me to describe my early experience of bonding patterns is a little like asking a fish to describe the water it swims in. That's how natural and seamless bonding patterns are when you're in them and don't know about it.

Yet, in some ways, they're no more invisible to us as any other part of our humanity that we ignore or disown. Because to be in relationship with anyone, be it friend, family, professional contact, spouse or lover, the soil is rich for harvesting what comes instinctively to us: the original model of the parent/child relationship.

176

However it was that one experienced the original model, it is imprinted in the psyche and will reproduce itself in any and all relationships until it's made conscious - and even then, it's like a weed you can't kill.

Even as I write this, my sense of competence and self-knowledge objects, as if what I have done in the past doesn't count and is no longer troublesome in the present. But if I brush that aside, because I know better, then I can see why changing behavior comes at such cost. I don't really want to change my behavior. Moreover, my experience tells me I have a lot of company in that. Let's just say that on some level, I want what I want. I have enjoyed that self-righteous anger and judgment that fuel my side of things when difficulties surface in relationship, as well as feeling justified in digging in and blaming the trouble on someone – no – anyone, else. Or at least I used to.

But then, like a lot of other things that have to do with reflection at depth and the Stones' work, the layers go deeper than my initial understanding. The contribution that the work with bonding patterns makes becomes pretty fascinating. First, in my repertoire, bonding patterns seem to appear in infinite number. Second, they are as available to me as the number of people with whom I'm in relationship. Third, the awareness of them is one of the most immediate tools to foster consciousness that is out there. They provide, in a nutshell, a built-in home study course for psychological growth.

Understood as a pattern for human relationship, based on the only model we have, which is the parent/child relationship, it's not hard to see how this all works. Embracing the multiplicity of the psyche like other schools of thought, especially Jungian work, the psychology of the Aware Ego Process reveals many options of attitude and action that present themselves in familiar and agonizingly tedious

177

repetitions until something brings us to consciousness about *who* in us is engineering all this.

What does this mean in everyday experience? It means it's me and my personal cadre of selves who manages to make almost anyone into my overly critical or protective mother. Believe it or not, it's me again who creates relationships like I had with my healer or all-knowing father. And what about helping the wounded birds of the world? Right again, on a certain level, any individual can become, in my trusty psychological viewfinder, my helpless and angry handicapped sister. What's even more astounding, and correct according to Jung's complex theory, is that in response to these inducted players on the stage of my mind, I will become the little girl I was in relationship to them. Fantastic so far! So much for the past being the past.

Now here's the best part. This bonding pattern situation has a predictable outcome. Instead of falling into the dreaded *"psychological stuckness,"* I'm guaranteed that this will change. Not only that, I can pretty much guess how. That little girl of mine will eventually become hurt or irritated with the experience of being criticized or over-protected, and as the pressure mounts, she's going to complain loudly enough for a Primary Self of mine to grab some of that power and become a Critical Mother herself; or a strong and All-Knowing Father, if the need arises as the Good (and silent) Daughter in me grows weary of taking all this in again.

Further, I can say with some certainty that the part of me that is a dutiful and compassionate, young, care-giving sibling will most certainty tire of seeing about her sister. At that time, she will, with the help of a Primary self, morph into an entitled adult rival and push back without a moment's hesitation. My opponents in this drama will flip to their opposites as well. Back and forth these patterns go in varying degrees of enjoyment and disaster, both people trying to find the energetic connection that drew them into relationship in the first place.

Now, if this doesn't remind you of every fight you've ever had in a long-term relationship then I question if you've been in one. Because while the characters in this particular drama may change description, the drama of the parent/child dynamic will not, unless someone in the relationship becomes conscious of the bonding pattern being presented.

If the bonding pattern is positive in nature, no one objects to anything. There's no negativity, no fighting, because no one talks about problems. No one wants to make waves. However, peace at all costs has its shadow. Relationship without the bumping up against opposites eventually dies of its own inertia and lack of fire. Everybody making nice becomes suffocating and dull. Because the psyche will not tolerate imbalance, as Jung described in the *enantiodromia*, the flip to a negative bonding pattern, described above, is predictable, if not inevitable.

How the Stones came to understand this dynamic is the meat of their work. Again, they worked on their process with each other. Once they married, these bonding patterns became not only obvious, but terrifically problematic, and educational. Their love story became the birthplace of the bonding patterns whose identification is the cornerstone of the working with people in relationship. The psychology of the Aware Ego Process steps onto the creative stage with no small fanfare.

CHAPTER THIRTEEN

The Work

LIFE AND THE AWARE EGO PROCESS

Although the seeds of the Aware Ego Process were there at the beginning, there was so much commotion around the discovery and facilitation of the Selves, Hal and Sidra could only see it indirectly. It was like not being able to see the wind, but knowing it was there by the movement of the trees. The Stones *felt* what happened when people separated from selves and found the opposite. But as a formal process, the Aware Ego Process wasn't at first definable.

By the 1980's, the work generated by Hal and Sidra's relationship began to find its home in larger venues. From early seminars in an L.A. restaurant, to more formal seminars near home, Hal's focus narrowed. Leaving his earlier concentration on energy work and field clearing, he began teaching Voice Dialogue to larger groups out of their Sherman Oaks home. Although Hal and Sidra learned fairly early on that therapists weren't yet open to the work, it became very popular with other professionals and laymen alike. Hal was busy. Many of the people involved in those early days remember them as quite different from the work known as Voice Dialogue today. Martha Lou Wolff, Ph.D. was one of the original participants.

"In the early days in the backyard," she said, "the Aware Ego Process hadn't really appeared yet. There was still a lot of energy clearing and facilitation of the 'heavy hitters', the Power Selves,[49] that came from the work at the Center for the Healing Arts. They were the selves that kept people trapped in an energetic space. Hal did the teaching. He was much more impersonal then ... very much more 'Dr. Stone' than he was a bit later on."[50]

As time went on, many professionals in all fields of healthcare became interested in the work. In fact, many of the early practitioners went back to school and became therapists themselves. Voice Dialogue continued in a process of expansion, looking in new directions, then further discovery for the Stones and those around them. New teaching modalities appeared, such as events called Summer Kamp and Voice Dialogue workshops out into an International community. Although it looked as though these may have been shifts in the work, Hal and Sidra remained true to learning from the process between them as it unrelentingly led them toward the largeness of their process.

Summer Kamp was one of those creative discoveries that took on a life of its own. Memories of these events are rich with anecdotes that still bring laughter to participants who attended them. There's a fondness that lingers in the air after the telling, no matter who the storyteller might be. Hal and Sidra enjoyed the creation of their work and allowed an irrepressible sense of humor free rein in the doing. The mood lightened, and people learned to play as well as deepen. Summer Kamp was, in fact, just that: a summer camp, but for adults. It was held in Philo, California, and became an educational and personal phenomenon. Structured as a live-in experience, people shared cabins, rituals and meals together, then split up in groups for discussion, facilitation, teaching, and art. A woman named Carol Bardeen prepared an open arts and crafts table where people worked through various personal issues with creative activities. Modeled after the groups Hal had run in the backyard of the Sherman Oaks house, groups assembled in the morning for dream work. Then there were one or two facilitators who worked individually with people on what might have come up for them in the morning. Hal's daughter, J. Tamar, remembers the events from the very beginning.

"The entire thing was electric!" she said. "There was huge energy in the field. I taught Body Dialogue there for the first time, and Larry Novick was there, too, teaching Aikido. The events ended with creative skits, art displays - it was a place where all the ingredients came together."[51]

Summer Kamp represented the middle phase of Voice Dialogue's evolution, a phase that eventually yielded to the Retreats at Thera in Albion, California. These then morphed into week-long training events called Intensives at Levels 1, 2, and 3. The essential elements of the future work came into being during these early groups, completed only by characteristic laughter that permeates any gathering of Voice Dialogue practitioners. J. Tamar continued to reminisce about the Voice Dialogue events of her past.

"One thing I always remember," she said, "was that Dad put a lot of time and energy into lunch. It was a big effort - a lot of work, really. I remember having these big Greek lunches at workshops even as far back as those held in the Sherman Oaks home and then the Sherman Oaks Church. I asked him once why he put all this time, money and effort into what could have been a relatively simple affair. He said, 'You want to feed all the selves. It's important that all of them be nourished and happy.' "[52]

Even in these early beginnings, Hal understood the importance of something so basic and essential. It set a template for tending to all the selves in this way until the Intensives held at Thera, which became famous for their great lunches and snacks until they ended in 2013. The social aspects of trainings and workshops gave Hal an opportunity to soften and become playful. Another long-time facilitator, J'aime Ona Pangaia, remembered the early days as wistfully as others who enjoyed the work's buddings.

"Early on, when I came to the work," she said, "Hal and Sidra didn't teach facilitation, they modeled it. They gave lots of demos. Then they gave people free rein to try it themselves, unless they wished for guidance. Then sometimes, we'd take a day off for us to take our Inner Children shopping. It was a creative time. We even moved into Selves and expressed them non-verbally, dancing the selves with Gabrielle Roth."[53]

Dr. Stone gave way gradually to the Hal people enjoyed in his personal life. He began to have a lot of fun with those lunches he deemed so important. His creative "recipes" were anticipated with delight during the early years of the Intensives that followed Summer Kamps, and on any given schedule for the week, one might have found announcements such as this.

1:35pm – 1:40pm – SPECIAL LUNCHEON FOR THURSDAY

SEPT. 20

LENGEN SCHMOOKLES:

Brought back by popular demand

The following ingredients are poured into a five-gallon pot of Aloe Vera and a specially prepared powder of green and mixed vegetable puree a la Garfield. Then

183

add a handful of sassafras leaves; a handful of cumin seeds; the bark of the African Lubong tree; one jar of fermented almond butter; two handfuls of boiled stinging nettles; one jar of Saskartoon seed mustard; two freshly picked organic zucchinis. Finally add onions, garlic and crushed oleander, then blend until thick but still moving. With a wooden ladle, we spoon the contents onto our special schmookle torte pans, which vibrate when heated. Bake these for 16 and ½ minutes. Then let contents vibrate without heat for an additional 10 minutes. We recommend not eating more than three of these schmookles at any one sitting. If you have more, we suggest you take two digestive enzyme pills to support the work of your intestinal spaces. These will be provided to you on an "as needed" basis. Bon Voyage.[54]

Many remember these recipes were so convincing, some participants took them literally, concerned about their allergies to some of the ingredients. It sounds like a lot of fun!

Stories abound about this period of time. It seems the work was experiencing its own Aware Ego Process as it struggled to find its balance in the early retreats and trainings. The experienced Voice Dialogue facilitators who now figure in a small cadre of "old timers" remember the old days like beloved family history. The selves they discovered came in all shapes and sizes, dragging behind them their opposites who sometimes sat at the table like the drunken uncle one has to invite, and everyone tolerates because it's family. It wasn't long before another aspect of the work appeared in time to balance things out. Marsha Sheldon, another of the very early crew, spoke with as much amusement and fondness as everyone else who attended or staffed these early events.

"When we did the first Summer Kamp," she said, "we wanted to highlight the Vulnerable Child. We made T-shirts with Vulnerable Child on them and wore them as the theme. Back then we didn't realize the shadow side of this self is a Demon Child, full of self-centeredness and rebellion. The staff had to deal with these awful belligerent, screaming children. The next year, the T-shirts read 'Aware Ego'."[55]

Still in the creative phases, Hal and Sidra shared the teaching sessions. Although Hal took the lead in most of the early work, and while Sidra took part in demonstrations, they divided the group work. Although Hal's facilitations of Aphrodite are memorable, (fifteen of the twenty-five people reminiscing at the Colorado Convergence in 2013 had done Aphrodite facilitations with Hal) Sidra embodied the strong feminine principle. Her early women's groups, facilitating and exploring the many aspects of Aphrodite, were also a favorite. Cynthia Hymowitz, another early participant who became a Voice Dialogue facilitator later on, remembered Sidra's groups with that same nostalgia that characterizes this unique history.

"Sidra's induction into Aphrodite energy was different than Hal's," she said, "but it was equally beautiful. She ran a group for just the women, in part talking and drumming, and then moving in Aphrodite energy. We all left the group finding the beauty in every woman."[56]

Sidra's presence and participation as a teacher became more and more obvious as she took her place in the retreats and trainings with Hal. In what seemed to be advance notice from the Trickster, it was during one of the early Summer Kamps that her future identity in the work was foretold in the form of a gift. Dorsey Cartwright, another early participant destined to use the work professionally later on, talked about this foreshadowing in a personal communication.

"We were at Summer Kamp in Philo, CA," she said. "The group decided to get a gift for Hal and Sidra, to present to them at the end of Kamp. Somebody went into town and found two pewter dragons, one larger than the other. We had them wrapped and labeled, the larger to go to Hal. When it came time to open the gifts, Sidra's gift box contained the larger dragon."[57]

It was as if something in the universe knew that a shift in responsibilities was to come. After Hal left the Center for the Healing Arts, he had a vision that a new project was coming to him. The project looked to be a world visionary group, named at the time, the Epidauros Project. But the wisdom of the psyche already had a reversal in mind. Epidauros was not to be. In the planning of this new program, Hal contracted an infection that required two successive surgeries. During his convalescence, he and Sidra began to talk about the purchase of a small property with a cabin, perhaps within a hundred miles of L.A. They hoped to use it as a retreat space.

Sharon Tepper, a friend and neighbor in Sherman Oaks, suggested Hal and Sidra visit her at her farm in Northern California, about one hundred miles inland of the city of Ft. Bragg. Unbeknownst to the Stones, Sharon had lined up a real estate agent who agreed to show them available properties nearby.

"We didn't mind," Hal said, remembering that first tour. "We loved looking at old houses." But when they came upon the property that was to become Thera, it gave new meaning to the term *fixer-upper*.

Middle Ridge Road was largely the same, minus the llama farm and a number of neighbors who hadn't developed their properties yet. Things were a lot more isolated. As they stepped out of the car, Hal and Sidra detected the faint smell of pot wafting toward them on a mild breeze. Their eyes followed the scent to the left of the house, finding its source – a young man sitting in a chair, a plume of smoke rising slowly from his lips. He was stark naked.

As they looked around, they saw what appeared to be an abandoned 1960's pothouse, which was pretty close to what it was. The original house had been built in 1870, but there was little left of substance by 1980. Trash lay piled or dropped randomly around the porch, and there were actual holes in the floor of the house. They had to step over them to

Thera, newly purchased in 1981, Albion, CA

enter and exit. The beautiful meadow in front of the house was overgrown with brush and dotted with a number of old cars, parked indefinitely, so to speak – contributing to more of a garbage dump look than a farm.

They continued their inspection and could see the place was filled with nooks and crannies, both in the house and the surrounding forest. They were all inhabited in some form, making it nearly impossible to tell exactly how many people lived there. But one thing was clear. The woman who rented the house didn't want it to be sold, and the initial tour was dogged by a hostile energy following Hal and Sidra from space to space as they tried to imagine a country retreat of the future.

It seemed impossible. The amount of work that would need to be done was daunting, not to mention the incalculable nose count of tenants who would have to be displaced. But as they pulled off the road to talk about it, they both had an impossibly strong sense that they were going to buy the place, and Thera, like so many endeavors they took on together, seemed supported by something larger than themselves. They looked at each other and said in unison, "we're going to buy it, aren't we?" And they did. They returned in December of the same year with a firm offer.

"We weren't traveling much then," Sidra said. "Recha, Claudia, and Tamar were living with us then. They were seven, fourteen, and twenty-one respectively. With Tamar there to babysit, Hal and I began working only three weeks a month in L.A. Then we would go up to Thera. It took several years of this before we had the place really livable."

So, the need to be quiet, away from L.A., and drop into retreat trumped the obvious shortcomings of the house that would become a haven for so many. Further, Hal and Sidra followed the underlying principle of their relationship as a guide to the future. "Again," Sidra said, "we trusted where the relationship was taking us. Whenever we held our breaths and took a chance, something really interesting would happen. It was like taking a deep breath, going down into the cave, and seeing what was there."

EXTENSIVE TRAVELLING

It was also in the early 1980's, and in the midst of all this training and creative discovery, that Hal and Sidra decided to take the work overseas. Over the Thanksgiving weekend in 1982, Hal taught solo during a very emotional Voice Dialogue workshop filled with actors and actresses, hosted by Anna Ivara in NYC. Then he and Sidra boarded a plane and left for England and then Holland. The international phase of Voice Dialogue's evolution had begun. Gabrielle Pollecoff, Homeopath and Voice Dialogue facilitator, reminisced in a personal conversation with me about these early European workshops.

Hal teaching, 1980's, London,

"Hal was on fire then," she said. "He was amazed by the selves and what Voice Dialogue work would offer people. He just wanted everyone to get it. He was beyond generous and giving of his time. Thank God Sidra came along to rein some of that in. He would have just given the work away in the interest of sharing his discovery."[58]

Although Hal continued to do most of the teaching at this time, Sidra was present with commentary or demonstrations. "I was uneasy speaking to a large group of people," Sidra said. "I wasn't bad at being on stage. I loved that part. But I had to have a script. But Hal was such a good, natural teacher, he couldn't work off a script.

189

He was inspired and charismatic and our audiences were ninety percent female. It worked. It's always been his forte."

Robert Stromboliev, another Voice Dialogue facilitator who was essential during these first excursions overseas, filled in some of the blanks in the story of the Stones' European beginnings.

"The most important difference in those early days," he said, "was that Hal did all the teaching. Sidra was there only occasionally and more in the background. But she was very important for the individual sessions. Hal as a solo teacher was characterized by the unexpected. He was more shaman-like then, shifting to a totally different topic sometimes than the one people expected. When he and Sidra began to teach more jointly, the programs took on a slightly different structure, more planned ahead of time. They were active in Europe for many years. When they stopped coming, it was truly the end of an era."[59]

It wasn't long before Sidra learned how to fit in, finding her own voice in the work and her place on stage in these earlier workshops. It was not an easy act to join. Hal was an experienced and gifted teacher. Sidra felt at first like she had to compete with Hal, instead of becoming simply more impersonal. "For me it was either compete and lose, or keep my mouth shut to avoid coming across as really second rate. And that wasn't just my opinion. Hal didn't trust me."

Sidra's teaching style was quite different from Hal's. She taught and presented the material quickly and in a distinctly different style. Although their joint teaching was to become a seamless interweaving of their respective attitudes and approaches, Hal was used to teaching alone at this time. He didn't really share the stage.

"Not only that," Sidra continued, "he wasn't really ready to share the stage with someone who wasn't seasoned. I wasn't necessarily a teacher, either. I had to learn not to come from such a competitive space. On his side of things, Hal had to learn to listen to what I said, so he didn't jump in and say the same thing in his own words. It was a big piece of learning for both of us."

It was a time of significant transition for everyone. Even familiar audiences objected to Sidra's appearance beside Hal. "A lot of people felt I was ruining Hal's life," Sidra said. "They feared I was ending his career, his calling. They thought I was distracting him, leading him into something less than what he was."

Hal's daughter Tamar talked about this time with honesty and the understanding of someone who lived through it. "The truth is," she said, "everyone wanted to marry Hal Stone at the time. I felt an allegiance with Sidra, as he was also surrounded by a great many women who lived out being a Good Daughter in relationship to my Dad. I had a lot of compassion for Sidra's situation. The solution for me? I finally chose to have a great many sisters!"[60]

The detractors of the day gained no ground. These transitions in the relationship between Hal and Sidra were as significant as advanced tutorials in consciousness. Every step of the way, Hal and Sidra looked at their relationship and took what they saw seriously. They reacted to one another, took note, and reflected on what these interactions could tell them about themselves and where they were going.

"You know," Sidra said, "although there were difficulties, I always saw who Hal was. It was hard to be with someone of his stature without struggling to find my place. It was just as hard from the other side, to make room for someone else."

191

So, the international debut of Voice Dialogue began in England, bringing with it a whole new area of learning. The Stones had done other trainings in the format of an introduction, teaching, and facilitations of selves - and then Sunday morning Dream Groups. But the English people presented Hal with something very different to deal with, and something important in the evolution of their understanding of the Selves and how they operate.

"This first training in England went decently," Hal said, "but it wasn't going as I had hoped. By Sunday morning, I stood in front of the group and asked if anyone had a dream. Now, this was a group of about thirty people. Dead silence. Then I tried asking if anyone had a dream from childhood they'd like to share. Again, silence. I was stunned."

Hal later consulted with the organizer, Lawrence Blair, whose mother, Lydia Duncan, now deceased, was a dear friend of the Stones. She had invited Hal and Sidra to introduce the work in England. What Hal learned in this conversation made a very big impression on him and led to a change in his understanding. Lawrence told him that asking an Englishman to share a dream in front of a group was tantamount to asking him to take off his clothes. The English were simply not open in that way. There had been another incident during which a Countess participated in the training but didn't want to work in front of other people.

"I had rules back then," Hal said. "I could have accommodated her, of course, but I told her I was sorry. It couldn't happen. I worked with groups. But I began to see very quickly that it wasn't only us individually who have Primary Selves. Cities, countries and cultures have Primary Self Systems as well. I saw that if I was going to spread the work, each Primary Self System in each country or city would have to be investigated, and then honored."

One of the essential tenants of Voice Dialogue facilitation is that one can't violate the Primary Self in a person. Change can't be initiated without the permission of this powerful sub-personality. The first lesson about this happened in England. "So, thank God, I'm a fast learner," Hal said. "That experience was very painful. I can tell you it never happened again."

For the next ten years, Hal and Sidra travelled all over Europe, essentially away teaching for six months and then home for six months. What started in England and Holland became a regular tour, expanding to Israel, Italy, France, Germany, Hungary, Norway, Denmark, and Australia.

Hal and Sidra teaching in Holland, early 1980's

As romantic and exciting as this might sound, it didn't come about by whim. Hal and Sidra never lost sight of the importance of their process with each other and its central contribution to the work. No outside feedback about the work they were perfecting was ever as important as the information they received from each other.

193

For Sidra, the turning point came a couple of years into the international work they did together. Always attuned to their individual processes as much as their joint experience, it was during one of the workshops in England that she realized she needed to change two things. The first was to develop a more impersonal energy when they taught together. A personal energy and connection was more natural for her. The second awareness was harder.

"I also needed to be able to project my own energy out into the room," she said, "taking over the room as Hal did. I had to learn to make my energy as physically big as his. I did that. Then things really changed for me."

Sidra came to understand that when she was emanating a very personal energy when they were teaching, and losing boundaries in so doing, Hal didn't feel safe. So, he had to hold the whole vessel. But as Sidra began to manage her energy differently, the whole teaching situation changed as well. The Aware Ego Process, as it developed between them, saw the light of day in their challenges and solutions to teaching together.

It was during these international conferences that Hal and Sidra began to explore and develop energetic styles. Large group exercises in energetic awareness yielded understandings they now call energetic linkage. Although this wasn't formally written about until their book *Partnering*, which came out in the year 2000, much of the thinking in that volume came from these years of travel, working with larger audiences.

For Sidra in particular, these years constituted the foundations of stepping up and into areas of the work for which she had a particular sensibility. After a couple of years of presenting the work overseas, Sidra's efforts to come into the teaching as an equal paid off.

"In the beginning," she said, "Hal would do the teaching and presentation. Then I would do the demonstrations with him. People were intimidated by Hal. His energy and his mind were intense. I was not a threat and could do really strong demos by that time. We were doing a lot of Inner Child work then."

In addition, another area of their work whose development had its roots in these international waters: the facilitation of couples. Actually, it was Sidra who jumped into this kind of work, which is now a seamless foundation to the path of relationship. It was in Holland, a couple of years after Hal and Sidra had begun traveling on a regular basis. Hal had shied away from doing couples' work. But Sidra, in one courageous moment, cut a new path into consciousness work through relationship.

"We were working for a group of Dutch psychiatrists," Sidra said. "They had brought with them a couple to work with. They were patients of theirs. When they showed up, it turned out the man of the couple was scared out of his wits and neither of them spoke any English. I had to work through a translator!"

As I listened to Sidra, I imagined myself in a foreign country. I don't speak the language. I've been hired to work with an obviously upset couple that doesn't speak my language. In this tense but personally vulnerable situation with a third person in the mix, there enters a fourth party in the form of a translator. Now really! This is the stuff of therapists' nightmares.

In those days, Sidra would engage with a couple and Hal would go to the back of the room. But once this demo began, Hal began going in and out of the room,

195

pacing, watching. Sidra remembered that he felt terrible having left her in this position, trying to do Voice Dialogue with a frightened man and his wife who didn't speak English. But then, Sidra began listening to a dream through the translator.

"So, there we were," she said. "Then it came to me. Rather than begin with the couple's Primary Selves, as was our custom, I would simply ask to speak to the part of the husband who didn't want to be there. The whole thing opened up. This generated a whole new idea in working with couples. And believe me," she said, "translator or no, that subpersonality had plenty to say."

Hal and Sidra continued to use each other for teaching facilitations, always learning from each other in the workshops and trainings. Their facilitations moved from actual facilitations, which proved to be a hair too vulnerable for them in the inner child work, to scripted demonstrations. Sidra took the opportunity to return to her love of the stage from her Barnard days.

"It gave me a different connection with the audience, and offered Hal a different energetic connection with me," she said. "It worked brilliantly. He was always a great teacher. Then I became something fun that came in from the side. I could be in the selves and teach about them at the same time."

As the early international groups got underway, Hal had a dream that refused to leave him. It proved to be not only inspirational, but life-changing. "I had a dream of a world teacher," Hal said. "He was travelling around the world with his younger assistant. He was helping people in many different ways, not necessarily workshops. Whatever they needed, he would do. If they were building swimming pools, he helped build them. The image of him simply wouldn't leave me."

At the time of course, what a world teacher was exactly, was pretty unclear. But the image of traveling around, teaching, and opening up centers was mesmerizing. He and Sidra had seen what happened to people when they separated from their primary selves in facilitations. They were committed to sharing this.

But the tension was building, and by 1984, Hal felt he was in a professional crisis in Los Angeles. "I just couldn't stand it," he said. "I couldn't stand the weather. I couldn't stand the smog. The whole culture felt like it was choking me. I felt I would have died if I stayed there." This awareness heralded the end of his private practice in Southern California. He and Sidra already owned Thera and they had been going up there to write on a regular basis. On their way north one trip, Sidra did a spontaneous, seven-hour facilitation with Hal's Mars Self, whose archetypal presence in the car was an experience not to be ignored. He represented the interests of Hal's power selves, his anger, his instinctual energies.

"He was a very heavy dude," Hal said, speaking of his Mars subpersonality. "He couldn't stand private practice anymore. He didn't mind seeing clients. But the idea of taking on another long-term analysis with someone seemed like a prison to him. It had to stop."

So, onward Hal and Sidra drove, only stopping the spontaneous conversation with this figure one time when they ate lunch. This angry sub-personality ranted on, telling them both that he was going to kill Hal if he didn't listen. He threatened that if Hal didn't stop working like he was doing, he would hurt everyone. Hal took heed. He never saw another regular client again after that. By 1984, he was done with traditional private practice.

He and Sidra continued to drive north to fix up the property the third week of every month. They began work on their first two books, *Embracing Ourselves* and *Embracing Each Other* in the room that would later become Sidra's office. According to Hal, they learned a lot more about bonding patterns during those one-room writing sessions, then editing each other's material. Sounds ripe for difficulties of more than one kind to me, but bonding patterns would top the list. Fortunately, an Aware Ego Process was in the works as well. The Stones and the manuscripts survived.

"We had no idea of moving up here," Hal said. "Thera was a retreat space … but a crazy retreat space, really. You don't travel five hundred and fifty miles to a retreat space. It made no sense."

But Sidra had been listening too during that long facilitation of Hal's angry Mars self. She heard that he was stretched as far as he could go. So, although they still had one child with them, Sidra agreed to make a change of location as long as her children's security wasn't jeopardized by the move. They considered relocating to London because they loved it there, and because the schools were wonderful for their twelve-year-old daughter. But when Recha decided to go live on a Kibbutz in Israel, Hal and Sidra looked at each other and for the first time saw Thera as a potential international base for their work.

It seemed it was fate that the Stones made their decision just before one of the biggest real estate inflations Los Angeles has seen. Within only months of selling the Sherman Oaks home, its value had doubled, and Hal and Sidra had missed the window. Although an international move might have been appealing, by August of 1986, Hal and Sidra had moved to Albion and settled permanently in at Thera.

Hal and Sidra, walking on Middle Ridge Rd. by Thera, mid-1980's

"It was a hard thing for people when we left," Hal said. "We had given a lot of time to a lot of people. We had to go back and do some teaching even though we lived up north. We couldn't just make it a total break." Hal's daughter Tamar was among those who felt the loss of their move.

"It was huge for me," she said. "I lived a mile away from them. I was shocked and vulnerable watching a huge moving van packing up their lives. But I can see the move out of L.A. saved and extended his life. The Source energy he talks about now was operating then. It plucked him out of a situation he needed to leave. His life depended on it. But what might have seemed like abrupt endings were always the direct result of my Dad's intuitions. These endings were the births of other things that were always life affirming for him."

The years of intense work prior to this decision had drained Hal's physical resources. The cost to his health had become considerable. He'd been diagnosed with diabetes and had experienced brief episodes of arrhythmia. By 1986, the problems came back and didn't go away this time. Hal had to explore a whole new path of keeping himself well and stable with diet, exercise, and mental health. So, the move north ushered in a time of intense self-focus for Hal. While Thera dressed herself up for company with renovations, Hal and Sidra began a period of traveling to teach. "We didn't do any teaching at Thera yet," Hal said, "because our intention was to travel. We just put the word out that we were … available; that we'd like to come and do trainings. Once it started, it never stopped."

It was during this early settling in period that Hal and Sidra made another important decision, a decision many therapists face if they live and practice in a small community. This had to do with seeing local people. They chose not to. Albion was a small community. Hal and Sidra chose not to be identified as therapists. If people came to them for help who were known to them, they decided to see them for a few sessions at no charge. Then if they needed more help, they would make a solid referral.

"Oftentimes," Hal said, "that was enough to solve a thing. If not, we steered them in the right direction where they could get the help they needed. We were generous about that. We never charged for this because these folks were not our clients. That was a great decision. We're comfortable here with people knowing we write books and do workshops. That's enough."

As rich and expansive as the 1980's was for Hal and Sidra personally and professionally, the opportunities to develop and practice an aware ego process continued to be plentiful. Each decision, presentation, and change of direction offered another pair of opposite selves to find a position between, another Aware Ego Process between another pair of opposites. The fundamental structures of Voice Dialogue were in place and Sidra was about to take her place in the work. As the dragon sculptures had predicted years before, she was to claim the larger dragon while Hal retreated to the sidelines for a time.

Hal's arrhythmia required an intensive period of rest, but Intensives at Thera had been underway for some time and they weren't inclined to stop the schedule. So, Sidra decided to go it alone. Hal would be there, but she essentially did the teaching, helped by some of the older staff.

THE AWARE EGO PROCESS

So, it's appearance and evolution noted in the Stones' personal experience, what does an Aware Ego Process feel/look like to the rest of us? People describe it differently depending on their orientation. Jungians might say that in deep processes, we stand between two opposite attitudes in the psyche, enduring the tension of flipping into one or the other until the transcendent function is activated. This produces a new psychological attitude containing something of both sides of the conflict. The tension is real and the goal essential. French Jungian analyst Elie Humbert wrote:

From 1916 on, Jung had the intuition that self-regulation was possible and began to explore this possibility in his essay "The Transcendent Function". The transcendence to which the title refers has nothing to do with metaphysics. Jung borrowed the term from mathematics and used it to designate an ability to shape psychic reality, made possible in a two-fold process: first, one makes unconscious factors speak, then one reacts to these unconscious factors by way of the ego's values and goals. An organization in tension, capable of proposing a new orientation to consciousness, is gradually substituted for resultant conflicts, particularly those that emerge between ego and shadow…. For Jung, it is in the activation of the transcendent function that true maturity lies.[61]

While this sheds some light on the history of the problem and Jung's attention to it, there is more to it than abstract descriptions can offer. One of the elements that is fundamental in the Stones' work is the energetic experience, that connection between thinking and feeling shared in connection with another person and experienced in the body. It yields a consciousness that looks different, more complex, multifaceted.

The best way I can describe it is to use my own experience as an example. Any creative process, be it book, musical composition, or visual art, invites a particular group of selves depending on your Primary Self System and temperament. For me, my Perfectionist duels with my looser, more creative, free-spirited Muse when I first sit down to, say, write a book.

I face my laptop screen with a kind of free-floating enthusiasm. My Muse hops from one grand idea to the next, thinking about the many things she finds exciting and fascinating about the work and the people who created it. This self begins to play with a couple dozen metaphors, anecdotes and fond memories. Then with great flourish and drama, she sends me to the keyboard, chasing my fingers lightly over the keys to immortalize these ideas in print. She *knows* Hal and Sidra will like this.

The minute the Stones' names appear in my mind, I am aware of a certain unbearable vulnerability that comes to me in the form of a question I can barely entertain: What if they don't like the book? This question stops all forward momentum. The big guns in my self- system take over immediately. Sensing my vulnerability, my Perfectionist stomps in and grinds the process to a halt. She slowly surveys my lack of punctuation, my faulty grammar and incomplete phrases. She looks for sense where there's only creative elan. She starts crossing t's and dotting i's before the paragraph is finished, reminding me that I wouldn't want anyone to think I write poorly ... so we should begin early cleaning things up ... line by line.

Like the process of holding the tension of the opposites, good Jungian that I am, I await activation of the transcendent function. I also appreciate that standing between these two opposite selves requires some doing. Hal refers to it as sweating the opposites. Sidra prefers the image of a hummingbird, hovering between two flowers. But the result should be that, according to Jung, a new psychological attitude forms, containing something of both opposing ideas: I'm a creative writing genius or a grammatical slob. Now, here's the place where the Aware Ego process distinguishes itself and rescues me from the inevitable flip-flop that leads to a dreaded-for-good-reason writer's block. The Aware Ego Process will give me a choice. Rather than stopping the action, or jumping helplessly from one viewpoint to the other, it will free me to move on. Here's how it works.

The Psychology of the Aware Ego Process holds that each of my selves has its own worldview, set of values, and a boatload of opinions about how things should be handled in my life. Much to any one self's dismay, when I stumble upon a self that holds the opposite view, a well-known tension begins. At the beginning, I have only awareness. I see both selves and realize they are entirely different. I usually flip from one to the other for a while. Most of us do.

203

In the above-mentioned example, my Muse throws off the grammatical shackles of the Perfectionist and runs ahead, breathlessly transcribing aesthetically pleasing words and phrases that cleverly bring the message home that Voice Dialogue yields results that touch the divine. Now, once the word "divine" hits the page, my Perfectionist can no longer stand it. She leaps in, cautioning me not to inflate things. Maybe divine isn't the best word, she counsels me. In fact, she will consult a thesaurus and get back to me while she looks closely at every single word in my last three paragraphs. She wonders if I've considered renting a studio where I could really concentrate on this project. In fact, the perfect place might be somewhere by the ocean. Peace and quiet … the sound of the waves hitting the beach …

This flip-flopping can continue indefinitely, until I close my computer thinking that at this rate I'll be finishing my book from a nursing home. But if I continue to look at these opposing choices, struggling not to hold either one as THE TRUTH, something changes. I begin to settle down. I take a deep breath. I see another possibility.

I pull my Muse closer to me, letting her whisper suggestions while my Perfectionist puts a light pressure on the brakes of my speeding fingers. My ideas no longer race across the screen. I have time to select the ones that have legs and let the others go. My concentration improves. I feel in charge of my own process while being called toward my own largeness. Now ideas come to me that I didn't even know I'd thought about. This is the Aware Ego Process. It moves me from inaction and frustrated conflict, to an exciting selection of possibilities. The next action I take, and I emphasize the word *action*, is informed by both selves and something more.

While I have a playful tone in the above description, it shouldn't belie the largeness of the experience. Like witnessing a birth, transformation of this kind brings with it a sense of awe and wonder. Not only do I act differently, I feel the expansion within me as I open to this new perspective.

The opening this creates at the level of personality is only part of the gift, although feeling less neurotic has its merits, to be sure. But like living mindfully, or consciously, as many of us hope to do, the Aware Ego Process offers a way to the top, to a consciousness loaded with all the goodies. Stories about this experience abound, from professionals of all disciplines. In a personal communication, His Holiness Lama Drimed Rinpoche recalled the value of the Aware Ego Process.

"While in a deep session of 'sweating the opposites' with Hal," he said, "he paused and said to me, 'A conscious choice is made when we choose to go with one side, while having full consciousness that we will carry the loss of what we have not chosen as well.' This was one of the sanest perspectives anyone had ever shared with me."[62]

Reaching beyond flipping back and forth between opposite selves opens the lid to a treasure chest of gifts. As time moved on, Hal and Sidra discovered just how big this treasure chest was. Their clear connection to the Higher Energies had begun. Things once again got very creative and very busy.

CHAPTER FOURTEEN

A Psycho/Spiritual Process

What makes something a psycho/spiritual process? How do we recognize that dimension of a path or body of work? From my earliest associations with the Stones, they were clear that the psychology of the Aware Ego Process had had that specific character from the beginning. Once they began exploring the phenomenon that drew them to each other, it was clear something larger was not only involved, but orchestrating or supporting them and their work together as well.

Jung identified a psychoid dimension[63] in the psyche, in which the boundaries between the reality of the psyche and the reality of the conscious world seem to blur. Jungian analyst Jerome Bernstein[64] called this kind of liminality "living in the Borderland." For some, such an experience is commonplace, and only troubling when it is wrongly identified as pathology and aberration. Jungian analyst Donald Kalsched[65] recently referred to this same phenomenon as a mythopoetic aspect to psyche's function in relationship to deep trauma. He used a term Hal and Sidra Stone had long recognized and used to describe their experience as early as the 1970's: a psycho-spiritual process of development.

When I think about what makes a process psycho/spiritual for me, and how I understand that to be a part of the Psychology of the Aware Ego Process, I rest on the idea of surrender. For me, this one word and the action attached to it, open all the doors to my understanding of largeness. I want to talk about it firstly because it's so central to the Stones' work and secondly, it's inherent in any psycho/spiritual process. Nonetheless, the act of surrender is a challenge. I started this chapter many times, but my perseverance kept slipping away from me. I wonder if the reason was that the idea of surrender is so abhorrent to my sense of power and agency, that my first reaction to talking about it is to push back.

Like a small child on the eternal playground of my personality, there is always a naysayer whose job it is to reject any form of giving in. Following any feedback that doesn't suit her, she is ready to deny, argue, or deflect said information in the hope of thinking about herself the way she wants to. Mature? No. Human? Yes. Truth be told, surrender is one of those actions that is just unpopular. Echoes of schoolyard taunting and struggling to win, mingle with old messages about being a quitter, or loser, or pushover. Why such resistance? Perhaps this is because the idea of surrender at first has a lot to do with accepting that you are not going to get what you want. Having to give in and go along with what comes to you is a lesson that starts very early in the socialization process and continues in varying degrees of intensity as we go forward.

It's a tricky thing, moving toward the thing you fear. Letting go of my personal desires, giving up on a goal, sacrificing my pride, all these so changed my sense of self as I grew older, it was hard to understand surrender in any other terms than defeat. Perhaps that's not too far off, except it only addresses half the picture. The first half of surrender, maybe the top half, has to do with not getting what I want. But as I understood it, the other half concerns what surrender really addresses: the nature of trust, the experience of willingness to be taught, and a decision to move ahead or stand still without knowledge of or clarity about what might be coming - a tall order! In short, I've learned to let my life experience be my teacher, understanding always that there is something larger orchestrating the process.

I don't remember exactly how old I was when I finally understood my relationship to this … maybe in my late thirties. But I thought I had a pretty good grasp on the nature of things, my relationship to the world, and people I cared about in it. I'd begun to make forays into the outskirts of Zen territory and consciousness literature of the day. I fast left behind the spotty and sporadic religious training I'd survived and rejected as a child. I was restless and depressed. Nothing was satisfying. If I'd been asked what would change this situation, I wouldn't have been able to say.

Then one midsummer night in Ohio, while outside waiting for my dog to return from his habitual "Chasing of the Imaginary Hare" in the field next to my house, I looked up at the night sky. It was very dark, but the night was clear, and the stars shone exceptionally brightly in the moonless sky. I stood behind a large brush pile and thought about the pointlessness of my life and struggled to hold onto the thread that gave my life the meaning I thought it should have by then.

Then, as I looked out at the night, suddenly the stars and the entire canopy of the night came down and touched me. My face felt the warm light of the stars because they were right in front of me. The night reached down and simply found me. I knew in an instant that I was part of this; that I belonged to the universe, to whatever power there was out there that reached down to touch me. I stood immobile for some time, held in the energy of the night sky. My dog returned and was lying at my feet when, weeping, I returned to my ordinary consciousness. I have never been the same since.

Whenever I think about this experience, I'm reminded most of all that I belong to something larger, that I have a place in a larger plan that is often none of my business. I surrender to it and assume that there is a plan out there that has to do with my wellbeing. So, I stay in touch with that.

The codicil to this testament about surrender is that lessons in it change the way we meet our lives. I mean, I plan plans, and I wait to see if the results match my plans. Often, they don't. But I surrender to a larger Intelligence that others, like Hal and Sidra Stone, speak of more eloquently. I didn't have to struggle to defeat my logical mind, or question my experience scientifically, because I knew it was authentic. That summer night in the field behind my house, I felt it.

So, when my plans and results don't mesh in the way I expected, I surrender to what's larger. I look around for what the results I actually get might mean. What it means thus far is that whatever comes to me has its shadow in its pocket. I don't have to know more than that on the front side. But I have to stay curious about it all, because I'm interested in the larger plan, how down the road, what looks like good fortune can yield disaster, and vice versa. I think this attitude gives me traction in my life while keeping me connected and surrendered to the larger Intelligence, who seems still curious about me.

Perhaps when I near the end of the life I've been given, I'll have some of that distant perspective that I see in Hal's eyes, or feel when Sidra drifts out to touch another dimension. Then I think perhaps I'll dissolve into the night sky again, like the first time, and live in service to those who needed what I did so long ago, at the edge of the field, asking the night sky why I was here.

The Stones have yet even different takes on the experience of surrender; different than mine and different from each other. But the essential giving over of control, resting into an understanding that one is not in charge, is an initial piece of the process. Their teacher was relationship, and they surrendered to it in their own unique ways.

209

SURRENDER TO RELATIONSHIP

Hal

Hal began talking in that very clear, direct way he's known for when I asked him to clarify his thoughts on surrendering to relationship. Although I poured over the original interviews, some of the transcript's material still eluded me. It wasn't really the concept that had changed, but Hal and Sidra continue to work on these ideas. They continue to be informed in different ways, and they language their ideas differently as time goes on and their understanding increases.

"There are two kinds of surrender," Hal said when I was with him in 2013. "There's conscious and unconscious surrender. Unconscious surrender is made by a *self*. Everybody knows how that works. Take falling in love. Let's say you meet somebody. You fall madly in love. You're completely besotted with this person - totally surrendered to them."

Hal maintains that it is a self that surrenders in this experience. It dissolves into the other person and gets completely lost there. It's not that this is a bad thing. To have that experience is a certain kind of surrender, but its nature is total. Surrender, like fusion, enmeshment, and other losses of one's own separate space, is unconscious ... and, in the case of falling in love, it feels wonderful. That's the best part. Except for the experience of being in the womb and infancy, falling head over heels in love is the only other experience that feels as good, close, and familiar.

"So, this is where the bonding patterns begin," Hal said. "The positive bonding pattern begins with a love affair between *good daughter* to *good father*, or *good son* to *good mother*. In the moment, no one cares which self is involved, because it feels good. That's why it's always a shock when it ends."

Talking about that honeymoon period of falling in love, or more accurately, when it ends, is opening the door to a room familiar to everyone. Suddenly, or so it seems, the person I adore most in the world begins to look different. The things I once loved about him begin to irritate me. Those cute little foibles that used to make me laugh, start to drive me crazy. In short, the idealizations of a self, fall apart. The relationship becomes alarmingly human. That's when a lot of relationships end, painfully and abruptly.

"That first surrender to love breaks down because it's done from a self who can only see and experience things through its own lens," Hal said. "Now, in the other kind of surrender, a conscious surrender in relationship, you don't surrender to the other person. Rather, you surrender to the process of interpersonal relationship. What happens between you and the other person is of such a nature that you can surrender to it, to what's going on between you. The process between you brings things to you that you didn't have before."

This description points toward the central idea of the Psychology of the Aware Ego Process. Relationship offers a new kind of consciousness. This doesn't have to be a primary relationship, either, which is the larger point. Any relationship, be it friend, coworkers, colleagues or lovers, contains within it the opportunity for greater consciousness if understood in this way. For example, I can go along for a long time in relationship with my closest friend. Then something comes along. We have an argument. I realize I've been in a positive bonding pattern with her. I then become conscious of something I need to see in myself.

Now, I can march off in a kind of righteous indignation, and that's the end of the friendship. Or, I can see the positive bonding pattern and surrender to the process of the relationship to show me my role in the pattern. I can stay and work it out. Sometimes that's easy and fun, and other times it's bitter, hard work to look at myself in this way. There have been times in some relationships when I wondered why I continued to try, they seemed so fraught with problems and difficulties. It wasn't until I was on the other side of the process that I understood what was in it for me.

"So, it's an important distinction to make," Hal said. "Surrender in the sense I'm talking about isn't to another person, no matter how much in love you might be. The real question is who in you is surrendering, which always leads back to the Aware Ego Process."

To understand the process to which Hal refers leads us to the core of what I understand to be a psycho/spiritual process. What he means is that essentially, one has to surrender to all the selves and their energies. That is on one level. But on another level, there is surrender to a higher intelligence that directs things. There is a process between the individual, the Aware Ego Process and some other knowing that goes beyond the Aware Ego Process. Hal sees this developing in us on earth, in a body, so we can appreciate other, higher energies.

"Otherwise, I surrender from a self," he said, "like a *loving son*, or a *frightened son*, or a *sick son*. It's easy to surrender to a higher power when I'm sick. Then when I feel better, I forget about surrender. At that level, I only surrender when identified with a self."

Hal's understanding of this process has changed over time. He can trace the evolution, as usual, through his dream process. At first, he surrendered to a spiritual process, to god, who's in charge of the spiritual pantheon. Then he got a sense that there was more going on. He began to have dreams that were not oriented to becoming more spiritual.

"It seemed to me that I had an on-going connection to a *spiritual* and/or *source energy*," he said. "I had a dream that I was dropped into god energy in an extreme way. I know I will die. I mean I just knew I couldn't live there. Then the *source energy* enters in and takes me out of the *spiritual energy*. It brings me back to consciousness and tells me it's not time to go out now. It tells me I have work to do to make this differentiation. I was given to understand I must remain here to tell others. I know now I've been taken back to the original molecules of creation, and since then, my intuition is that it's source energy that has created the universe, and god as well."

This idea came from a dream, which suggested that surrender comes at another level or dimension, as in surrender to energy that has something new to bring to us; something we don't have already. For Hal, it's not just a connection to a higher energy that brings about change. He recognizes that human relationship effects change as well. "The *other* in our human relationships continues," he said, "until the hole they occupy in me is filled."

Hal pauses frequently when talking about this topic, in a kind of reflective humility. He tells me often that this is only one man's intuition. I'm reminded of Jung's frustration at the end of his life, feeling that no one truly understood what he

213

discovered. Perhaps he was right. Perhaps, too, Hal won't know if his intuitions have legs until the rest of us get there with him. He continued describing this vision of things.

"It's not just one universe for me anymore," he said. "I think there are other universes than this one, with different designs than the one we know. The dream process becomes clearer, and through it, I can see that the *source energy* values the world as much as spirit. It values a cup of coffee as much as going out to God."

Hal is well known for his exaggerations and his examples in teaching are peppered with them in a delightful way. He especially loves talking about spiritual experience, and often does so with delight. He even talks about enlightenment as a way of identifying with a self.

"So, take a Zen priest who sits in meditation," he said. "Suddenly he gets hit on the head by God. Or the Buddha comes down and kisses him on the mouth. Ha! I don't know. But he's in ecstasy. He thinks he has found IT. He comes out of the experience completely identified with enlightenment. This is all fine until his wife comes in and shouts at him, 'Take out the goddam garbage. It stinks in here!'"

From this I conclude, as did Hal, that the details of living are important. He feels that the unconscious has driven him to understand that the goal, the reason we're here, is to learn to live life as simple human beings. This means to value everything, as well as that which God brings.

It occurs to me that there is no shortage of gurus and spiritual teachers out in the world, many of whom teach a specific and regimented course of action to achieve what they themselves have experienced. But just like many gifted people, there's always another side to every gift. Talk to their wives and children. What is their experience of the enlightened one's path?

"Source energy doesn't have rules and traditions," Hal said. "It has to do with *rebalancing.* It will unhook you from the marriage to a cherished ideal. Source energy functions like a divorce court. So, when I pray, I pray to God and the source energy at the same time. In addition, I might pray to Christ, to Buddha, and sometimes recite the Hebrew *"alohim, adonai* ... Different things resonate with me at different times. But I surrender, over and over again to the dream and what my relationship with Sidra teaches me."

Sidra

As convincing as Hal's perspective can be, Sidra sees it differently. In short, she resists the whole idea of surrender. As added proof of their respect for their individual differences, Sidra responded quickly about how she sees this concept of surrender in the process of their work and lives together. I introduced the discussion with her, stumbling around trying to summarize, in my own words, what I had talked about with Hal. Then, I tried to give her the short form of what I understood her position to be. That was when she really started to laugh, as I finally landed on "Just where do you guys meet on this issue?"

"Well," she said, "in some ways, it's a question of semantics. I have a different sense of it, meaning I feel it in essentially two ways. One way is that surrender is like feeling an energy flow, like the movement of a river. For me it's a feeling of whether or not I'm moving with the current of a river I belong in. I don't think of it as surrendering to 'Thy will not mine dear God.' For me, it's much more about going with the flow of energy that's meant for me."

215

When I pressed her for how she relates to the hierarchical ideas of *higher energies* or how to connect with them, Sidra told me she was simply more connected to the evidence from inside herself. She doesn't see this as coming from outside or above. "These energies vibrate with a part of me," she said. "I can feel if I'm aligned with that vibration or not. When I am, I have a sense of, 'Phew! I can relax now.'"

Hal had been clear that his connection came from the Aware Ego process in relationship, and Sidra's perspective seemed to align with that. She had always seen relationship as the vehicle for many gifts. Hal had brought in a whole different context for her at the time they met; a context that included energies that weren't tangible.

"Remember," she said, "I was identified with the rational mind and believed that science would win out. What I discovered had more to do with experiencing things energetically *now*. When I need help, I ask. 'Okay, guys, I need some help.' It's really as simple as that. Then I have a sense that they respond."

There seems to be very little about Sidra's perspective that is hierarchical. She rests into feeling three kinds of energies. The first is a holding energy that surrounds. She recognizes it as belonging to the property, the land they live on. Then she talked about an influx of energy that comes to her through her crown chakra. When guidance is needed, she lets those energies come in, resting into it. Lastly, when teaching or writing, Sidra connects with a third kind of energy. This, too, comes through the crown chakra, but it is met by energy bubbling up from her depths.

"I also connect to these energies through dreams," she said. "Three days ago, I wanted to do some revision on an article that I'd written. I woke up with the whole picture of what I needed to say spread out before me, as if it had come to me in the dream."

Of course, the topic of working with dreams fascinates me, as I spend much of my waking life doing just that, working with my own or others' dreams. But further, which is what keeps me at it, is that the unconscious never fails to impress me, and impress upon me, the infinite variety and creativity in its own expression, with some arguable intentionality. The incredible uniqueness of peoples' dreams, and my own, never fails to amaze me. I don't think we could ever make anything up as creative as a dream that comes to us without effort on our part.

For instance, some people are blessed with, and/or burdened by long, narrative dreams in which a lifetime of a story unfolds. One could work on such dreams analytically for an entire month. Others receive what we call "big dreams," suggesting a striking life change or attitude adjustment. Still others get small snippets of a dream, whose meaning through associations and timing expand our understanding exponentially about something we struggle with or will need to know in the future.

So, when Sidra spoke about what comes to her from the unconscious it seems that dreams have yet another form. "Sometimes information from these higher energies comes to me in a dream in the form of sentences," she continued. "or even commentary. When I was writing *The Shadow King* in 1998, the dreams just popped in to help me, not to mention the initial dream that gave me permission to even begin writing. What it feels like to me is that I have the support of an energetic cloud, as opposed to any embodied beings."

The tricky part of this whole topic of surrender is a basic contradiction. Something that seems to be so intimately connected and consonant as the way Hal and Sidra live in relationship to one another, can be resting on such disparate understandings of the same, very important experience.

217

"I think the place where we really meet in this," Sidra said, "is in the feeling and the understanding that these energies exist. We agree on that. I just don't have the sense that they have genders. Maybe it's a male/female thing. I'm sure Hal doesn't think of the higher energies as a group of women. I certainly don't think of them as gendered at all. Although when I first met Hal I was very connected to Gaia, and now have included Kwan Yin in my personal pantheon. But we simply language and experience the energies differently."

What it seems to come down to is that Hal and Sidra share a *knowing*. The perception of this knowing and the information derived from it is then processed through their individual conceptual structures and language. Much like psychics who get a hit on something or an image that they then interpret, the Stones understand that what comes to them may or may not fit for them both. I'm reminded of the psychics who predicted that Hal and Sidra's relationship would never last in a form other than a work relationship. "As if passion, friendship, and work couldn't happen in one bundle," Sidra said wryly.

I reasoned this error in prediction was because the psychics in question hadn't seen the picture of Sidra riding on a mule in the summer heat of Santorini, Greece. Had they glimpsed what should stand as an image of Aphrodite herself that Hal would have been a fool to let go of, they'd have understood that anyone would work to have the whole prize. But indeed, psychics can be wrong and not everyone believes them anyway. For that reason, Hal and Sidra only put out in writing what they come to agreement on.

The essential part of this surrender, for either Hal or Sidra, is the relationship, and when either of them feels it's off track, then they lose connection with the higher energies. "The relationship is the key," Sidra said. "When that's clicked in and the bonding patterns are cleared, we're automatically moved into an Aware Ego Process and away from the selves, where we find the connection to the higher energies. There's a way in which we're forced toward an Aware Ego Process that keeps us on track. Both of us feel the flow of that in relationship. There's no power dynamic in it. It's a flow of consciousness."

This seems to me to be a big statement, "relationship with no power dynamic in it." Not only have I long understood and participated in power-based relationships, I know very few people who can or want to give them up. But Sidra was clear about it, repeating that whenever there was a glitch in their connection, it had to do with leaving that particular flow of consciousness and falling into a power mode.

"It was very hard for me in the beginning and that understanding came to us slowly," she said. "But in a power relationship, either it's all your fault and I have to change you, or, it's all my fault and I feel so awfully guilty. But that's still a power play, even if I'm saying it's all my fault, it means I am powerful. I am powerful enough to do such a terrible thing. It keeps the weight in the relationship on my side. That's the part that's hard to catch."

What a perfect description of many, many marriages and friendships and professional relationships that never seemed to evolve past "who's in charge." The cost and difficulty of surrender in this context becomes understandable, but exponentially more desirable. This would be the reason that everyone who meets and works with the Stones wants what they have. If you can't feel it when you're with them, you can see it as they smile when they connect energetically. And if you're fortunate enough to be sensitive to energies in general, or even in specific, then what they hold can almost launch you to a broader understanding than you can imagine alone.

I've certainly wondered in the course of this writing, and listening to them separately, if part of the depth and success of their lives and work rests on their differences, as much as the similarities. Perhaps that's true, at least in part. In keeping with their thought, I have to believe that everything counts. But in combination, I think they have offered something that furthers our understanding of consciousness, and perhaps creates a bridge to a brighter future than one might predict for humanity at the moment. It would bear reflection.

CHAPTER FIFTEEN

Spokes of the Wheel

Although I'm not inclined to favor western motifs, the image of an antique wagon wheel pesters my consciousness as I think about the various aspects of the Psychology of the Aware Ego Process. The Stones and their relationship have certainly served as the hub of an ever-enlarging wheel. The steel rim of this wheel heats up and expands as the Higher Energies crowd and shape it to accommodate a consciousness of the future. How they talk about it now, and how they've taught it over the years is worth looking at. Like all other aspects of the Stones' work, the methods of presenting the material has undergone its own and equal evolution. As the audience and location grew, the Stones adapted, forming new ways of dealing with new demands and new understandings as they came upon them.

Originating in the long dialogues Hal and Sidra had as they rebounded from the effects of their connection, the early model of Voice Dialogue was facilitation. Voice Dialogue facilitation consists of an actual conversation and energetic connection between facilitator, client and the selves that show up. These sessions can last anywhere from an hour and a half to three hours, moving between opposite selves to find first an awareness of their respective views and a separation from identifying with either one. Then an Aware Ego process develops between these opposites from which an Operating Ego can make a choice about what information it uses, from "whom," and to what degree it will be expressed.

An example would be if an introverted client entered complaining that she just got a call from a friend who attended the same party as she, laughing at the big show she put on after a drink or two. A facilitator might then observe that there seemed to be a part of this client who is more introverted, and another part, who when invited or allowed some expression, had the capacity to be the life of the party. A facilitation would thus begin perhaps by saying, "what if we were to talk to that part of you who feels embarrassed about the party last evening?" An actual conversation would then take place, first with the more introverted self, who is likely to be the primary self, followed by the self who thoroughly enjoyed herself the evening before.

Teaching the work continued in an evolving forum as well. Contained at first in small group sessions, Voice Dialogue's early structure and method of communication surfaced as informal but structured groups in the backyard of Sidra's home in Sherman Oaks, CA. These groups morphed into groups of eighty people and a cadre of early staff members when Summer Kamp arrived on the scene. When the Stones expanded their horizons to include international locations, a small staff traveled with them. Group training experiences hosted by Voice Dialogue practitioners all over Europe and Australia became another forum for the experience and dissemination of their ideas.

Although the 1980's had started the ball rolling internationally, and personal and professional travel broadened the Stones' sphere of influence and learning, the 1990's opened even more important doors. In 1986 Hal published his autobiography *Embracing Heaven and Earth*. By 1989, both *Embracing Ourselves* and *Embracing Each Other* had come to light, books then becoming another medium in which to spread knowledge of their work.

The 1990's brought particular challenges for the Stones. Hal's heart condition pressured him yet again to make changes he might have preferred to ignore. Serendipitously, it offered Sidra a chance to bring that larger dragon she'd acquired at the end of a Summer Kamp, out into the sunlight. She took charge. Cathryn Keir, one of the Voice Dialogue staffers in the early years, reminisced with me about that time.

"They almost cancelled Summer Kamp in the 1990's," she said, "because Hal's heart had gone through a major process. Hal had always been the stronger teacher of the two, but they didn't cancel it. He talked about surrender to the feminine at the time and we watched Sidra move to the forefront and take charge. It was surrender for both of them."[66]

Sidra remembered those first few times of running things with much less participation from Hal as pretty rough. She laughed about how caught up she was at first in trying to please everybody. However, it wasn't long before Sidra found her stride, and the transition was seamless enough that some participants didn't know it had ever been different. Iudita Harlan, another long-time teacher of the work and participant in these early Summer Kamps, remembered the progression of things from another perspective.

"When I first went to a training, Hal wasn't active at all," she said. "He kind of hung around putting logs on the fire while Sidra did the teaching. My first real energetic connection to the work or to either of them was with her. Then the following year, Hal was more present, and I thought, intrusive! So, when I went to my private session with Sidra, I said to her, 'Look, Sidra, before we get started, I just want to ask you why you're letting Hal interrupt you all the time. I mean, really, why would you let anyone do that? Who is he anyway?' And Sidra looked at me quietly for a minute, like she does, and said, 'Well, Iudita, that's something I'll have to look at. Now let's talk about you.'"[67]

In many ways, the late 1980's and early 1990's made space for Sidra to blossom in a space that had at one time been only big enough for Hal. Teaching opportunities opened in Europe in 1986 with Lydia Duncan, and in Australia in 1987 with Ana Barner, Christopher Sanderson, Cristobel Munson, and David Condon, who produced the Stones teachings for their first trip there. The Stones returned to Europe again in 1996 and then there was another period of calm while Hal rested. Sidra dropped down into a serious project that had been demanding her attention.

Although she had spent years leading breakout groups with women in Europe and the United States dealing with the Inner Patriarch,[68] and being encouraged to write about it, Sidra was hesitant to write her own book. "I didn't feel ready to stand alone behind my theories," she said. "I wanted it to be free from both judgment and rebellion. I also feared it would alienate most women – not only those with strong Inner Patriarchs, who basically agreed with them – but also the feminists, who unbeknownst to themselves, had really strong Patriarchs as well!"

Like Hal, Sidra also attends to the promptings from her unconscious, and finally she had a dream that freed her to begin the writing. In the dream, Sidra found herself facing a semi-circle of impressive, serious, obviously important white-robed older men with beards. They looked like the patriarchs of biblical times. One of them spoke for all of them and turned to Sidra with tears in his eyes.

"He told me that they hadn't meant it to turn out this way," Sidra said. "He said it was okay to write the book; that they knew about my ambivalence about the outer patriarchy. He assured me it had been worked through; that they knew I would be fair to them. They knew I would honor them for what they had brought to the world and correct some of the problems that had arisen. I began to write the next day!"

In a touching dedication to her book, Sidra not only takes her place solidly beside Hal in the work, but as a talented writer with a contribution to make to literature geared to the growth of women in particular.

This book is for every woman who has put aside

her own wisdom, deferred to others,

and waited for permission to speak.

It is also for her sister, the woman of power,

who has learned how to speak up,

but fears that in doing this she has sacrificed

some intangible but

precious aspect of her essential femininity.

It's important to remember that all this happened as a part of a full life. There were children's marriages, the birth of grandchildren, developing the property in Albion and a travelogue that contained the Far East for fun and most of the countries in Europe for professional seminars. Their travel trunk would have stickers from France, Italy, Ireland, Wales, Switzerland, Holland, Germany and a host of towns in Australia. They lived a big and full life and relied on what was between them to inform their next moves.

Eventually, of course, things begin to wind down. Hal's son Joshua died unexpectedly in the late summer of 2005 and his death had a profound effect on the family. It precipitated a pulling in of the energies the Stones had poured out so freely all over the world. The Seattle Conference of that year marked the last of the major group teachings in the U.S. By 2007 they had completed their European tours and the Intensives at Thera became the central location for people from here and abroad who wanted to pursue experience and training in Voice Dialogue and the Psychology of the Aware Ego Process. Hal was then eighty years old, and Sidra, seventy. It was time. Genvieve Cailloux, a facilitator who was introduced to the work during this time of transition, remembered the experience with fondness.

"We, Pierre and I, were first introduced to Voice Dialogue in 1990 by Shakti Gawain and her staff,"[69] she said. "We had been deeply immersed in studying and working with Jungian typology, which I enjoyed, but felt I was missing something in it. Then when we started going to Thera and met Hal and Sidra, it was like discovering a colored film inside a black and white picture or playing the music instead of just reading the score. We found the missing piece and above all, a deep personal and loving linkage with the Stones."[70]

People came from all over the world to the trainings at Thera. International energy and vocabulary became part of the fabric of the summer events. Voice Dialogue spread its wings wide as the excitement for the work gained breadth and strength. But not all experience hit people the same way. For Pierre Cauvin, the other half of the preceding anecdote, first impressions came with a little attitude.

"My first session with Sidra, some fifteen years ago, began with a few bumps," he said. "I don't remember exactly what I said, but Sidra commented that I sounded very mental. I, or what I would come to know as my Operating Ego, jumped up from my seat and started to the door. 'I didn't come ten thousand miles to listen to that crap!' I said with a flourish. I was already at the door when I heard Sidra's gentle voice behind me, saying, 'Maybe you didn't come ten thousand miles to leave right away.' Since it sounded quite rational, as you might guess, I stayed."[71]

For the last twenty years, at least until 2013, the Psychology of the Aware Ego Process has been offered to these smaller groups in programs called Intensives. The Stones provided a safe learning environment at their home in Albion, and people came to further explore their competence with the work, or their own personal process working with Hal and Sidra and a select staff. Progressively letting go of big teaching programs either in the U.S. or abroad, in recent years getting into one of the Intensives at Thera was the only direct teaching happening with Hal and Sidra themselves. At this writing, Hal has stopped working with people professionally all together. Sidra continues working privately with people they've worked with for years, but the day will come when they will simply concentrate, as always, on their own processes.

But many of the people who trained in the original groups, and many who have been trained along the way, have started their own institutes and organizations. Voice Dialogue centers exist in many parts of the United States from east to west coast and north and south. Trainings continue to be held in models similar to the original, and international institutes continue to function and attract people interested in this consciousness process.

STORYTELLING

Group teaching and the experience of facilitation are only two aspects of the method the Stones use. Their skill resources reach much further back when it comes

227

to teaching. They are master storytellers, a tradition that not only predates the written word, but also engages the student on multiple layers of consciousness simultaneously. Hal and Sidra know how and when to use it to make a point.

The reason I'm even talking about this is that I see a similarity in the styles of guided meditation and the way Hal and Sidra teach through storytelling. Although different from one another, they can lead you through a story like the best of them, and in keeping with the experiential nature of the work, their way of teaching is like being guided in meditation.

Some years ago, I spent a session with Hal, whining about the place I lived in. I make no apology for whining. There's nothing quite so satisfying as a good whine, and someone listening intently to it. Anyway, I didn't like the neighborhood I lived in. I wasn't crazy about the house I rented. I hated the traffic.... you get the picture. Rather than give me advice or sympathy, Hal took me on an energetic ride, beginning with this particularly effective introduction.

"I once knew a woman whose husband was in the furniture business," he said. "He had a big store in a *schlocky* part of town. He was kind of a *schlocky* guy himself." Hal began to laugh a little, playing with the word, enjoying using it in a way that the sound of it transmits the meaning. "So, anyway, he had this store that covered an entire block in this *schlocky* part of town, and he made lots of money … millions.

"One of his top salesmen came into analysis with me, and always complained about the job. He hated the guy that owned it, hated the store and how it was run, and hated where he had to work there. He complained all the time that the place was dirty and messy. When I suggested he clean it up, he would get angry and say he wasn't spending his time cleaning up some other guy's business, especially a guy like this *schlocky* guy."

Now, I listened to this story, engaged by the element of an unfamiliar and comical word. Hal's deft use of it pulls me in to the feel of the situation. I could see the store, the guy who ran it, and the salesman rubbing up against it in disgust. Hal paused watching me step into his tale. Knowing that he had me fully engaged in his story, he continued.

"So, this goes on for about a year," he said, "yet the analysis seemed to be going nowhere. There weren't many dreams and the process just felt stalled. So, he came in one day, again complaining about the job, the awful conditions, and his boss, and I again say to him, 'Look. Why do you make yourself live like that? I mean, you spend eight to ten hours a day at this store and you surround yourself with stuff that makes you feel worse. Why treat yourself like that? If you fixed it up, you'd be helping yourself, not the owner. I think it would make a difference.'"

My imagination was following every word by then. I was in the store with the salesman, watching him clean things up and arrange the space so that it looked great. Hal told me that everyone noticed, and the sales went up, and the owner was, of course, very happy about all this. The salesman also felt very differently about going to work, even if it was still in a *schlocky* part of town.

"So, one day," Hal continued, "a man stopped by this salesman's department and asked him who organized it. Was there a store manager who was responsible for setting this up? Naturally the salesman said that no, he had done this himself, and thanked the guy. The guy left his business card and suggested the salesman call him if he ever wanted to get out of this store.

229

"There was no big incentive to leave," Hal went on, "so the salesman waited and after a couple of months, the guy who'd seen him at the store called him up. He said that he was the owner of a very large chain of furniture stores. He said he would like to hire the salesman to reorganize each one of them, just as he had done in the small space he managed in the bad part of town."

Hal paused, letting the image linger, allowing me to begin to fill in the end of the story. When I think I know how it's going to end, he steps in. "So, naturally the guy accepted the job. But before he left, he had the following dream. In the dream, he sees himself attending a funeral, but he didn't know who had died. This worries him, as he's standing in line to view the body, and has no idea whose funeral this is. As he approaches, his anxiety increases, and he looks into the casket. There he sees his boss's penis, lying on the silk pad, and the dream ends."

The end of this dream had the desired effect on me, and Hal was waiting for it. I was shocked, then delighted, then amused, then so appreciative of the wisdom of the unconscious. What a bang-up ending! And Hal loved telling it.

On another level, the skill he demonstrates here makes a broad stroke. In this simple and amusing story, he offers a subtle analytic reflection, as well as an example of his favorite tools, humor and the dream. His sense of humor is delicious, and love of working with dreams underscores his teaching and consciousness work. Indeed, it's rare for Hal to tell a story about anything that isn't summed up by an offering from someone's unconscious or his own. His passion for it has never left him.

The storyteller in Hal is skilled and inducts with delight, usually humor. He punctuates his tales with pauses that hold you in, or explosive laughter that keeps him from talking at all sometimes. The effect is much like that of the yogi who makes you wait and wait for the next word in a guided meditation. He delights in sustaining the connection to see where it takes you; then winds things up with a surprise ending. This ending so often incorporates the use of a dream as icing on the cake, it's hard to tell if the story showcases the dream or if the dream showcases the story. Regardless, the effect is wonderful.

Sidra's stories, on the other hand, are like plot-driven movies or books that are real page-turners. Listening to Sidra tell a story is something like watching good theatre when the actress turns to the audience and speaks directly to them. They call it opening the fourth wall. Equally compelling, she weaves a story that she carries you through by herself, supporting you with enthusiasm and energy, clearly seeing for herself the images she wants you to imagine. She punctuates the theme with small details, some seemingly tangential until you feel how completely you're running after her, attached to her narrative and energy. Then she brings it home.

We had been chatting one afternoon in front of a crackling fire. Sidra was musing about the many synchronicities that surrounded her early years with Hal, tracing a sense of being observed and supported by the larger forces at work in the universe, even before they had the language to speak about it. The energy of it was clear. Inviting me into the landscape of her favorite spaces, Sidra talked about a place in Guatemala she visited during her first marriage. She found it so compelling and powerful, she couldn't wait to share it with Hal when they were first together.

"We did a lot of travelling in my first marriage," she said. "There was an extensive Mayan ruin called Palenque we wanted to see. The destination was unreachable by any ordinary means of transportation. We had to take a commercial flight to Villahermosa, then a two-seater plane, and finally an off-road vehicle!" she finished triumphantly. "I used to love those kinds of trips. My first husband did too.

231

Of course, we were very young and very brave," she added laughing, "…still immortal."

So it began. Sidra started to paint the picture in my mind with the deftness of a psycho/spiritual artist. Before I could drift off with my own touches of imagination, she jumped back in the story and pulled me in with her.

"There were no roads going in. We took a commercial airline to Villahermosa, Guatemala and then got seats on the weekly mail plane to Palenque," she said. "We sat on mail sacks in the back of a two-seater. Then we landed on a mowed strip in a cornfield! 'Don't worry,' the clerk at the airport had told us. 'There will be someone there when you land.'" Without waiting for the visuals to completely form, Sidra rolled right on without taking a breath.

"It was Pierre La Croix, that 'someone', sitting in a Jeep with a big machete laying across his lap. He took us back to his lodge in the woods, where we spent a few very exciting days and nights." The image of a stranger in a Jeep with a machete, taking anyone into the woods of Guatemala began to feel like a modern Hansel and Gretel fairytale.

"So, when Hal and I were first together, I really wanted him to have the experience of Palenque," she said. "By the time we got there, many years had passed since my initial visit. Palenque had turned into much more of a park. They had started to clear the Mayan ruins, and had just discovered the tomb in the temple of the pyramids. Also, by that time we could get there by bus. Also, by that time there were a number of places to stay, and a little village off to the side. The grass was cut, and it was all cleaned up. It was beautiful," she said. "Of course, we were very interested in exploring energies and energy fields in those early days, and the energy of the place was palpable. It just hit you. So did the heat!" she said laughing.

All the senses accounted for in the telling, I was all in. As she went on to describe an ancient observatory near the village, she added detail and history to seal my attention. I began to visualize a tower built in the corner of a square surrounded by a wall of stone. The locals called it an observatory, opening my imagination to questions and wonderings about astrology's beginnings. In my mind I followed Sidra, walking around the top of the wall and going up into the tower.

"There was a big stone table in the center," she said, "maybe seven feet long. It was under a roof of curved arches. The archeologists thought the building had been an astrological observatory. The Mayans were great astronomers. They also discovered absolute zero. They were great mathematicians."

Rather than having the effect of distracting me from the thread of the story, these asides engaged me further. The fourth door opened and whisked me into the monologue. So, I added the Mayan math skills to the list of things piling up about this tower, this square in the middle of nowhere, and the energetic pressure that's building in the room from the telling. I feel the hair rise on the back of my neck as Sidra moves on.

"Hal had me hop up on that table. God knows what it was for when the Mayans used it but judging from its placement in the room and the fact that there was nothing else in there, clearly it was important. So, there we were. No one else was around. They were all off taking their siestas. Hal had me lay down on the table and began to do an energy clearing on me. Suddenly, I felt a huge trembling, like an earthquake under me. Mind you, nothing at all was moving on the outside, except Hal

233

swatting at a bee that had been bothering him, but I felt what I felt. I jumped up and said to Hal, 'We've got to get out of here!' So, I jumped off the table. When I looked down there were two drops of fresh blood on the floor just in front of the place I stood. I knew they had not been there before and there was nothing bleeding on either of us."

Now, at this point, I'm so caught up in the story I'm right there in the tower with them. I feel the charge of electricity in the room, both the tower room and the one I'm in with Sidra. The suspense she has created builds as she pauses in the narrative to add a couple of details.

"At this point in our relationship we were having a lot of experiences of synchronicity," she said. "I remembered that the Mayan royalty offered drops of their blood in some rituals as offerings to their gods, and I was looking down at a drop of blood for each of us. Suddenly I was filled with a sense that this was a deeply sacred place; that an offering had been made for us, and that we'd better hightail it out of there. It was one of the really striking experiences of synchronicity we witnessed as we moved through those years of intense change."

Now, the broader point of Sidra's story becomes clear. So, after the winding thread of the story line, the details, both factual and functional, and the sidebar comments, Sidra glides smoothly to the idea that this story is a teaching about recognizing the presence of the Higher Energies they talk about today. They both felt their relationship was not only approved of by the higher energies, but that they were being protected and used by them for the expression of a larger and evolving consciousness.

"From the beginning I felt really protected, even before we had decided to get married. I have felt that same sense of protection again in these last couple of years, particularly that six to eight-month month period of Hal's illness in 2014. All during those months, what we've needed has simply shown up. I have learned to walk through life with a sense that everything I need is in place. I just have to notice it. All I have to do is pick up what's there, rather than force things to happen. I think that's true for all of us if we become sensitive to it."

Like anyone who listens to a good story well told, I linger in the silence with Sidra, reflecting on the panorama of experience I've just witnessed. I think about the impact of the dream at the end of Hal's story and recognize the same resting place found from another direction. This is teaching the way they do it: above all else generously, layered deeply and delightfully with their energy and unswerving dedication to sharing their experience and expanding consciousness.

THE DREAM

The dream process is another part of the method of Voice Dialogue, although in some ways, that understates its importance. In the early days of writing this book, I strung a clothesline, and then another, from the stairs in my den to the doorway of the mudroom. On it I hung the chapters of THE PATH OF RELATIONSHIP as they came to me ... hot off the presses as it were. Then I tried placing a chapter about dreams on it in different places. After a lot of hemming and hawing, I came to understand that there's simply no right place to put a chapter about the dream process because it resists being a separate chapter. I realized that the dream process was, in fact, the clothesline itself. The entire story hung itself along the stretches of these long, cotton roadways. Nothing in the Psychology of the Aware Ego Process is now, nor ever was, disconnected from the dream.

235

From the beginning of his Jungian work, Hal's fascination with the dream has continued uninterrupted to the present. It was the place in which he met himself from his earliest connection to psyche; in which Sidra joined him from her own history of transpersonal experiences and visualizations. Throughout their lives first separately and then together, the Stones never doubted the connection they formed with the unconscious, nor its intention to support the work they pursued together. The dream rests, like the center and circumference of a mandala, as the form around which the art is both inspired and contained.

In the early years, Hal and Sidra used the dream process and Voice Dialogue interchangeably. When a client would bring in a dream, it was invaluable to be able to identify a self and be in actual dialogue with it. Although this is much like the active imagination engaged in nearing the traditional end of an analysis, Voice Dialogue is a shared process. There is actual, active, energetic engagement with the facilitator, and an energetic induction into selves one might not have experienced before.

"You get a mixture of benefits," Hal explained. "That's really the primary issue. The other thing is that the Organizing Intelligence, (later Source) seems to know a great deal about relationship. If you work with a couple in this way, they begin to recognize the selves involved in their relationship. They separate some from the Primaries and the Intelligence responds to that. It brings them very strong teaching dreams. It usually happens in the first few months of work."

Hal added a story about a bonding pattern he and Sidra were in once when her children were visiting. They wanted to go shopping and wanted him to come along. He added that all children can smell a Good Father when he's around, and that self is very strong in Hal. Sidra wanted him to go along as well, although in recent years she is clear up front that she doesn't want his company if suffering with the Bad Father comes on its heels.

In any case, this time Hal's Good Father lasted for a portion of the shopping trip and then he began to get tired, worrying privately about a lecture he had to write. "I began to get snippy with Sidra," Hal said. "She continued to deflect it all, but by the time we got to bed that night, we were in a pretty good negative bonding pattern. Now, it's not unconscious. I know I'm being a schmuck, but I couldn't stop it."

That night, Sidra had a dream that it's morning and she comes into the bedroom. Hal begins to throw lighted matches at her, which she's deflecting. They aren't doing much damage, but she has to fend them off. We both began to laugh when she told me this dream," he said. "Here the unconscious comes in and gives us this amazing image that reflects what's happening in the relationship."

Where does that understanding of relationship come from? Hal and Sidra believe that a larger Source drops these dream ideas on them all the time, because they do so much relationship-oriented work with couples, so much work on bonding patterns. This kind of work then interacts with the Higher Energy field in its relational function.

Another way of seeing the dream as central in this work is to recognize that the dream ego is really a picture of the primary selves in operation. "Well," Hal said, "not always but very often. A guy has a nightmare that he's driving down the freeway at a hundred miles an hour. Clearly there's a part of his personality that goes too fast through life. I can tease that out. I ask to talk to the guy who's driving the car. Knowledge of the disowned selves is so important. So, if you think it's clinically relevant or appropriate, you might say to this guy, 'Bubbala, Bubbala, Bubbala.[72] Do

237

you realize how hard you're pushing the pedal down?' Finding that out is a therapeutic gold mine."

Hal's dedication to psyche's waterways is famous. To be in a dream process with Hal is to follow a labyrinthian thread into deep recesses in the unconscious not visited before. Many people treasure their work in the dream landscape with Hal. Neil Mieli, a poet and longtime Voice Dialogue facilitator, commented on his experience with fondness.

"I was once working on the progression of a dream with Hal," he said. "I could tell Hal was enjoying it as much as I was. He wasn't working. He was enjoying himself. When he finished, he said, 'Well, you're clearly in the hands of the gods.'"[73]

Perhaps the thing for which I am most grateful to Jung is his capacity to be open to the immense variety of psyche's expression. While my path into such appreciation was formal analytic training, I was deeply involved in my dream life from an early age, but I had no context for my nightly adventures until I discovered Jung. While not nearly applauded enough in his lifetime or even now, he added fantasy, visual arts, drama, transpersonal and paranormal experience to my psychic repertoire. All of these became for me the stuff of personal investigation, leading to understanding my humanity in continuing depth.

Although Sidra would say today that Hal has always taken the lead in the dream work, she'd been exposed to the terrain herself from early childhood. This is one of the remarkable things about their work together. It almost seems they were destined to cross paths, although they started from such different directions. While Hal's love affair with the dream process began in his twenties when he started a Jungian analysis, Sidra had already found the transpersonal world, many years earlier.

"My process was neither psychological nor spiritual from the beginning," Sidra said. "I was never on a 'spiritual' path. It was psycho/spiritual from the beginning and then was carried by the relationship to Hal. We were equally each other's teachers and therapists. I had dreams, transpersonal experiences and *knowings*, but I didn't pay much attention to them until I met Hal and began to focus on them."

Before then, Sidra's spirituality and process were just a part of her life as she lived it. Her spirituality was inextricably intertwined – and expressed in – her relationship to other people and to the earth itself. She viewed her process as a fascinating, but very private, narrative. Visions and other worldly understanding had been her companion since the age of two. Although she wouldn't have called it that, Sidra's first transpersonal experience happened one morning when she, at the age of two, wandered out onto the porch of her family's country home.

She was small, her head not reaching the top of the railing. "I was all alone," she said. "I watched the sun rise and saw the brilliant magical play of the light on the dewy grass. It sparkled like diamonds. I felt a strange answering sparkle inside myself. I felt absolutely happy and excited, but at the same time, at peace. I knew I had experienced something special."

Sidra was remarkably aware as a child, as earlier chapters have illuminated. On this dimension, she continued to record in memory, many more such liminal, or transpersonal sights and sensations. When she was ten, she saw the Rocky Mountains for the first time. She was deeply moved by the way the clouds and the snowy peaks seemed to blend into each other. She felt transported to another realm. When she was older, she saw the same mountains again in one of the first Cinemascope movies. They made her weep. "I remember laughingly telling my mother that I never cry at movies," Sidra said, "… except when I see mountains. These tears came from a different source, and I knew it. They were my first tears of the heart.[74] They opened something new in me that I would come to understand as my deep connection to the world and the people in it."

Before she had even heard of Hal Stone, Sidra had begun to wonder about and work with her own dreams, recognizing images from them appearing in her outer life. In one such dream she was saved from death by grabbing onto a large Deodar tree rushing down a flooding river. She found a safe place between its branches and rode it to safety. Within a year of this dream, Sidra moved into a house in whose back yard grew the tree she saw in the dream.

In 1968, Sidra had the near-death experience traveling in Guatemala that she spoke of earlier. She recognized right away that there was definitely something else at work; that there was palpably something more -something she knew nothing about. It was following this experience that Sidra took real interest in exploring what she called "realms that existed beyond appearances," to learn things beyond the grasp of her rational mind.

Although Sidra's attention to dreams and things mystical is no less illuminating than Hal's, her relationship is more private, or at least it used to be. In recent years, she acknowledges that things have changed since the early days. All those years of facilitating selves and relying on the unconscious to guide them have given way to more practical concerns related to teaching and managing their lives in their maturity.

"We always shared our dreams," she said. "But our process back in the 1970's was much more private, and separate. I relied on my own dream process early on. My take on things was often different from Hal's." Sidra's expansive dream landscape parallels Hal's. While his concerns focused on the Center for the Healing Arts and his larger world task, Sidra reminisced about how her dream process reflected the enormous change she was facing in her own evolution.

"I remember having a long series of dreams in the early years of our relationship," she said. "The images surfaced one after another telling of the exploration of new places, new vistas, new landscapes. I had endless dreams about the third floor of my house. It was filled with unused furniture and treasures I could bring down into my life. There were attics filled with magical antiques and books with secrets in them I couldn't yet read."

But that kind of independent process around their dreams is no longer so private. Sidra sees their relationship as so powerful, they now share their dreams and rely on the unconscious as objective feedback. As early as the mid-1970's, Sidra received dreams that seemed to indicate support from other dimensions around their relationship. In one such dream, Hal and Sidra were sitting together facing a semi-circle of eighteen men in white robes. The nine on the left were from the Himalayas and the nine on the right were from the Andes.

"They spoke to us at length about relationship," Sidra said. "and remained surrounding us for what seemed like an eternity. They held us in their energy fields and let us know they were there to protect us. They were clearly blessing our work."

By the 1980's, Hal and Sidra travelled to Ibiza, where they stayed with an old friend, Lydia Duncan. Sidra remembers being very clearly swept up in a feeling of "immanence". She awakened with the following song running through her mind.

241

Songs that I sang before come

Softly once again.

And the shadows of uncounted journeys

Cross my way.

This visit, the one she was enjoying at the time, and perhaps the one that came to her from the realms behind the appearances, led directly to expanding their teaching to Europe, England and Australia in the years that followed.

"Now I have what I call 'consciousness dreams,' in which the unconscious brings me back to the basic structures," Sidra said. "They're Aware Ego Process dreams, with an experience of the selves with me as a player in the drama. There's a commentator of Awareness giving me a blow-by-blow account. 'Oh look. There's your Primary Self doing its usual thing.' It's a psychological commentary without the judgment."

So, Sidra's hit on psyche's offerings is different than Hal's, while just as unique, with its own flow and history. Together they offer a picture of the wisdom and infinite variety in the world of dreams ... and they have taught, from the early Intensives on, what they've come to understand between them. One longtime Voice Dialogue facilitator and participant in many of the Intensives, Judith Hendin, recalled an exact experience of the richness of the Stones' separate perspectives.

"One time at an Intensive," she said, "I had a dream that I didn't share in the morning group. Later I shared the dream with Sidra and she gave an interpretation. Everything fit. Then I saw Hal was in his office, so I went in and shared the dream with him. He offered me an interpretation that was absolutely perfect and completely different. It taught me there is never one "right" way to see a dream."[75]

CHAPTER SIXTEEN

The Evening of Life

Describing the stages of life, Jung said:

> *[Aging is] ... a deep-seated and peculiar change within the psyche. I ... take for comparison, the daily course of the sun – but a sun that is endowed with human feeling and man's limited consciousness. In the morning it rises from the nocturnal sea of unconsciousness and looks upon the wide, bright world, which lies before it in an expanse that steadily widens the higher it climbs in the firmament. In this extension of the field of its action, caused by its own rising, the sun will discover its own significance; it will see the attainment of the greatest possible height, and the widest possible dissemination of its blessings, as its goal. In this conviction the sun pursues its course to the unforeseen zenith – unforeseen, because its career is unique and individual, and the culminating point could not be calculated in advance. At the stroke of noon the descent begins. And the descent means the reversal of all the ideals and values cherished in the morning. The sun falls into contradiction with itself. It is as though it should draw in its rays instead of emitting them. Light and warmth decline and are at last extinguished.*[76]

In this almost poetic reflection, Jung offers a way to frame the inevitable trajectory that human life must follow. With neither fanfare nor regret, he pays tribute to the great cycle, the stuff of mythologies the world over. Facing the aging process requires a courage and consciousness we have to learn, for we are surely not born with it; nor, would such preoccupations be appropriate during our early years. Attention to decline isn't relevant while we're still growing. Moreover, it seems it is just as easy, and often preferable, to ignore it later on.

As I listened to Hal and Sidra talk about their experience, I felt my own discomfort dogging my thoughts. I recognized the faint rustling of frustrations unfamiliar to me in my mid-sixties, the ones I'd kept at bay until recent years. The small tasks that used to be automatic now require some concentration, like unscrewing jar lids, kneeling to pull weeds and getting up again. Although I still ride and train my horse five days a week, and keep up with a steady yoga practice, I'm aware of the frequent self-diagnoses of viruses that are just as likely plain fatigue from doing what I've always done when my age might dictate doing less.

Hal and Sidra talk about aging a lot now. They tell you up front they're old, and how that is for them. It shakes my denial about the future right to the bone, even though I love them more for lasting this long, and planning to be here longer. I like to know the details of their experience. It simply feels good, having the chance to be empathetic, to look at them tenderly, to laugh with them about their frustrations and vulnerability … and more importantly, learn from them about what's coming, how to deal with it.

Sidra Stone, 2015, Albion, CA

It's funny how this goes, the dialing down of life. I hope I do it with as much grace and openness as they do, but I can't imagine it will be as interesting somehow. Watching them now reminds me, in an instantaneous replay, of how they used to look and move when I first met them. I'm certain it's like that for a great many people who have known them for a long time. I remember times when Hal would challenge me, with a force of energy that would make me want to back out of the room slowly, not taking my eyes off him. His point was of course that I should push back, but it took him time to teach me how.

Sidra used to leap up in the middle of conversation to show me things that pertained to what we were talking about, sometimes giving me a wall ornament or small sculpture to take home with me. I remember her rushing to give me a hug in greeting, whereas now, she walks, even if the hug is the same in energy and strength. In the end, it's the body that has changed, although the energy is interrupted more frequently now as they both clear their throats more often, and we all run to the bathroom after one cup of tea.

While Jung's ideas are solar in inspiration, like much else about Hal and Sidra, their ideas on aging are a blend. Sidra adds that lunar, feminine quality to most of what she brings to their work and that is not lost on Hal. He appreciates it more as time goes on, for conscious aging is more than an art. The discipline they apply to just starting the day is impressive. They're quick to talk about its importance on a broader scale as they run through the simple routines of getting started in the morning. Some years before this writing, as is their way, they had already begun to talk openly about what was happening to them.

"You know," Hal said, "aging is a very strange process. We get up in the morning. By the time we have breakfast and are ready to 'do' something, it feels like it's nine o'clock at night. We look at each other and wonder where the time went."

Sidra agreed. "I can't remember how we used to get up, go to the gym, get breakfast and get to work on time. I'm serious. I don't know how we did it! And … raise five children."[77]

The dialogue about aging has not only continued, it's deepened, reorganized itself into manageable categories. Hal and Sidra sit with a similar amazement, but greater understanding of the process has replaced the wonder of earlier times. There have been health crises, recoveries, surgeries and emergencies for them both. Each one offered them the opportunity to learn more, prepare more thoroughly for a life with different demands.

We sat at the dining room table again in the fall of 2014. I had spent more time with them, filling in the holes in the first draft of my manuscript. If their generosity has lessened with age, I surely can't detect it. The sun was illuminating the garden behind the house. The red and gold and purple blossoms waved silently through the windows, bobbing and weaving like the heads of tiny children wearing caps, playing hide and seek beneath the windowsills.

247

"The Primary Selves and the Bonding Patterns that have ruled your life, no matter how much work you've done on separating from them, come back like gangbusters as you get older," Sidra said. "You just have to face the challenge of not knowing if you're going to live another week or for another twenty years. It makes planning incredibly difficult!" she added with mock melodrama. "So, in spite of the fact that you have physical changes coming in, you just don't know. That question is a constant. If you died next week, what would you wish you'd done today?" And conversely, "what if you did it all today, and then lived for another twenty years!" They enjoy the joke for a minute and then move to what's underneath.

Hal in Sidra's garden, age 88.

The point they make is that as life progresses everything needs to be reexamined. The solutions of youth no longer work. Perhaps that's why there is so much discussion between them about even simple decisions. How much travel will they look forward to now? What precautions need to be in place if Sidra leaves to visit her children? How does Hal feel about visiting his daughter? Do they make a trip to San Francisco just to see the museums? These become real questions with more complicated answers as time goes on. Aging demands new paradigms, as Jung suggests, again in "The Stages of Life":

Ageing people should know that their lives are not mounting and expanding, but that an inexorable inner process enforces the contraction of life. ...After having lavished its light upon the world, the sun withdraws its rays in order to illuminate itself .... [There are] inevitable consequences of the delusion that the second half of life must be governed by the principles of the first.[78]

Hal and Sidra would definitely agree, but it's not as simple a decision as Jung might imply. In fact, it's not a decision at all, it seems, because the process has us, not the other way around. Because we aren't ultimately in charge of the journey, the level of vulnerability ratchets up dramatically. In the end, we return to a level of helplessness akin to infancy, when we needed the help of someone else to see about our needs. "Real vulnerability begins," Sidra said, "when you can no longer trust your body to sustain you. It's a whole different game then."

The notion of vulnerability moved the conversation to issues of limitation. Contrary to my expectations, what Hal and Sidra mean by limitation is that people who age consciously have to provide limitation. This means changing your life and life style. As old age approaches, people need to set boundaries to respond to the ever-changing landscape of vulnerability.

"I was fifty years old when I was diagnosed with Type Two diabetes," Hal said. "It wasn't a surprise. It was in the family gene pool. But then I had to deal with limitation. I mean, lots of people can't do it and usually bad things happen. Others go way into the medical end of things, give themselves shots, and don't change consciousness. But really, it's an opportunity to make one's life more conscious."

In truth, if Hal had the choice, he acknowledged he'd have preferred to have fewer illnesses as consciousness-changing experiences. Perhaps in his next incarnation things will go a little more smoothly. But he's clear about getting things in place for help before you need it because there's such a range of physical things that happen.

One of the things Hal and Sidra strongly recommend is to get the group of people together that are going to support your health, both traditional, for hospitalization etc., and alternative for nutrition and acupuncture. The task is to get both systems in place. For those who are very oriented toward either one, they stress it's a terrible missed opportunity.

"I promise you," Hal said, "the one you don't have is going to bite you in the ass. If you don't have traditional medicine, you miss the gift of longevity. Without alternative practices, you have to do without the gentler, more subtle remedies. But I had the will to take responsibility for what was happening to me," he said. "I changed my diet and exercise and learned to monitor things. Life can really be a teacher in that way. But as you age, the question is always this: when do you push through a physical process, and when do you stop?"

As always, Hal and Sidra are quick to give a practical example from their own experience. Hal followed up with an example from his seventies. "It can be as simple as getting out of the car," he said. "As I did that one day, my left foot gave out on me. It just stopped working. I didn't fall but I had to hop to the house. It was fine the next day. But that's what it's like. You push yourself one day, and the next, your arm is really sore. As you age, your muscles and tendons are developing a new life style. By your seventies, a lot of people get hit by it. But when it really comes ..."

Just then, Hal's hearing aid began to buzz. Sidra began to laugh, saying, "That's perfect! When it really comes, you have to change your battery more often!" Laughter fills the room now. "You realize your husband has been telling you to stop mumbling for days," she said, "and you remember to ask if he's remembered to put his hearing aids in."

That's one of the joys of spending time with the Stones. They model how they cope with the things the rest of us fear or stigmatize, and they laugh at it. They fold you right into their process and invite you to laugh with them. It's infectious and delightful, even the hard parts ... and they seem to know how to make those the funniest of all. Hal's daughter, J. Tamar, has watched it all from the beginning and the inside. She commented in another conversation with me.

"What they've done for me is debunk the negative field surrounding aging. I mean, if this is aging, bring it on! They're so present and have such fun with it. They make the process so organic. My Dad is like a magician when it comes to putting in his hearing aids. He's so unself-conscious, it comes off like a sleight of hand, totally organic. I think in part it's also because he's so grateful. He saw the toll it was taking not getting them.[79]

In a mania and youth-crazed culture such as ours, there's tremendous pressure to avoid aging itself as long as one can. In fact, modern science has made tremendous strides to that end. Life expectancy has been increased because of them. But the inevitable changes come down to a pair of physiological opposites that Sidra identifies as "irreversible breakdown" and "manageable breakdown".

"There's a certain amount of acknowledgement that some things just aren't working anymore", she said. "But then the question becomes 'Are my veins popping because there's something really wrong, or is that normal at my age?' With all the medical advances, there are ways to look and feel forever young, even though aging is taking hold of the body."

251

How one avails themselves of those advances then presents another pair of opposites with a different set of questions. The Stones try to find balance between the psychophysiological and the psychological.

"What it boils down to," Sidra said, "is a simple question. Are we looking for the fountain of youth to deal with a body that isn't forty anymore? Is the fountain of youth a cure for the tremendous vulnerability that comes with aging?" She describes the process as watching the river of life go by quickly. People who are familiar have died. The world one grew up in, in which one's consciousness developed, has long since passed. These changes are inevitable and powerful.

"We're constantly in process," she said, "constantly changing, like tectonic shifts happening under our feet while we try to stay upright. The vulnerability we experience is ratcheted way up because of this. Our work is built on how you take care of your vulnerability."

Hal had been nodding his head the whole time. "And believe me," he added, "if you haven't learned how to deal with vulnerability before now, it will take you down. It means that your Primary Selves will be dealing with it, so you don't have to feel or accept aging. But going into your advanced years that way changes relationships."

He explained that when the vulnerability is accepted, you feel at home with people. Without it, with Primary Selves dealing with things, you can't be with people on an energetic level. Vulnerability then becomes the doorway to the fruit of spirit in relationship. "Energetic linkage is the most important thing," Hal said. "It offers us the ability to connect to the heart and essence of others."

Hal and Sidra enjoyed the morning, teaching, commenting, laughing at their misunderstandings and reflecting on their many years of working with people and themselves. Of course, if there's an opportunity for Hal to find a fairytale that pertains to things, he's on it. This was no less the case when the focus turned to sexuality and aging.

At a certain time in their marriage, Hal began to ruminate about the future, the likelihood that he would die before Sidra. When the idea came to him that she might find someone else, his fantasies plagued his consciousness. The thought of her with another man troubled him deeply and he had to deal with it.

"There's a fairy tale called 'The Golden Child'," Hal said. Sidra and I both settled in, awaiting the spell he was about to cast in the room. "There's a wonderful king and queen. They have this marvelous son. All is good and wonderful and kind. Through the middle of the kingdom flows a river of milk. Anyone can come at any time and fill up their flask."

So, setting the stage, the tale naturally goes on to break up the perfect setting. The king gets sick and is dying. He calls his wife to him and tells her he's dying. She responds that she knows. He asks her to promise that she will never take another partner. She so promises.

"Now, this king is an innocent," Hal continued. "He's never done any psychological work. So, the king dies and it's only a short time before a very dark king comes into the kingdom. Before long, the queen is married to him. Predictably, he doesn't like the son at all. He also stopped up the river and refuses to let the people take any milk from it."

253

The tale continues, telling us that there is one old man who refuses to be shut out. He sneaks down to the river and steals milk at five in the morning. The dark king is outraged and chooses to make an example of him. He has the old man captured, puts him in a cage and parades him through the kingdom. When the wonderful son witnesses this, the old man gets his attention and asks to be freed. Of course, the boy refuses because he knows his stepfather would kill him. He knows he's crazy. But the old man is persuasive, and eventually the boy yields and frees him. The boy then naturally has to flee the kingdom, and his story begins. His adventures include solving the problem of good and evil.

"In a way, I had to go through a similar process," Hal said. "When I thought of Sidra being sexual with another man, it was very, very painful. But I also knew that the positive bonding pattern between us was dissolving. She couldn't promise to never take another partner, and I couldn't control what was going to happen after my death. It was my issue alone. Eventually, I just walked out of it, but it took a while."

Sexuality is, of course, a core issue in relationship. When it declines in the aging process, is very individual and how people confront that is often not talked about. But characteristically, the Stones don't avoid it.

"Sidra and I have been blessed with both a work relationship and a sexual relationship," Hal said. "But as I got into my eighties I wasn't feeling as good about it. What I mean is I was forcing it. Like many men, I knew I could take something that could support being sexual. The idea of giving up sexuality in a relationship is not a popular thought. But, it began to feel like forcing things was the wrong path."

Again, our culture dictates an opposite attitude. There is tremendous pressure to stay young and fit and sexual. A paradigm shift is obvious in what's expected, in the images we see "That's great, but I won't be going there, because I couldn't do it when I was twenty!"

But their commitment to the deeper connection between them, the energetic linkage, is clearly what they most value. "What I've always done with Source or God is demand clarity," Hal said. "'If you want me to give something up, you have to make it clear.'

I once got a dream that told me directly to stop drinking or we would lose the ability to move together in the higher spheres. So, I did for a period of time. I want clarity and I ask for it. The point is you never know where limitation is going to take you. It might not always be a bad thing."

Although Hal talked about his sexual drive going down earlier than Sidra's, he thought that other connections were more complete. The spiritual and energetic connections are beautiful and fine.

"Changes in sexuality are expected," Hal said. "I chose to think of it more as I had a great run. Everything changes. The question is more about how much to fight it and how much to accept it. Honestly, it was a relief to me to stop pretending we're young."

As usual, it's not that the Stones give people advice. The choice is always out there to continue as long as you want. They simply model both sides. Again, the cultural norm is slanted toward the side of being young and sexual as long as possible. Sidra began talking about a woman she worked with who actually asked when a woman has the right to say no to sex.

255

"The way the culture is going," Sidra said, "the answer is never. But if we do make that decision, we don't all have to get into rocking chairs in an upstairs bedroom in our children's house, either. We don't have to apologize or worry about what people will say about you and think about you if you decide not to have sex anymore. Furthermore, when that pressure to continue to be sexual disappears, it can make room for an exquisitely delicate and sensual energetic intimacy."

Hal had been nodding his head again, thinking. He joined in. "People need to know that when they get into limitation, death isn't the only alternative. If sex is all you've got going for you in relationship, that's another thing. But if you touch into the unconscious, it opens whole other vistas."

In the end, whether it's about sexuality or other areas of the psychophysiological process, the Stones recognize aging as an archetypal and genetic event. They rely heavily on the unconscious and the attention to dreams to guide and respond to the inevitable changes. While they both nod as I restate their ideas, Sidra jumps in quickly, delighting in her thought. "Your knee might give out," she said, "but your unconscious can come through stronger and quicker."

As the discussion progressed, it was naturally impossible to avoid my own ruminations about loss and how it was handled in my family. Memories I didn't know I had bubbled up unbidden as I listened to the wisdom in the room. When I was in my mid-teens, I remember an evening when my father's attorney came to the house. This was odd because we seldom had visitors during the week, and when we did it was a special dinner or party affair. So, the atmosphere was a little tense. My mother seemed very upset.

I wasn't invited into my father's den that evening as my parents dove into organizing their wills. That was the agenda. I listened from a hidden distance in the stairway. My mother was crying in spite of my father's insistence that talking about dying didn't make one go any quicker. It was clear that wasn't the comfort she was looking for. But somehow the papers were drawn up, signed, and stored away for what was to happen a quick four years later for my father. He died suddenly before my twenty-first birthday. None of us guessed he was ill. None of us were prepared. We never talked about death.

Some twenty-five years later, and several decades after Jung's death, I was exposed to his thoughts about it. Again, in the *Collected Works,* Jung offers wisdom that I certainly find more helpful in my sixties than I ever would have in my twenties. He said:

> *I am convinced that it is hygienic – if I may use the word – to discover in death a goal towards which one can strive, and that shrinking away from it is something unhealthy and abnormal which robs the second half of life of its purpose. ... From the standpoint of psychotherapy, it would therefore be desirable to think of death as only a transition, as part of a life process whose extent and duration are beyond our knowledge.*[80]

257

In what has become a recognizable pattern, Hal and Sidra next turn their attention to this matter that many people avoid, even up to the last minute of a life. They began discussing with earnestness and clarity the importance of dealing with issues of death and dying in the aging process. Of course, having your affairs in order was at the top of the list. Wills and medical powers of attorney, though sometimes complicated and tedious, need to be in place or the vulnerability that becomes so acute as we age, gives us no peace.

"The other thing," Hal said, "is that many people have selves in them that want to die. It's shocking to facilitate these selves. They say things like 'I don't know …it's boring. The body is breaking down. I have to deal with all this maintenance. It doesn't feel worth it.' Believe me, if you don't get hold of these selves, you'll lose it."

Hal went on to explain that aging for the extrovert can be the pathway to introversion, a version of just letting yourself die there in the chair. Or, they can go inside themselves maybe for the first time. Out of that might come the realization of how trapped they've been in doing for others and the world.

"On the other hand," Sidra said, "for someone who's introverted and tends to isolate, the deterioration forces them into increased isolation. It can make them not want to live anymore. Studies show that unless you are able to maintain outer connection, people die sooner."

The idea of keeping connection with others surfaced over and over again. The Stones acknowledge a pull to isolate as we age and advise against yielding to it. Just as the body moves toward contraction, so does the psyche. The task is always balancing these opposing draws, the natural sense of wanting to isolate with a real need for the feeling that comes from connection with others.

Hal and Sidra had an opportunity to review all of this in the spring of 2014. The Prologue of this book attests to the result, and the Introduction to the necessity. Before they understood that he had a serious blood infection, Hal simply turned to Sidra and said, "I'm dying." They were instantly put to the test of their beliefs. She spoke softly, remembering the previous spring's experience, reflecting on it from the perspective of having avoided the worst.

"When Hal turned to me and said, 'I'm dying,' I had two distinct reactions," Sidra said. "It felt as if they happened in two different dimensions, using two different sets of perceptual equipment. On the one hand, I felt if it's time, he should go. I don't want to hold on to him for selfish reasons. I know he's fascinated with what happens after death. He's been doing a lot of reading about it. I don't want to hold onto him when his natural flow would be to leave. I felt that way about my mother too. When you love somebody, your tendency is to hold onto them. But the greatest gift you can give them is really to say to them, 'Go on. Fly free. I will be fine.'"

As she told the story, what followed were a number of very practical concerns related to some acceptance of Hal's situation and Sidra's desire to make it as easy for him as possible. She tried to be aware of what he might want, what he would like. Also, she began to think of what she should get ready. What needed to be in order? She thought of getting on the computer to see how they set up special websites for people who have just died. Questions of who to notify and how, were at the forefront. What to do with the ashes? Should there be a memorial gathering? Sidra wrestled with her desire to honor him and her natural shyness around that. They talked about having a ceremony at their home.

"As we moved into *that* conversation, about 'it's okay to go,'" Sidra said, "I had another reaction that was equally strong. Maybe it wasn't his time. It didn't feel

259

like it to me. So, I decided to make things as nice as I could. I made some fires, and thought we'd just be together, connected through the linkage."

Hal was feverish by then but didn't want to go to the ER. It was Sunday and they agreed that taking him then wouldn't have been a good choice anyway. It would have been too intrusive and controlling. Sidra chose to simply hang onto the energy between them, make him comfortable, love him, and keep the linkage without making it an anchor.

"So often in our relationship we've held on to the energetic connection between us without knowing what the next step was going to be;" she said, "getting in touch with ourselves first. In a way, it was a very precious day. Physically I just held onto him with the full realization that it might be his last day. There was an exquisite intimacy in all this. I can still feel it in the pit of my stomach. The sense of that day hasn't left me. It made us both aware that each day was a gift. We live it like we live it."

An internist's appointment the following day confirmed a blood infection, but what kind would take a few days to discover. Hal's fever had broken but it turned out not to be the good sign we might expect it to be. His body had simply given up. It was shutting down. While Hal and Sidra were deciding if they should go to Santa Rosa to a hospital or stay local, Hal began falling asleep in the car.

"But it didn't feel like sleep to me," Sidra continued. "He was slipping into a coma. That made the decision for me. We went in. He was in very bad shape. I could feel his energies moving elsewhere. I stayed with him because I knew his hold on life was tenuous, holding the tensions within myself of allowing him to go, but holding onto the idea that if he could heal, he should stay. It was an incredible experience of holding the experience with an open hand," she said with a sigh. "...So touching! It was my most intense experience of the Aware Ego Process. According to Hal, it was utter surrender to what would come."

While Sidra would say she still might not have a clear picture of a particular Higher Power, she clearly surrendered to the flow of energy, to what was unfolding. "It was so clear and sure," she said. "There was a deep stillness about being there, a sense of awe. I knew I wasn't in control of this. In the end, what is, is. The river flows without me pushing it."

It's hard for me to imagine being bored with life, although there have certainly been periods during which I would describe my status as stalled. Sameness is a slow and insidious killer. It dulls the senses and blocks creativity below the radar of consciousness. In part, I'm sure my Jungian studies were motivated by the fact that when working with dreams, there is never a chance for things to get old or repetitious. But Hal and Sidra warn against letting it creep up on us, especially as we age.

"The danger," Hal commented, "is that you can become bored with what you're doing and not know it. You keep talking about the same thing over and over again. The part of you that wants to die can get stronger through this, and you won't even know it. Jane Roberts,[81] the New Age author and psychic, wrote about contacting a number of world thinkers, among whom was William James," Hal said. "He died in his early sixties and it was a complete shock to him. She said that he contacted her from the other side and told her that his book, *Varieties of Religious Experience* had defined his life. He never entertained the possibility of doing anything else. He simply had no knowledge of how bored he was until he got to the other side. The trap of sameness and boredom supports leaving this life, not living it."

The next item on the Stones' list would deal with the importance of separating from your Inner Critic in the aging process. Although separating from this self is a constant for most of us, it takes on larger proportions as we age. The Critic's relationship to our increasing vulnerability is, of course, the key. While our capacities to function normally after sixty or seventy years require more time and attention, our patience with ourselves diminishes unless we stay connected to how vulnerable the process makes us. Again, the Stones return to dealing with vulnerability, and the many ways we can lose the battle.

"If we have not dealt with the Critic and separated from it, we will continue to face the aging process as a victim via the inner child," Hal said. "Everything becomes frightening. If you forget something, the critic goes wild. 'Why didn't you take those courses? Why didn't you do that during the last five years?'"

"There is just a lot of pressure to remain young," Sidra said laughing. "'Why are you not young and gorgeous? Did you forget your teeth?'"

"Yes," Hal joined in, laughing as well and then getting serious. "It's like blaming the victim for getting cancer. Between what genuinely goes wrong physically and all the things you might have done, the critic just goes crazy. You have to have some separation from this or you can't work out a reasonable program."

As the sun made its way high above the house, the brightness of the day highlighted the contrast between the setting and the topic. But in truth, learning from the Stones generally comes in that way. If their reflections were a piece of music, the refrain would have an amused tone, set in counterpoint to the depth and power of the theme. Growing old is inevitable. There are ways to do it with grace. It's good to know.

The clock was ticking in real time for me. The hour of my departure from the coast loomed large that last morning. I felt into my resistance to leaving the stillness of the bubble I had entered, trying to get the last of my topics covered. Just then, Hal remembered a message he's forgotten to share with Sidra.

"Oh, the robot called to confirm your appointment," he said. After a short pause, he added, "I fell in love with her."

Sidra picked it up right away, laughing. "You love those impersonal gals," she said.

"Yes," Hal said. "I've been feeling bored in my love affair with my primetime robot. I feel like she's boring. I just wish she would say something different. It's such a good teaching. No matter how much a robot can give you, she can't give you energetic linkage. She just can't think outside the box. But that's okay."

The playfulness Hal and Sidra continue to have with each other is a delight to witness. It's reassuring that a sense of humor doesn't have to be sacrificed on the altar of physical decline. It's rare that one or the other of them isn't finding a way to make discussion juicy in that way.

One of the last areas Hal and Sidra focused on during their reflections on aging was the need for psycho/spiritual change. What they mean by that is that aging requires moving into a new consciousness. This includes exploring other realms beyond the spiritual.

In his book published in 2013, Jungian analyst James Hollis, like Hal Stone, turns his attention to the power of a dream and begins a line of questioning pointing in a similar direction.

I have also learned, by personal experience, professional training, and clinical example, that there is a deeper intelligence than our egos at work in the lives of all of us. (What, after all, produced such a weird dream? I certainly did not conjure it forth from any conscious frame.) … we recognize that there were other factors at work than those of which we were conscious at the moment…. The invisible in the midst of the visible world.[82]

"You see," Hal said, "Millions of people hate this or that religious doctrine and have to move to Perth to get away from it. They flee the old forms."

Then Sidra chimed in. "That's one of the things about aging. You just can't go to Perth anymore. So, you have to take the next step on a whole different level than the one you've been identified with. It's not a question of fighting being Jewish, or Buddhist, or Christian. It's about finding something larger that you don't have to fight against."

Hal was quick to elucidate. His process in finding a name for this immense change in his understanding has taken up and abandoned several forms and continues to be subject to revision. From Intelligence, the Organizing Intelligence, Source Energy, then Source alone to Source Field, Hal and Sidra continue a dialogue with each other and other energies to wrap their minds and hearts around a process that continues to expand. In the end, although Sidra never liked the idea of higher intelligences, they agree that there are Higher Energies available to us, and Source Energy is the tool used by them to intervene on life processes.

"We understand now that the Aware Ego Process is literally a new consciousness," she said. "You can't describe it to someone who's still in the old one. It brings with it access to other dimensions that were not accessible earlier. The more we do the work, the greater the number of dimensions and knowledge we discover; knowledge that hasn't been perceived or articulated yet."

Hal described this process as vibrational, operating outside of the body, but accessible through vibrations received by the mind and body. "For me," Hal said, "there is an outer god energy that sends energies to us. If there weren't receptors in my brain and other parts of my body, I wouldn't receive this at all. There is god energy. If you don't believe it, that's fine with me. The term simply describes the fact that there are realities outside of the physical system that are operating in the universe. The more we do the work, the more the Aware Ego evolves; new dimensions and new knowledge become available to us. We are exposed to mysteries for which we currently have no words."

Hal thinks of it as coming in from the oldest molecules of creation, the oldest of energy systems. These molecules behave in an intelligent way, but also seem to interact with what we, as human beings, bring to it. There is a sense in this that we all come into the world with the basic equipment to connect to these energies. The first of these energies were instinctual, supporting survival as physical beings. But certain individuals seemed to be wired differently. Perhaps they were less skilled as hunters or gatherers but compensated in ways that offered dreams of larger impact and

265

knowing that influenced the tribe. These people then opened a spiritual reality to life. They became holy men.

"They were the only two choices people had," Hal said. "Live in physical reality, relationship, instinctual needs and the physical demands of life itself. Or, people could choose the opposite. Over identification with either side has increased exponentially over the last hundred years. In general, the consciousness process has become much more associated with the spiritual side of things. Even when I began my analysis back in my twenties, Buddhist teachers were coming over to the U.S. The yogic movement was on the rise, with teachers coming over from Tibet, India and China. Anything that had to do with Higher Energies was labeled spiritual, even psychic events."

For Hal and Sidra, this is not the last transition in their thinking or experience. For them, the Aware Ego Process is totally different than a spiritual process. It's a different path, because it is relationship oriented. The ability to stand between opposite shifts in energy is the key, but not the last word.

"It's not just standing between the opposites," Sidra said. "It's relational on lots of levels. It's relational to the earth, others, family, strangers, and to energies from other dimensions whatever they are. We don't even know yet what all that means. There's a sense of awe and familiarity. It may not always feel good, but it all belongs to me. It's like being in touch with your psychic fingerprint up there in the sky and down here at the same time."

The morning drifted into early afternoon, with little to no diminishment of the light surrounding the property or the three of us on it. I have to wonder if I'll be as present when I'm ten or twenty years older than I am now, as interested in and able to take care of myself as Hal and Sidra. I watch how carefully they talk to each other, how gently they move around the house. I think about the lightness of being that must descend upon us or develop from within if you're connected correctly to Source. I like the thought of connecting in a more direct way with the higher energies, or the energy field that enlivens Hal and Sidra so when they feel into it.

It's always been my experience that people want what Hal and Sidra have. All you have to do is meet them and listen to them talk about their relationship. You can feel envy creep in the room, brushing up against everyone, listening like an old, beautiful cat, purring quietly while watching what you most hope for and haven't found, unfold in simple conversation. Their humor always permeates the story of their life together and their ability to laugh at themselves isn't diminished by the physical challenges of aging.

Hal and I were sitting having a cup of tea one afternoon and he began talking about the intricacies of scheduling surgical appointments. His then recent cataract procedure had come at an inconvenient time when Sidra was needed elsewhere and was on his mind as an example of what aging requires. He was explaining to me that since they live at least an hour and a half from their major hospital, they made the trip and stayed overnight at the Hilton in Santa Rosa for each procedure.

Hal begins to laugh in this out control sort of way, like someone who knows the punch line of a joke and thinks it's so funny they can't stop laughing themselves long enough to get it out, so you can hear it and laugh too. So, Hal starts to laugh, and he explains that every procedure requires a preoperative visit. So, they go down and spend the night at the Hilton. Then they go home and return two weeks later for the surgery, and they stay at the Hilton again for the procedure and the next day post-op appointment.

Then two weeks later, he explains to me, there's another post-op visit, for which they go down, stay at the Hilton, and make the appointment for the next preoperative visit for the coming surgery on the other eye. By this time, Hal is weeping, finding all this so funny, not because the schedule is funny, but because keeping all these appointments straight is a huge deal now. They overlap, and the potential confusion around what's pre- and post and how post and pre- and post for which eye ... unbelievable ... and pretty funny in the telling.

Now he comes to the best part. The part that he really enjoys is this: all this requires that Sidra make all these trips with him, allowing him to reflect to her recently, "Boy you can't say I'm a bad husband. I take you to the Hilton every other week!" By now, Hal's beside himself with delight. I know she would have joined him in her quick laugh and comeback had she been sitting with us. To watch them play with each other is a dance not to be missed.

So, I watch this during our afternoon tea, thinking about and admiring the life they bring to their aging process, and remember the incredible economy of the psyche, in which nothing is wasted. It takes more than one thinks to meet life on life's terms, and clichés, like the last one, abound about how we hope things will go when it's our turn to move into the music of the end. That's the gift of being with the Stones, watching them live their lives at any age, while they tend to the watching of yours ... because that's part of it. While you're with them, they're just as delighted to take you for the ride they've found so incredibly enlightening.

CHAPTER SEVENTEEN

The End or the Beginning

Early on in the creative phases of this book, an analyst colleague of mine encouraged me. He insisted, in the face of my doubts and early disorganization, that it's a valid pursuit to preserve the stories of our predecessors, who, inspired by Jungian thought, take his work and ride its energy into their own directions. Jung might well approve of that himself, if he were here to see what has sprung from his fertile beginnings.

Hal and Sidra at Hendy Woods, 2015

As the "King and Queen" of Voice Dialogue step slowly and carefully away from the lead, Voice Dialogue and the Psychology of the Aware Ego Process become the object of speculation. Where will it go from here? Hal and Sidra have no predictions to put out there. I might add that they have no attachment either. In fact, they expect that Voice Dialogue as it exists today may not look the same at all twenty years from now. But of course, there are other speculations.

As is true for any group, there are some whose hope it is that the work would be preserved in the classic way it originated. Fantasies of lineage and purity meld with a kind of birth order structure among those who have been steeped in the work for decades. Perhaps it will be so for some.

Others see the work pointing beyond where it rests now. Not only have these folks seen the work grow beyond its early structure, but they also speculate that its application will broaden into areas other than psychological. One longtime facilitator, J'aime Ona Pangaia, speculated about Voice Dialogue's projected usefulness in a personal conversation with me.

"For the future, I see Voice Dialogue and the Aware Ego Process as having two levels of service: The facilitation process will be helpful in working out conflict, intra-personally and inter-personally. This can become very valuable for coaches and therapists alike. On the more spiritual side, I see the Aware Ego Process speaking to the mystic. This process renders the mystical more available to us and is in harmony with Buddhist and Vedic traditions."[83]

Still others speculate in different directions, even different dimensions than consciousness rests in for most of us. But who knows for certain? Miriam Dyak, another facilitator with many years' experience with the work, also spoke to me privately about her thought for the decades to come.

"In discovering the Aware Ego Process, Hal and Sidra discovered something for the next generation. If we're living in the third dimension, then the Aware Ego Process becomes a fourth dimensional process; one that takes us toward the center. I would look forward to it becoming a more evolutionary normal state."[84]

For me, it is my sincerest hope that exposure to this work offers generations of the future what happened for me the last night I was at Thera in 2014. I went to bed grumbling that I wanted an experience of Source Energy; one like Hal or Sidra seemed to enjoy so easily. In a response from a new dimension, so direct it startled me, I was given the following dream:

I saw myself lying on the bed. I was above, looking down. Then I was taken up and out onto another world. The land and atmosphere were like nothing I'd seen before. Then I woke up. When I went back to sleep, the same thing happened. I was again taken out onto another planet, this time with different and unfamiliar terrain. The atmosphere was a color I didn't recognize either, and then I woke up. I spent the entire night being drawn out in the dreams to different worlds and then dropped back into consciousness. Not one planet was the same as the others. Not one world had the same landscape or atmosphere.

EPILOGUE

The years of carrying this project have come to an end. I've folded up the interviews, returned the photos, and boxed up the early drafts to be stored somewhere for posterity. And yet, I linger over the early questions that propelled this work. What kinds of people make contributions to consciousness? How do they come to do so? At this juncture, the answers to those questions seem more and less complex than I had once imagined.

I look back at some of the now famous photos of Jung at his tower retreat at Bollingen. He stands stirring a pot over an open fire in the corner of his tower home. Without electricity and the amenities of the city, Jung returned to his origins, allowing his psyche to drop into the less complicated lifestyle of his youth, the simplicity of his more primitive experience and instincts. Beneath the largest of his contributions to consciousness, there was Jung the man, living his life, reflecting on what it brought him, and how to understand his relationship to it.

Five plus decades later, I stood in the dining room of Hal and Sidra's home one last morning before returning home. The house was quiet, and I stood feeling into the silence. The view out the back windows of the house is as soul stirring as the view out the front. In the distance beyond the back driveway is an expansive pasture belonging to a neighbor who keeps horses. The sightline sweeps out to the coast over rolling hills covered with the beige grasses of late summer. Sometimes I can even catch a glimpse of riders on horseback meandering over the terrain.

The picture evokes a kind of nostalgia in me. Images of my youth remind me I had that kind of freedom in my early life, wandering across acres of pasture and trails through the woods on horseback. The memory makes me smile. I began riding again not long ago. This view and that decision remind me why. It's the way I come home to myself.

I linger over the view from a distance for a bit until my gaze slips closer in. The second line of fencing is thinner wire and high enough to keep the deer out. It surrounds Sidra's garden that borders the back deck. I call it Sidra's because it's she who selects the flowers in the arrangements found throughout the house. She chooses what's planted so that blooms are always available in rotating colors and fragrance as the West Coast seasons slip their way through the year.

The garden had a new design this year. Flowing like a cedar-colored river, new pathways of wood chips separated the flowerbeds. The fragrance coming from the damp wood was softly spectacular all by itself. The deep greens and reds I thought were flowers from a distance were simply late summer foliage, supporting buds almost ready to bloom. Off to the right I saw Sidra's silver hair trying to reach the ground over her shoulder as she bent to cut a few select blossoms for her morning's bouquet.

She looked like a graceful Gypsy gardener. Already dressed for work, her long, flowing skirt hid her feet, giving the impression that she hovers over her flowers in a trance or ritual only she can tap into. Knowing her, I suspect that's actually true. Her shawl fell across and behind her shoulders as she moved from pot to pot, clipping a long stem here, a shorter one there, a small burst of contrasting color mounting in her half-closed fist. I felt like I was watching a beautiful, private dance. Suddenly embarrassed at my intrusion, I looked away.

273

I reflected on the image of myself working in my yard in summer months. Like Sidra, I, too, prefer flower gardens to vegetable, but the similarity between us stops there. I've spent many hours trying to organize and plan what nature offers me in my own backyard, a much smaller version of what I've mistaken as Versailles, if the time and focus I've devoted to its creation is any indication of its worth and fame. And then there's the look of the gardener ... definitely a different image.

I saw myself in my backyard hovering over wildly spreading irises so big they're almost scary, and some shade grasses that will soon complete a takeover of an entire bed. I wince to recognize my baggy, stained painter's pants and a wrinkled T-shirt of undecipherable color. A pair of leather work gloves finishes off my gardening outfit, except for a very worn-out baseball cap that keeps my hair from throwing itself into my eyes every time I bend over. My dislike of hats shows in the selection of this cap: dull brown with an insignia whose meaning I've never known.

Then I looked back at Sidra. I already anticipated the fragrance of the wild ginger blooms she would place in the house. It must be what heaven smells like, and if not, God should plant some there. There's a mix of wildness and order in her bouquets. It speaks to the depth of her aesthetic and the openness of her consciousness. I bore witness to it in a larger sense that morning in the garden. Who contributes to consciousness and how do they do it? Sidra Stone does it this way, metaphorically and concretely. She moves back into the psychic space of her childhood country boarding house in Yulan, New York. She tends her own garden here now, slowly, and from a dimension only she can touch. She finds the aesthetic in her life and work, in her relationships, and the things that come to her. She remains open to collecting and considering ALL of it as part of the larger plan ... and then, she'll share it with you in a heartbeat, smiling, because she knows it will change again, and there will be more.

I think in part, people who contribute to consciousness do so from a place of grace, like Sidra selecting the blooms she finds in her garden and her life. And how does Hal do it?

I sat drinking coffee at the little dining table in the Thera apartment I occupied one of the last mornings I was there. I did it every morning during my last visit, savoring the sight with the awareness of time passing too quickly for all of us. The early morning view of the meadow never loses its magic for me.

I waited for and was rewarded by the mist travelling inland from the ocean. It dropped in great swells from the grey sky. Floating down through the branches of the dark pines and great cedars, it brushed through the plum and apple trees to rest on the brown summer grasses. It moved like a great living thing, rolling over the ground toward the woods at the northern line of the property. As it passed, it revealed several hen turkeys and a couple of does foraging for breakfast in the day's dampness. Another swell covered them quickly, making me wonder if I had really seen them at all.

Out of the corner of my eye, I caught a glimpse of something white; a shiny ball of silver bobbing across the drive, in front of the Stones' house. As I turned my head to identify it, it disappeared like a ghost behind the woodshed. After a long moment, it reappeared. I saw the ball of silver was a thick head of hair belonging to Hal, who was making his way across the field. "Ah," I say to no one, "a dawn water level check".

We had talked about the draught in California the day before. The gardener, whose name was appropriately Lichen, and Sidra, were lobbying for an increased drip in the watering system for some of the plants in the back garden. Hal was judiciously

275

resistant but agreed as long as the water levels in the wells remained constant. I listened to this like a passionless tourist in a foreign country.

I had already spent days listening to Hal and Sidra welcome me into their private thoughts about other topics, less ordinary in nature and focus. They spend equal time talking about how the cosmos operates, the higher energies and how to access them, and experience in additional dimensions. My mind was still stretched from these sessions. I needed time to adjust. I relished my quiet mornings and evenings to come back to myself slowly. The sight of Hal moving to the wells grounded me.

I began to smile when he came into full view. His shining head of hair bobbled above a black terrycloth bathrobe and some clog-like shoes. He must have gotten out of bed and started directly out to the wells. He had the gait of an older man who knew the terrain, but walked carefully because he also knew his limitations. His ginger movements and the curvature of his back reminded me of his age, which I readily forget in the presence of his energy. He, too, was only visible in moments as the mist swirled around him. I thought he could as easily have been a gnome I imagined in the morning's reverie as I watched out my window.

In a few minutes, I saw Hal on his way back to the house. His slender bare legs stood out under the black robe. They carried him faithfully back along the path he'd taken to check the wells, missing some clumps of tough grass, avoiding holes only he could see near his feet. It struck me that for all the explorations of our minds and spirits, for all the passions that inspire and carry us to great heights, there is, in the end, a "dailyness" to life that balances out the higher realms. For me, this early morning, it was my coffee and the quiet time gazing out a picture window. For Hal, it was checking the water levels in the wells whenever the thought came to him to do so. Just life.

Who contributes to consciousness? People who straddle the cosmos with its demands for expansion, as well as the ditch by the driveway, because it needs to be clear of brush and debris so the waters can flow freely. For the Stones, relationship has been the forum for the greater work of the Aware Ego Process, which will rest comfortably among its Jungian ancestors and consciousness seekers of generations to come. May their experience and generosity in sharing it, educate us all.

ENDNOTES

¹ **Abbey Rosen,** Voice Dialogue facilitator, Annapolis, MD.
² **Ruth Berlin,** Voice Dialogue facilitator, Annapolis, MD.
³ The tension of the opposites refers to a concept described in Jungian thought as "Whatever attitude exists in the conscious mind, and whichever psychological function is dominant, the opposite exists in the unconscious. As the aging process continues, it is necessary for the unconscious contents be brought to consciousness to produce a tension of the opposites, without which no forward movement in the personality is possible. (Paraphrased from *C.G. Jung Lexicon, A Primer of Terms and Concepts, Daryl Sharp, Toronto, 1991.*
⁴ This another Jungian idea related to the tension of opposites. Endured without flipping from one psychological possibility to another when in conflict, Jung proposed that a new psychological attitude is formed containing something both opposing choices.
⁵ I am reminded of Jung, who addressed a 1958 memoir to his children, saying that he would be "telling [them] what little he can recall from the darkness of [his] youth," Shamdasani, *Jung Stripped Bare by his Biographers, Even,* 2005, p. 26.
⁶ Translated from the German *biergarten* is an outdoor area in which beer, other drinks and local food is served. Beer gardens originated in Southern Germany (especially Bavaria). They are usually attached to a beer hall, pub, or restaurant.
⁷ From the unpublished manuscript of the Fireside Chats 2011, held in Mendocino, CA, April 1-5, 2011, presented by Iudita Harlan and Dianne Braden. P.74.
⁸ **Hollis, James**, *Hauntings, Dispelling the Ghosts Who Run Our Lives,* Chiron, North Carolina, 2013, p. 25.
⁹ **Jung, C.G.,** *C.W. XV,* "Paracelsus", 1934, pp.2,
¹⁰ This game was played in many countries and cultures. It is a kind of game of tag with near-military strategy, also known as Prisoner's Base and Manhunt.
¹¹ **Stone, Hal**, *Embracing Heaven and Earth*, a Personal Odyssey, California, 1985, p. 35-41.

[12] According to the Jewish Virtual Library, **Yisrael Baal Shem Tov** (Master of the Good Name) was a Jewish mystical rabbi. Born Yisroel ben Eliezer in August of 1698, he lived in the small town of Okopy, which over the centuries has been part of Poland, Russia, and now the Ukraine. He was orphaned early and cared for by the community. Educated within the mainstream of the day, he showed early signs of difference and spent much time wandering the fields and forests, secluding himself and talking to God. He developed an unusually strong emotional relationship to God, which would later stand as the defining characteristic of the religious approach he founded, *Chassidus,* or Hasidic Judaism. Copyright 2012.

[13] Plasters were used to relieve congestion and fever. However, the most common of these was the mustard plaster, first recommended by the father of medicine, Hippocrates, as a treatment for pulmonary illnesses and rheumatism. Although there are various recipes for making a plaster, all basically use ground mustard seed, preferably from the pungent black variety, and flour mixed with water. The paste is then wrapped in a flannel or other cloth and placed on the affected area, the original theory being that the heat caused by the substances in the mustard would draw out poisons from the body.

[14] **Stone, S.,** THE SHADOW KING, The Invisible Force That Holds Women Back, NE, 1997.

[15] According to Hal, a core process has to do with a continuity of events that may exist on an outer level or an inner level or a combination of both. After his first analytic session, Hal's dream life exploded. He had the immediate experience of knowing that there was an Intelligence guiding his process; that there was in him an unconscious and the he was experiencing this process in his nightly dream life, as well as in events that were occurring in his daytime living.

[16] Editor/Recorder of Memories, Dreams and Reflections, Jung, C.G.,1961, Random House, New York.

[17] Hal Stone was given an award in 2003 for his contributions to the field by the Southern California Group Therapy Association.

[18] ***Encyclopedia Britannica:*** Entelechy, (from Greek entelecheia), in philosophy, that which realizes or makes actual what is otherwise merely potential. The concept is intimately connected with Aristotle's distinction between matter and form, or the potential and the actual. He analyzed each thing into the stuff or elements of which it is composed and the form, which makes it what, it is (see hylomorphism). The mere stuff or matter is not yet the real thing; it needs a certain form or essence or function to complete it. Matter and form, however, are never separated; they can only be distinguished. Thus, in the case of a living organism, for example, the

281

sheer matter of the organism (viewed only as a synthesis of inorganic substances) can be distinguished from a certain form or function or inner activity, without which it would not be a living organism at all; and this

"soul" or "vital function" is what Aristotle in his *De anima (On the Soul)* called the entelechy (or first entelechy) of the living organism. Similarly, rational activity is what makes a man to be a man and distinguishes him from a brute animal.

[19] From the French meaning the vital force or impulse to life; a creative principle that Henri Bergson held to be immanent in all organisms and responsible for evolution.

[20] **Gottfried Wilhelm Leibniz,** a 17th-century German philosopher and mathematician, called his monads (the ultimate reality of material beings) entelechies in virtue of their inner self-determined activity. The term was revived around the turn of the 20th century by Hans Driesch, a German biologist and philosopher, in connection with his vitalistic biology to denote an internal perfecting principle, which, he supposed, exists in all living organisms.

[22] **Jung, C. G.,** C.W. IX ii, para 126.

[23]Operant conditioning is a method of learning that occurs through rewards and punishments for behavior. Through operant conditioning, an individual makes an association between a particular behavior and a consequence (B. F. Skinner, 1938).

[24] **Stone, H. & Stone, S.,** *The Fireside Chats,* ed. D. Braden, 2011, p. 152-160. This section is paraphrased and reprinted with the permission of the authors.

[25] Sandplay is a hands-on psychological work. It is a powerful therapeutic technique that facilitates the psyche's natural capacity for healing. In a "free and protected" space provided by the analyst, a client creates a concrete manifestation of his or her imaginal world using sand, water, and miniature objects.

[26] A bonding pattern is a psychic dynamic structured like the parent/child relationship, moving back and forth in roles defined by authority and vulnerability. Bonding patterns can be created between people, objects, animals, and inner figures and voices.

[27] From a personal conversation with **Dr. Marvin Spiegelman,** Jungian Analyst in Los Angeles, CA in the Fall of 2012.

[28] These are part of a multi-volume series entitled *The Red, Blue, Yellow, Green, Brown, Violet, Crimson, Orange and Grey Fairy Tale Books*, and more, *Dover Classics*, Unabridged and Illustrated, edited by Andrew Lang, Dover Publications, Inc., New York, 1965.

[29] Symbolic visualization is a technique used to access images that can yield information from the unconscious. Much like working with the figures and images in a dream, minus a specific focus on meaning, the process includes guided meditation and forms of active imagination or dialogue with inner figures that come to the participants.

[30] Esalen Institute, first founded in 1962 in Big Sur, California, became a retreat center and humanistic alternatives educational institute that continues to offer programs to date. Known for its open and free-thinking perspectives, it became a haven for residential scholars and philosophers including George Leonard, Ida Rolf, Fritz Perls, Stanislav Grof, Joseph Campbell and Virginia Satir.

[31] **Roberto Assagioli,** was a 20th Century Italian psychiatrist and pioneer in the fields of humanistic and transpersonal psychology. He founded the psychological movement known as Psychosynthesis. His work emphasized the possibility of progressive integration of the personality around its own essential Self through the use of the will.

[32] **Daryl Sharp,** *C.G. Jung Lexicon, a Primer of Terms and Concepts,* Inner City Books, Toronto, 1991. "Psychologically, the incest archetype is the innate regressive longing for the security of childhood and early youth. Jung interpreted incest images in dreams and fantasies not concretely but symbolically, as indicating the need for a new adaptation more in accord with the instincts.

Also, in "Symbols of the Mother and of Rebirth,", CW 5, pp. 351. Jung said "so long as the child is in that state of unconscious identity with the mother, he is still one with the animal psyche and is just as unconscious as it. The development of consciousness inevitably leads not only to separation from the mother, but to separation from the parents and the whole family circle and thus to a relative degree detachment from the unconscious and the world of instinct. Yet the longing for the lost world continues and, when difficult adaptations are demanded, is forever tempting one to make evasions and retreats, to regress to the infantile past..."

[33] **Jung, C.G.,** *The Red Book, Liber Novus,* Sonu Shamdasani, ed., p.8-9. During the same time period, Theodore Flournoy published his work on the medium Helene Smith, and William James and Frederick Myers contributed to a new climate of understanding of the human psyche using methods automatic writing, trance speech and crystal vision. Jung's medical

283

dissertation focused on the psychogenesis of spiritualistic phenomena relying on the works of these other pioneers in depth psychology.

[34] **Jung, C.G.,** Memories, Dreams, and Reflections, 1961, p. 187.

[35] **Serrano, M.,** *C.G. Jung & Hermann Hesse, A Record of Two Friendships,* Schocken Books, New York, 1966, p. 57-58.

[36] **Marsha Sheldon,** Voice Dialogue Facilitator, Reseda, CA.

[37] **Dr. O. Carl Simonton,** (1942-2009) originated the idea of helping cancer patients through psycho-social oncology. He understood and taught the importance of family and personal support in the treatment of cancer. Founder of the Simonton Cancer Center.

[38] **William Brugh Joy** was a physician whose training came from respected traditional institutions, interning at Johns Hopkins and finishing at the Mayo Clinic. When he experienced an attack of pancreatitis, Brugh Joy turned to alternative medicine. He turned to energy healing, Jungian work, and the dream process. He left his medical career and began leading self-development workshops. He is quoted as understanding that working with the body is a valid spiritual path.

[39] See "A Bio-Medical Treatment Approach to Autism Spectrum Disorder, Including Heavy Metal Detoxification. www.alternativementalhealth.com

[40] **Jack Zimmerman** is the founder of the Ojai Foundation, organized in 1975, exploring the interface between science and spirituality. He brought the idea of the Council Circle to light, dissolving the barriers between hierarchical titles in community, through group witnessing and processing, and passing the talking stick.

[41] **J. Tamar Stone,** Voice Dialogue facilitator, founder Voice Dialogue Connection, Boulder, CO.

[42] **J. Tamar Stone,** Voice Dialogue facilitator, founder Voice Dialogue Connection, Boulder, CO.

[43] **J. Tamar Stone,** Voice Dialogue facilitator, founder Voice Dialogue Connection, Boulder, CO.

[44] **Martha Lou Wolff, Ph.D.,** Voice Dialogue Facilitator. San Francisco, CA.

[45] **J. Tamar Stone,** Voice Dialogue facilitator, founder Voice Dialogue Connection, Boulder, CO.

[46] **Larry Novick,** Voice Dialogue facilitator and Aikido Master, Los Angeles, CA.

[47] **Larry Novick,** Voice Dialogue facilitator and Aikido Master, Los Angeles, CA.

[48] A facilitation is a Voice Dialogue session in which the selves of any given personality engage in actual conversation and reflection with a trained voice Dialogue Facilitator. In such work people learn to identify and separate from their Primary Selves, identify their opposites and Disowned

Selves, and develop a sense of psychologically standing between them in an Aware Ego Process.

[49] **Stone, H., and Stone, S.**, *Embracing Ourselves: The Voice Dialogue Manual,* "The Heavyweights:" The Pusher, The Perfectionist, The Protector Controller, The Responsible Self, The Psychological Knower, 1989, p. iv.

[50] **Martha Lou Wolff, Ph.D.**, Voice Dialogue Facilitator, San Francisco, CA.

[51] **J. Tamar Stone**, Voice Dialogue facilitator and originator of Body Dialogue, Boulder, CO.

[52] **J. Tamar Stone**, Voice Dialogue facilitator and Originator of Body Dialogue, Boulder, CO.

[53] **J'aime Ona Pangaia, Voice** Dialogue Facilitator, Portland, Oregon

[54] Thanks to **Martin Pollecoff,** Chair, United Kingdom Council of Psychotherapy, London, England, for saving and retrieving one of the few remaining recipes from the Intensives held at Thera, in this case, in 2005.

[55] **Marsha Sheldon,** Voice Dialogue Facilitator, Reseda, CA.

[56] **Cynthia Hyymowitz,** Voice Dialogue facilitator, Santa Rosa, CA.

[57] **Dorsey Cartwright, Voice** Dialogue facilitator, Austin, TX.

[58] **Gabrielle Pollecoff,** Voice Dialogue facilitator and Homeopath, Church Lane Near Liss, Hampshire GU33 6HT

[59] **Robert Stamboliev,** Voice Dialogue Facilitator, Netherlands, Italy, Turkey.

[60] **J. Tamar Stone**, Voice Dialogue Facilitator and Originator of Body Dialogue, Boulder, CO.

[61] **Humbert, Elie G.**, *C.G. JUNG, Fundamentals of Theory and Practice*, trans. Ronald G. Jalbert, 1984, p. 124-125.

[62] **His Holiness Lama Drimed** Rinpoche, Dechen Rang Dharma Center, San Jose, CA.

[63] **Sharp, Daryl**, *C.G Jung Lexicon, a Primmer of Terms and Concepts*, Toronto, 1991, p.108. A concept applicable to virtually any archetype, expressing the essentially unknown but experienceable connection between psyche and matter.

[64] **Bernstein, J.,** Living in the Borderland, the evolution of Consciousness and the Challenge of Healing Trauma, New York, 2005.

[65] **Kalsched, D., Trauma** and the Soul, A Psycho-spiritual approach to human development and its interruption, New York, 2013.

[66] **Cathryn Keir,** Voice Dialogue Facilitator, Seattle, WA

[67] **Iudita Harlan**, Voice Dialogue Facilitator and Hellerworker, Solon, OH

[68] The Inner Patriarch is a self, found in women and men who represents and operates as a harsh, dominant masculine authority in the system. There is a corresponding Inner Matriarch as well in which the primary authority is a powerful and judgmental feminine authority.

285

[69] **Shakti Gawain** is a spiritual teacher, author, and Voice Dialogue facilitator now living outside of San Francisco, California.

[70] **Genvieve Cailloux,** Voice Dialogue facilitator, Vernou La Celle sur Seine, IDF.

[71] **Pierre Cauvin,** Voice Dialogue facilitator, Vernou La Celle sur Seine, IDF.

[72] **Bubbala** is Yiddish for "little darling" or "little one". It is an intimate diminutive term of affection. It is also used in jest when talking to an adult who may be clueless about something, as in "Bubbala, listen to me. I'll tell you what's really going on."

[73] **Neil Meili,** Voice Dialogue Facilitator and poet, Austin, TX.

[74] **Guan Yin** was a Chen Dynasty empress, whose Buddhist nun name was Guanyin, a bodhisattva associated with compassion, and known as the deity of mercy. Guanyin is short for the name Guanshiyin, meaning "Perceiving the Cries of the World". When a Buddhist adherent departs this world, it is thought that it is Guanyin who places them in the heart of a lotus inwhich they are sent to the pure western land. Sidra's remark refers to frequent statuary depictions of the goddess with a pearl of wisdom in one hand and a vial of pure water or tears of compassion in the other.

[75] **Judith Hendin,** Voice Dialogue Facilitator, Easton, PA.

[76] **Jung, C.G.,** *The Collected Works,* XIII, "The Stages of Life", pp. 778.

[77] **Stone, H., and Stone, S.,** *The Fireside Chats,* ed. D. Braden, 2011, p. 1.

[78] **Jung, C.G.,** *The Collected Works,* XIII, "The Stages of Life", pp. 778.

[79] **J. Tamar Stone,** Voice Dialogue Facilitator and originator of Body Dialogue, Boulder, CO.

[80] **Jung, C.G.,** *The Collected Works,* VIII, "The Stages of Life", pp. 792.

[81] **Jane Roberts,** 1929-1984 was a resident of Saratoga Springs, N.Y., a graduate of Skidmore College, and a New Age author, psychic and medium. She channeled an energy personality named Seth and published a number of works, most notably *The Seth Material, The Oversoul Seven Trilogy.* She also purportedly channeled the worldviews of several other people, including philosopher William James, the author of *Varieties Of Religious Experience*, Rembrandt, and painter Paul Cezanne, using a process she described as using a typewriter to write "automatically"

[82] **Hollis, J.,** *HAUNTINGS, Dispelling the Ghosts Who Run Our Lives,* Chiron, Asheville, N.C., 2013, p. xvi-xvii.

[83] **J'aime Ona Pangaia**, Voice Dialogue Facilitator, Portland, Oregon

[84] **Miriam Dyak,** Voice Dialogue Facilitator, Seattle, WA

BIBLIOGRAPHY

Bernstein, Jerome S., *Living in the Borderland, the Evolution of Consciousness and the Challenge of Healing Trauma,* New York, Routledge, 2005.

Encyclopedia Britannica, https://www.britannica.com.

Hollis, James, PhD, *Hauntings, Dispelling the Ghosts Who Run Our Lives,* Asheville, NC, Chiron, 2013.
Humbert, Elie, *C.G. Jung: The Fundamentlas of Theory and Practice,* Wilmette, IL., Chiron, 1996.

Jewish Virtual Library, https://www.jewishvirtuallibrary.org/

Jung, C.G., "Paracelsus," Vol. XV, *The Collected Works of C.G. Jung,* Princeton, NJ, Princeton University Press, 1934.

Jung, C.G., "The Stages of Life," Vol. XIII, *The Collected Works of C.G. Jung,* Princeton, NJ, Princeton University Press, 1930.

Jung, C.G., "Christ, A Symbol of the Self," Vol. IXii, *The Collected Works of C.G. Jung,* Princeton, NJ, Princeton University Press, 1959.

Jung, C.G., *Memories, Dreams, and Reflections,* ed. Aneila Jaffee, New York, Vintage Books, Random House, 1961.

Jung, C.G., *The Red Book, Liber Novus,* ed. Sonu Shamdasani, New York, W. W. Norton & Company, 2009.

Kalsched, Donald, *Trauma and the Soul, A Psych-spiritual approach to human development and its interruption,* New York, Routledge, 2013.

287

Serrano, Miguel, *C. G. Jung and Hermann Hessee, A Record of Two Friendships,* New York, Schocken Books, 1966.

Shamdasani, Sonu, *Jung Stripped Bare by his Biographers, Even,* London, Karnac Books, 2005.

Sharp, Daryl, *C.G. Jung Lexicon,* Toronto, Inner City Books, 1991.

Stone, Hal, *Embracing Heaven and Earth, a Personal Odyssey,* Marina del Rey, California, DeVorss & Company, 1985.

Stone, Sidra L., *The Shadow King, the Invisible Force That Holds Women Back,* Lincoln, NE, iUniverse.com. Inc., 1997.

Stone, Hal, and Stone, Sidra, *The Fireside Chats with Hal and Sidra Stone,* ed. Dianne Braden, Albion, CA, Delos, Inc., 2011.

Made in the USA
Lexington, KY
25 July 2018